UNI WISSEN

English Idioms for University

Richard Humphrey

Ernst Klett Verlag
Stuttgart · Düsseldorf · Leipzig

»Every speech hath certaine idiomes and customary phrases of its own.«
HOWELL, 1642

»Languages are the pedigree of nations.«
SAMUEL JOHNSON, 1773

»While a translator endeavours to give his work all the ease of original composition, the chief difficulty he has to encounter will be found in the translation of idioms, or those turns of expression which do not belong to universal grammar, but of which every language has its own, that are exclusively proper to it.«
ALEXANDER FRASER TYTLER, 1790

»The one stream of poetry which is continually flowing is slang. All slang is metaphor and metaphor is poetry.«
G. K. CHESTERTON, 1920

Die Deutsche Bibliothek – CIP-Titelaufnahme

Ein Titeldatensatz für diese Publikation ist bei der Deutschen Bibliothek erhältlich.

1. Auflage A 1 5 4 3 2 1 | 2004 2003 2002 2001 2000

Internetadresse | http://www.klett-verlag.de

Bildnachweis | © William Roberts, „Bank Holiday in the Park". Englische Kunst im 20. Jahrhundert: Malerei und Plastik, hrsg. von Susan Compton. München: Prestel, 1987. In einigen Fällen ist es uns trotz intensiver Bemühungen nicht gelungen, die Rechte-Inhaber zu ermitteln. Wir bitten diese, sich mit dem Verlag in Verbindung zu setzen.

Gedruckt auf Papier, das aus chlorfrei gebleichtem Zellstoff hergestellt wurde.

Redaktion | Margit Künzel
Umschlaggestaltung und Layout | Christine Schneyer
Satz | Hahn Medien GmbH, Kornwestheim
Druck | Gutmann + Co., Talheim. Printed in Germany.
ISBN 3-12-939586-5

Inhalt

Vorwort

Einführung

Nichts sitzt so gut wie die triftig platzierte Redewendung. Sie ist das Salz in der Gesprächssuppe, das Tüpfelchen auf dem Essay, die Hefe der Journalistik, der Senf des Werbetextes, eine Hauptingredienz der Literatur – allerdings eine, mit der häufig dichterisch neuformend umgegangen wird. Nur: Für Anglisten und Anglistinnen sind Idiome oft eher Sand im Textgetriebe, Auslöser von Irritation, gar Mißverständnis. Man liest und lernt über sie hinweg, weil man nicht an ihnen entlang zu lesen und lernen vermag. Die Beherrschung der englischen Idiomatik gehört somit zu den unumgänglichen, wenn auch anspruchsvolleren Aufgaben des universitären Englischerwerbs.

Konzept

Der vorliegende Band setzt sich zum Ziel, systematisch in das so facetten- wie umfangreiche Gebiet der englischen Idiomatik einzuführen. Er will animieren, sensibilisieren, instruieren. Vermittelt werden die Idiome, denen heutige Studierende im Laufe des Studiums inklusive Auslandsaufenthalte sowie im künftigen Berufs- und Sozialleben begegnen dürften. Die Spannbreite der im Band berücksichtigten Diskurse reicht somit von der Literatur über die Medien bis hin zum gesellschaftlichen Miteinander und zur Praxis der Geschäftswelt.

Definition

Der Band geht von einer eng abgesteckten Begriffsbestimmung aus. Idiomatik wird hier weder als 'korrekter Sprachgebrauch' – '*So woulde I wish you to frame all sentences in their mother phrase and proper Idioma*' (Gascoigne, 1575) – noch als 'standesspezifischer oder regional bedingter Sprachgebrauch' – '*That Dialect or Idiome which was familiar to the basest clowne*' (Holland, 1601) – aufgefaßt. Vielmehr gilt Idiom hier als '*a peculiarity of phraseology approved by the usage of a language, and often having a signification other than its grammatical or logical one*' (OED).

Inhalte

Darüber hinaus ist die Auswahl der hier behandelten Idiome stark zielgruppenorientiert. Sie entspricht den oben umrissenen – zwar vielfältigen aber dennoch speziellen – Bedürfnissen der Studierenden der Anglistik. Die getroffene Auswahl beschränkt sich daher weder auf Literarisches noch auf Umgangssprachliches, weder auf Historisches noch auf postmodern Gängiges. Es wird vielmehr eine Synthese angestrebt, die sich als studiumbegleitend und alltagssituationsrelevant erweisen dürfte. Dass das Material dabei gelegentlich ins Triviale, gar Vulgäre abrutscht, ist weder gewollt, noch zufällig, sondern unabdingbar. Die Auswahl ist einerseits auf dem neuesten Stand und berücksichtigt z.B. die aktuellen *Dictionaries of New Words*, andererseits aber bestrebt, ephemere Neuprägungen nicht aufzunehmen.

Einheiten

Von den 25 Einheiten des Bandes behandeln 21 ein eigenes Wortfeld, wobei die behandelten Idiome jeweils ihre Herkunft – nicht aber ihre jetzige Bedeutung – in dem genannten Wortfeld haben. In den übrigen vier Einheiten werden Idiome nach Strukturmerkmalen gruppiert. Jede Einheit besteht aus vier bis acht Übungen, die je ein Teilgebiet behandeln. Alle Einheiten sind in sich abgeschlossen, man darf sie sich in beliebiger Reihenfolge vornehmen. Innerhalb jeder Einheit wird indes eine Progression berücksichtigt, nach jeweils leichtem Einstieg führt der Steilheitsgrad der Übungen nach oben.

Übungen

Wie die Parallelbände *Grundkurs Übersetzen* und *Aufbaukurs Übersetzen* ist auch dieser Band den Prinzipien eines entdeckenden Lernens verpflichtet. Jean Piaget steht erneut Pate. Seine Hauptforderung – dass nämlich *toute vérité à acquérir soit réinventée par l'élève ou tout au moins reconstruite et non pas simplement transmise* (dass jede zu erwerbende Wahrheit von den Studierenden neu erfunden oder zumindest rekonstruiert, und nicht bloß vermittelt werden soll) – wird hier ernst genommen und eingelöst. Sämtliche Idiome werden folglich weniger 'frontal' dargeboten als in eigens entwickelten Übungen entdeckend gelernt. Die Übungen dienen der Bestimmung und Kontextualisierung der Idiome und sind so angelegt, dass sie Vorwissen aktivieren und Halbwissen mobilisieren. Insbesondere geben sie einer oft unterschätzten menschlichen Fähigkeit gebührend Freiraum: dem *intelligent guesswork*. Die Übungen, die sich sowohl für den Einzelgebrauch als auch für die an dt. Hochschulen häufig praktizierte Lernform der studentischen Arbeitsgemeinschaft eignen, sind nicht zuletzt mit Blick auf die vielen Pausen, aus denen ein Studium zwangsläufig besteht, konzipiert. Mit dem Studium ist es wie mit dem Leben: beide bestehen „zu zwei Dritteilen aus Warten [...], und das Beste ist, was man sich verstohlen gönnt" (S. Freud). Das leicht Verspielte der Übungen ist Absicht. Es entspricht der Überzeugung des Verfassers, dass das Sprachenlernen, wie jeder andere Erkenntniszuwachs auch, zum richtig verstandenen und praktizierten *joie de vivre* gehört.

Lernerfolgskontrolle

Nach allen sechs Einheiten erfolgt eine Lernerfolgskontrolle, die es Lesern und Leserinnen ermöglicht, den gerade eingeführten und geübten Lehrstoff zu wiederholen und festigen.

Antwortteil

In einem ausführlichen Antwortteil befinden sich die Lösungen zu allen Übungen und Kontrolleinheiten sowie auch weiterführende Hinweise zu Herkunft und Gebrauch der behandelten Idiome.

Schlussbemerkung

Dem Band liegt zudem die Auffassung zugrunde, dass der Idiomatik nicht der Platz in der anglistischen Sprachpraxis und Linguistik eingeräumt wird, der ihr gebührt. Idiome sind mehr als farbenprächtige Redewendungen. Ein Idiom kommt mit dem Hauch der Jahrhunderte und des Zeitgeistes daher. Idiome sind Fenster in die Üblichkeiten und Sehensweisen, die Vergangenheit und das Selbstverständnis einer Fremdkultur und deren Sprachgeschichte. Ein richtig praktizierter Idiomatikunterricht ist ein ergiebiger Bestandteil einer anglistischen Sprach- und Kulturwissenschaft. Fest steht: Ein Anglist ohne aktive englische Idiomatik ist wie ein Theseus ohne Ariadnefaden.

1 UNIT Idioms of the Cosmos and Earth

Field 1: The Heavens and Heavenly Bodies

Your Task

Complete the idiomatic sense of the sentences below by selecting the appropriate word from the options beneath, taking care to use it in a correct form. The answers are to be found on page 142.

Sentences

1. Yes, culture is what makes you a stranger when you're away from home. Go abroad – and suddenly you feel you're talking to people from another ___.'
2. Her lecture was far and away the most original and seminal – the ___ turn of the high-flying conference.
3. 'How much are you prepared to spend, Madam?' – 'Any amount, my good man. Frankly, for me the ___ 's the limit. But it's a question of quality: I won't pay the ___ for rubbish, you know.'
4. Some authors, like Richard Hughes, have done their writing in the early morning. Others would still be dead to the ___ at eleven.
5. 'And how would you like your egg, Sir? ___ side up?'
6. 'As red-nosed as the reindeer, Dennis. Too much of the gin, eh?' – 'Nonsense, old boy, just caught the ___ in the solarium, what?'
7. There was no way they could pay the rent and they were already deep in arrears. There was nothing for it – a ___ flit it had to be.
8. She strode from success to success, carrying the ___ before her.
9. 'He's a real ___, I must say! What a misery-guts!'
10. 'A top job!! With his finals!! That's crying for the ___! Pie in the ___. He must be a loony, a complete ___ cadet to think that!'
11. 'Oh, what an embarrassing mistake! I do apologise. But you look for all the ___ like my great aunt Ethel!'
12. 'Done much today, Samantha?' – 'No, to be honest I've just been ___ around waiting for something to happen. – And it hasn't.'
13. 'What was it like to score that goal, Gary?' – 'Oh, just great, great, mega, brilliant, out of this ___, I mean, you know, just – wow. Wow. I'm over the ___.'
14. Some 5m citizens ___, not paying taxes on spare-time jobs.
15. 'Their manifesto is vapid nonsense, fantasy, mere ___, the ravings of naive, ___-eyed youngsters.'

Options

earth – moon (3x) – moonlight (2x) – moonshine – planet – ray of sunshine – sky (2x) – space – star(ry) (2x) – sun(ny) (2x) - world (4x)

> ***Idiom*** *A sequence of (more or less) fixed words having a meaning not deducible from the individual words.*

SYLVIA CHALKER/EDMUND WEINER, eds, *Oxford Dictionary of English Grammar* (1998)

Field 2: Astronomy and Astrology

Your Task

Complete the crossword below, noting that the first letter of each word and the number of letters in each word are given. The correct answers are to be found on page 142.

Crossword

Clues

1. It was written at the height of her creativity, the (6) of her powers.
2. The 1990s saw the end, or at least the (7), of Soviet power.
3. After the roof tile had hit her, she saw (5) for several minutes.
4. She could thank her (5,5) that the accident was not far worse.
5. Her rise to fame was dramatic: she was the (8,4) of her generation.
6. The bleeping of his alarm clock finally brought him back to (5), back from wild dreams.
7. If her rise was dramatic, that of her yet more talented sister was simply (8).
8. 'No, you're miles off target, totally off beam, right off (5).'
9. With three internationals in each team, it was a really (4–7) line-up.
10. Disgusted at the ref's decision, the player lowered his shorts and (6) him, the crowd jeering at this display of bare buttocks.

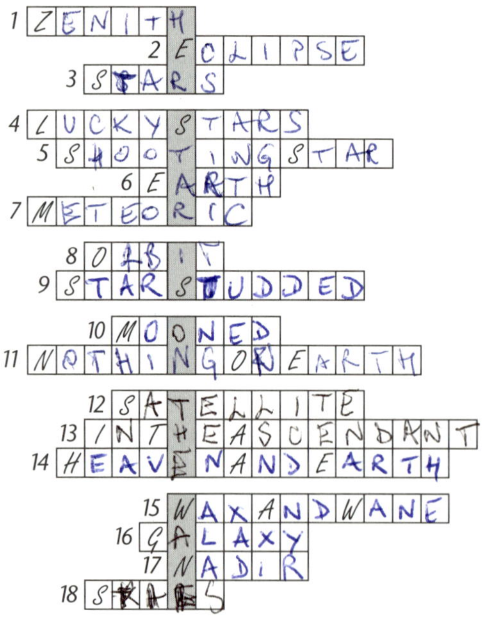

11. 'She has no sense of style. Not one bit. Not one iota. She often looks like (7,2,5), my dear!'
12. The former (9) state sought independence from the central power.
13. Her fortunes were on the up. Her star was (2,3,9)
14. 'We've tried everything. We've moved (6,3,5) to get the Council to reverse their decision. But no. They're intransigent.'
15. His timely book shows how all major empires are likely to (3,3,4), being subject to similar patterns of growth and decline.
16. 'With so many stars, there is a rich (6) of talent on display here.'
17. Their popularity sank to an all-time low, a (5) support.
18. 'I knew my paper was superb, but the prof. praised it to the (5)!'

Key Phrase: Things are on the way down for her. (3,4,2,2,3,4)

Field 3: Features of World Geography

Your Task

Study the idioms of geographical features on the left below and then decide which best expresses the concepts or situations listed on the right. The correct answers are to be found on page 142.

Idioms

to channel
the coast
a creek
an Everest
a/the field
the four winds
the hill
the hills
the tip of the iceberg
the island
the lie of the land
the landslide
a mountain
an oasis
the ocean
a pass
to peak
a pond
the rang
the slope
the slough
the tide
the summit
the tide

A. One's area of competence is one's ___.
B. to reach a high point
C. Nobody exists alone. 'No man is an ___.'
D. just the surface appearance of something that goes deeper
E. To be in a grave situation is to be in dire ___.
F. To be past one's best is to be over the ___.
G. spectrum
H. To be deeply depressed is to be in the ___ of despond.
I. ultimate test/achievement
J. a blessed haven
K. 'Time and ___ wait for no man.'
L. irretrievably heading downwards to degradation: on the slippery ___.
M. to be scattered far and wide: scattered to ___.
N. in a desperate situation: up ___.
O. far too little to help – just a drop in the ___.
P. a 'big player': a big fish in a small ___.
Q. We can escape now. The ___ is clear.
R. a clear electoral victory
S. this dilemma: this ___.
T. to direct money
U. to reconnoitre: to discover ___.
V. as old as the ___.
W. meeting of world leaders
X. Don't make a ___ out of a molehill.

Field 4: Countries and Nations

Your Task

Complete the idiomatic sense of the sentences below by selecting the appropriate country from the options beneath, taking care to use it in a correct form – the country, its adjective or its inhabitant. The answers are to be found on page 142.

Sentences

1. 'Such a delightful ending to the warm season, my dear! The dog days of the year – a real ___ summer!'
2. She refused to let any man pay for her, insisting on going ___.
3. 'The doctoral viva will be a real struggle, then?' – 'Absolutely. Cynthia knows what she's talking about. But the outside professor is said to be a real expert, and when ___ meets ___, you know ...'
4. 'Never. I wouldn't do it for all the tea in ___. No!'
5. Before the years of condomania, such articles were more decorously and delicately termed ___ letters.
6. The language of these computer freaks is the latest example of pseudo-scientific gobbledygook, the latest double ___.
7. He was afraid of going to face his accusers, but a couple of stiff – *very* stiff – drinks eventually gave him enough ___ courage.
8. They were both perpetual day-dreamers, real Quixotes, forever projecting, always proposing, ceaselessly building castles in ___.
9. 'I don't understand a word of it. Not a word. It's all ___ to me.'
10. Sick and tired of the routine, she just upped and went without so much as asking permission – took ___ leave for a whole month.
11. A *rive gauche* intellectual, he led a ___ life, dissolute and deviant.
12. In the years after 1962, the leading British parties held a ___ auction in illiberalism, outdoing each other on immigration control.
13. It was a total risk, the utter gamble, like ___ roulette.
14. 'As far as I'm concerned, he can **** well go and **** – pardon my ___.'
15. Most of the wedding gifts were not only superfluous but a damn nuisance, almost every one of them a ___ gift.
16. 'My grandfather knew Dickens, Gladstone, Disraeli *and* Lloyd George, you know.' – 'Oh, yes – and I'm the Queen of ___! Pull the other leg, it's got bells on!'
17. 'She *says* she's 39, but if she's a day under 55, then I'm a ___!
18. 'She's superbly witty in a cerebral way, full of ___ humour.'
19. 'We've got some bread, cheese and a tomato or two, so I'll make some ___ rabbits under the grill.' – 'Mmm! Delicious!'
20. The new Faculty members were real young ___, bent on change.
21. 'These new guidelines and regulations from Kassel are pettifogging!' – 'You can say that again! The old ___ thoroughness!'

Options

Bohemia – China – France (3x) – Gaul – Greece (4x) – Holland (5x) – India – Russia – Sheba – Spain – Teutony – Turkey – Wales

Field 5: Areas, Cities, Towns, Rivers

Your Task

Study the situations listed below and then decide which of the colloquial idioms of geography listed beneath would best express your message. The correct answers are to be found on page 143.

Situations

You You You You You You You You You You You You You You You You You

1. regard something as a dangerous intrusion that bodes ill.
2. consider that you have taken a decisive, even momentous step.
3. call on your fellows to exhibit a resolute, never-say-die attitude.
4. consider that a person should be outlawed, not even spoken to.
5. think that something is, all in all, a bit of a flop.
6. find a place hellishly noisy, a hullabaloo of noise and disorder.
7. refer to the high-tech transformation of the British newspaper industry, forced through by Rupert Murdoch in the 1980s.
8. consider someone to be a real Cockney (and not just a 'mockney').
9. note that many are flocking, making pilgrimages, to a certain spot.
10. remark that a room or flat is neat and tidy, all in tip-top order.
11. think that certain people are bores and boors, insufferable.
12. predict that something will be someone's ultimate downfall.
13. suggest a snap-decision marriage without any formalities.
14. refer to the IMF (International Monetary Fund) bankers.
15. are sceptical and demand evidence for a claim or remark.
16. consider a room or life-style very frugal, almost ascetic.
17. consider an action wholly unnecessary, superfluous.
18. deplore someone being inactive during an emergency or crisis.
19. declare a place to be a possible source of great wealth.
20. believe that a place is an intercultural quagmire, a confusing and confounding cacophony of languages.
21. declare that you have one final wish to be satisfied.
22. refer to someone's perpetual grin.
23. refer to a far-flung place where someone is living at the back of beyond, right out in the sticks.
24. protest that you have been abducted, press-ganged, 'bounced'.

Options

You Say You Say You Say You Say You Say You Say You Say You Say You

A. It's like Babel / B. This is Bedlam / C. He/she was born within the sound of Bow Bells / D. All ship-shape and Bristol fashion / E. Like a Cheshire cat / F. Send him/her to Coventry / G. Show the Dunkirk spirit / H. It's an Eldorado / I. Off to Gretna Green / J. It's a Mecca / K. Show me, I'm from Missouri / L. See Naples and die! / M. Coals to Newcastle / N. They are beyond the Pale / O. Fiddling while Rome burns / P. The Rubicon is crossed / Q. We've been Shanghai'ed / R. It's Spartan / S. It didn't set the Thames on fire / T. Timbuctoo / U. It's a Trojan horse / V. the Wapping Revolution / W. It'll be his/her Waterloo / X. the gnomes of Zurich

Field 6: Specific Streets

Your Task

Read the thirteen alliterative biographies below and then decide which life is most connected with which of the idiomatic streets listed beneath. The correct answers are to be found on page 144.

Biographies

1. Archibald abandoned the Army and afterwards asked for and acquired a civilian job.

2. Big shot Basil is a bigwig banker in the Bank of England.

3. Catherine underwent a conversion to a new creed.

4. Désirée is dreadfully, direly in debt, due to be hauled before the judge.

5. After Black Friday Philadelphian Fred made a fast fortune in futures on the frenzied and frantic financial markets.

6. Graham is gay and gains great pleasure from campaigning in ginger groups for gay rights.

7. Hilda is high up in the Home Office, a high-ranking civil servant.

8. On his national newspaper Neil was a real news-hound.

9. Patrick became Private Secretary to the Prime Minister.

10. Rosalind is rolling in money after raking it in at roulette.

11. Sam became a sought-after surgeon, a specialist in sarcomas.

12. Tracy tapped out some foot-tapping tunes that took her into the Top Ten.

13. Will would write a lot, but with little worldly wisdom or success.

Options

A. Carey Street
B. Christopher Street (Parade)
C. Civvy Street
D. the Damascus Road
E. Easy Street
F. Downing Street
G. Fleet Street
H. Grub Street
I. Harley Street
J. Threadneedle Street
K. Tin Pan Alley
L. Wall Street
M. Whitehall

2

UNIT **Idioms of Time and Number**

Field 1: Long and Longish Durations

Your Task

Complete the crossword below, which is made up of eighteen idioms, each of them having something to do with long or longish stretches of time. The correct answers are to be found on page 144.

Crossword

Clues

1. eine recht lange Zeit (1,5,2,7)
2. es verkürzte ihr Leben um Jahre (4,5,3,4)
3. Lebensabend (6,2,4)
4. vor sehr langer Zeit (poet.) (4,5,3)
5. Feierabend sagen (2,4,2,1,3)
6. Lichtjahre entfernt (5,5,4)
7. Sommerloch (5,6)
8. es hat ausgedient (2,3,3,3,3)
9. frühe Morgenstunden (5,5)
10. seit unvordenklicher Zeit (5,3,4,3)
11. Tagesthemen, 'Marschroute' bestimmen (3,3,6)
12. Nachtschicht haben (2,2,6)
13. versteckte Ziele (6,6)
14. eine menschenunwürdige Stunde (2,9,4)
15. seit urlanger Zeit (3,5,3,5)
16. Testament, in dem um Beendigung des Lebens bei chronischer Krankheit gebeten wird(6,4)
17. seit einer halben Ewigkeit (3,7,5)

1	AMONTHOFSUNDAYS
2	TOOKYEARSOFFTHEM
3	AUTUMNOFLIFE
4	MANYMOONSAGO
5	TOCALLITADAY
6	LIGHTYEARSAWAY
7	SUNNYSEASON
8	ITHASHADITSDAY
9	SMALLHOURS
10	SINCETHEYEARDOT
11	SETTHEAGENDA
12	BEONNIGHTS
13	HIDDENAGENDA
14	ANUNEARTHLYHOUR
15	FORAEONSANDAEONS
16	LIVINGWILL
17	FORDONKEYSYEARS

Key Phrase: lebensumspannend (4,6,2,5)

> *Jedermann weiß, dass man beim Englischlernen auf die zahlreichen idiomatischen Wendungen zu achten hat.*

ERNST LEISI, CHRISTIAN MAIR, *Das heutige Englisch* (1999)

Field 2: Time Idioms involving 'Time'

Your Task

Read the eighteen alliterative biographies below and then decide which life is best described by which of the idioms of time listed beneath. The correct answers are to be found on page 145.

Biographies

1. Alan and Alice arrived ahead of their appointed arrival time.
2. Avant-garde Amanda has always been in advance of the age.
3. Betty is a bustling, busy-as-a-bee business woman – but never so busy she can't be bothered.
4. Clever-clever crook Clint is now locked up in the clink.

5. Debbie and Dave were definitely in dire difficulties.
6. Indolent Eileen is eternally idle.
7. Fanny's having such fun – never had such a fine time.
8. Hesitant Herbert must now hurry to hand in his *Hausarbeit*.

9. Canny Ken considers he should keep up with current developments.
10. Lackadaisical, lassitude-lulled Larry always lingers too long.
11. Ninety-nine-year-old Nancy is now expecting Death to knock on her door and sound the knell.
12. Norris has now done his necessary nine years in the Navy.

13. Paul and Priscilla postponed, prevaricated and procrastinated.
14. Prudence plays patience to pass away the interim period.
15. Savvy Sally's so advanced she's standing still in the school's Second Year.
16. Toby tapped out the tempo so that the trumpeters could trumpet the tunes.

17. Weak-willed Wanda will waste away her weekends.
18. Wary William is waiting for a wiser moment.

Options

A. to be ahead of one's time
B. to do time
C. to have a hard time of it
D. to have time on one's hands
E. to live on borrowed time
F. to make good time, arrive in good time
G. to mark time
H. to take one's time
I. to serve one's time
J. to bide one's time
K. to fritter away one's time
L. to have the time of one's life
M. to kill time
N. to make time
O. to march with the times
P. to play for time
Q. to be pressed for time
R. to beat time

Field 3: Low Numbers – Nought to Nine

Your Task

In each of the sentences below, insert one (or more) of the numbers listed beneath to complete the idiom and the sense. The correct answers are to be found on page 145.

Sentences

1. She's accident-prone – but like a cat, she's got ___ lives.
2. 'Did you see Ulla at the party?! Dolled up to the ___ !' – 'They don't call her the Lone Ranger for nothing. She always gets her man.'
3. 'That's ruined it! That really has hit our plans for ___!'
4. It was a standard divorce case. Both partners had felt the ___-year itch. Each had ___-timed the other. And not only on ___-night stands.
5. '___'s company, ___ 's a crowd.'
6. Perhaps tastelessly, the snack bar at the centre of the Pentagon is called 'Ground ___' – a reference to the centre of any nuclear explosion.
7. After each successful rally the beachball players gave each other the high ___.
8. 'How did you know we were in the local?' – 'Easy, Friday night, hot day, Sue and Bert – I just put ___ and ___ together.'
9. 'Mummy, Mummy!! Wanna go wee-wee!!' – 'All right, dear. Number ___ or number ___?'
10. 'You're both equally to blame. It's ___ of one and ___ of the other.'
11. They had given up serious study long ago: the ___ deadly sins were simply far more fascinating and absorbing.
12. 'He's pissed!' –'Well, he's had ___ or ___.' – '___ over the ___ more like it!'
13. 'No, after that record no-one ever heard of her again as a singer. She was just a ___-hit wonder.'
14. 'I'm almost ready – I'll be with you in ___ shakes.'
15. The plane crossed the continent with ___-league boots.
16. 'That new shopping centre on the town periphery must be deadly for the old town retail trade.' – 'Got it in ___: it's a disaster!'
17. 'To reject the treaty now is folly, a ___-way ticket to the abyss!' – 'Yes, there's no ___ ways about it. Rejection means disaster.'
18. 'The great success of our new course is that its graduates are both linguists and economists. They've got ___ strings to their bow.'
19. 'It'll soon be forgotten. It's just a ___-days' wonder.'
20. He's the typical old Scottish laird – tweed jacket and plus-___.
21. 'Are there no other candidates?' – 'No it's just a ___-cornered fight between Conservative, Labour and Liberal Democrat.'

Options

eight – five(s) – four(s) – half a dozen – nine (2x) – nines – one (7x) – seven (3x) – six (2x) – three (2x) – two (9x) – zero

Field 4: Further Low Numbers

Your Task

Consider the idioms of number below and decide which of the explanations beneath is likely to be the genuine meaning. The correct answers are to be found on page 145.

Idioms

1. **a goody two-shoes**
   = a A. good dancer B. smart dresser C. obtrusively virtuous person D. nice but poor person

2. **to be six feet under**
   = to be A. under-privileged B. short C. miserable D. dead

3. **a four eyes**
   = a(n) A. inquisitive person B. circumspect person C. glasses-wearer D. currant pudding

4. **to be at sixes and sevens**
   = to be A. confused B. fit C. young at heart D. good with kids

5. **to have a quick one**
   = to have A. a drink B. brief sex C. a quick temper D. a ready wit

6. **You're a one!**
   = you're A. witty B. a fool C. useless D. foolish to say that

7. **to look after number one**
   = to A. do things in the right order B. be self-centred C. prefer one's first child D. be money-minded

8. **the old one-two**
   = A. two quick punches B. a double pass at football C. a typical relationship D. a veteran bicycle

9. **one in the eye**
   = A. a snub B. a bitter blow C. a direct hit D. a good drink

10. **to be one can off a six-pack**
    = to be A. incomplete B. standard, stereotyped C. slightly mad D. inclined to heavy drinking

11. **six of the best**
    = A. a win on the pools B. a caning C. a group of friends D. a happy family

Field 5: Number in Dialogue and Proverb

Your Task

Imagine you are involved in the mini-dialogues below. Which of the idioms of number listed beneath would best fit which situation? The correct answers are to be found on page 145.

Dialogues

1. – The man's a complete fool to invest *all* his money in the Euro!
– Well, ***.
2. – Hurry up, John! We'll be late if you go on like this!
– ***. I must just find my scarf, shave and phone Bill.
3. – You mean we've got to start all over again?
– Yes, it's ***, I'm afraid. Start again from scratch.
4. – And then they admitted that they'd made a mistake in my case and would have to re-consider my application for more grant!
– Wow! Super! ***, Sue!
5. – They're *forever* talking, aren't they?
– Absolutely. They're unstoppable! On and on and on! They talk ***.
6. – ***.
– Heineken, Tolly Cobbold or Real Ale, madam?
7. – Let's repair this rickety fence before the next storm comes.
– Good idea. After all, ***.
8. – You're resigning! But I thought you really liked working for such a dynamic, young, can-do firm.
– No. *** for them really, you know.
9. – That's a good order. That should keep the firm in business, shouldn't it?
– ***. I'm afraid it may not be enough.
10. – Have a last drink, old man! Bottoms up, what! – No thanks. This 'Don't drink and drive' campaign has left me very wary of ***.
11. – You're not going to do your exam with him?
– No, ***. Wouldn't touch him with a barge-pole, arrogant devil.
12. – Children, if I've said it once I've said it ***...!!
– Oh, Mummy, pleeeaaase!! Mummy!!
13. – Now, look, Mr Pratt, your randy son's got our Judy pregnant!
– I'm sorry, Mr Sidebottom, but remember: ***, you know.
14. – Joan refuses to move office for the new woman?
– Yes, simply refuses. She's been there three years and she says ***.
15. – Well, what do you think of my new pad then?
– Hmm. I'd give it *** for originality. About tidiness I'm not so sure!

Options

A. Half a jiffy / B. Half, please / C. There's one born every minute / D. nineteen to the dozen / E. One up to you / F. I don't give two pins / G. Possession is nine points of the law / H. one for the road / I. Back to square one / J. ten out of ten / K. A stitch in time saves nine / L. One swallow doesn't make a summer / M. It takes two to tango / N. umpteen times / O. not in a hundred years

Field 6: Higher Numbers – Ten and Above

Your Task

In each of the sentences below, insert one (or more) of the numbers listed beneath to complete the idiom and the sense. The correct answers are to be found on page 145.

Sentences

1. 'What a day! I've got ___ things to do! Talk about hassle!'
2. 'Where's your father?' – 'Taking ___ winks. He often likes a little nap, a little snooze after the Sunday lunch.'
3. 'Can the government still cling on to power after this latest fiasco?' – 'Well, who knows? That's the ___ dollar question.'
4. 'I feel great this morning. Fabulous. Like a ___ dollars.'
5. 'If the robbery comes off, we share the loot, ___-___.'
6. 'Buy twelve rolls, not just ten. Perhaps we'll get a baker's ___.'
7. 'England needs a new cricket team. Who'd be in your ideal ___?'
8. 'The only way to get a discharge from the Army is to be mad. But if you say you're mad and that therefore you want a discharge, well clearly you can't be mad. No way out! It's a Catch-___ situation.'
9. 'He was bribed to betray us?' – 'Yes, he took the proverbial ___ pieces of silver.'
10. 'That woman's going to be a star. She's a woman in a ___!'
11. 'And where did all this happen?' – 'Well, in a certain town not a ___ miles away from here...' – 'Good heavens! Not in *****?! If the mayor hears about it, he'll have ___ fits!'
12. Mrs Astor invited only the *crème de la crème* of American society to her parties, only the now-proverbial ___.

Options

dozen / eleven / fifty (2x) / forty (2x) / a hundred / a hundred-and-one / four hundred / a million (2x) / sixty-four thousand / thirty / twenty-two

Field 7: Ordinal Numbers

Your Task

Study the cases and situations below and then decide which ordinal beneath, linked to which substantive or verb, correctly expresses the meaning. The correct answers are to be found on page 146.

A. overjoyed state
B. acutely burned skin
C. underground grouping working against the good
D. ironic reference to 'achievement' of friend
E. *ad nauseam* repetition
F. to receive a raw deal
G. to anticipate a decision
H. the last possible minute
I. top degree at university
J. the press

Options

fourth / eighth / eleventh / fifth / first / second (2x) / seventh / third / umpteenth // column / to come off / degree burns / estate / (to) guess / heaven / hour / time / wind / wonder of the world

3 UNIT Idioms of Colour

Field 1: The Basic Colours

Your Task

In each of the phrases below in Part A, insert one of the colours listed beneath to complete the basic idiom and the sense. Then move on to Part B. The correct answers are to be found on page 146.

Phrases

Part A

A. aristocratic: ___-blooded
B. bookish woman: ___-stocking
C. bureaucracy: ___ tape
D. naive and inexperienced: ___
E. rhetorical language: ___ passage
F. wire-puller: ___ eminence
G. royal: born to the ___
H. appear sea-sick: look ___
I. almost never: once in a ___ moon
J. celebrate: to paint the town ___
K. cowardly: ___
L. catch in the act: catch ___-handed
M. fed up and bored: ___ off
N. deeply engrossed: in a ___ study
O. made a cardinal: raised to the ___
P. extremely hot: ___ hot
Q. to blush sharply: to turn ___
R. to 'cover up': ___-wash
S. to get angry: to see ___
T. big day: ___-letter day
U. go-ahead: ___ light
V. ashamed: ___ with shame
W. to squander: to ___
X. envious: ___ with envy
Y. harmless lie: ___ lie
Z. in debt: in the ___
AA. environmentally aware: ___
BB. evergreen record: ___ oldie
CC. cinema: ___ screen
DD. brain-power: ___ matter

Options

blue (4x) – brown – browned – crimson – golden – green (5x) – grey (2x) – pink – purple (3x) – red (6x) – silver – white (3x) – yellow

Your Task

Part B

In the following sentences, insert both a colour and a substantive from among those listed beneath to complete the idiom and the sense.

Sentences

1. For the arrival of the bigwigs, they really rolled out the ___ ___.
2. The policy was the latest great ___ ___ to save local industry.
3. Acutely drunk, he saw a few ___ ___ on his wayward way home.
4. Many of his arguments were specious, just ___ ___ to distract attention from the real issue.

Options

pink – red (2x) – white // carpet – elephants – herring(s) – hope

> *Idiom: A lexicalized phrase which is semantically non-compositional.*

KONRAD KUIPER and W. SCOTT ALLAN
An Introduction to the English Language: Sound, Word and Sentence

Field 2: Colourful Phrases

Your Task

Read the twenty alliterative biographies below and then decide which life is best characterised by which of the idioms of colour listed beneath. The correct answers are to be found on page 147.

Biographies

1. Ada is active and alert at eighty-eight.
2. Archy argued, advised and admonished – but all to no avail.
3. Bianca, that brainy, brilliant beauty, even knew where Bothwell was buried.
4. Carlo the caring Catholic could one day become a cardinal.
5. Cautious Constance constantly counselled moderation.
6. Cowardly Christopher was always called 'Cowardy Custard'.
7. Donald saw it as his duty to educate 'deep and darkest Africa'.
8. Evelyn is exerting enormous energy on the eve of her exam.
9. Fido is feeling fit – never been fitter.
10. Frank is frightfully frightened and can't face the future.
11. Lucy received a large lump sum on leaving Lloyds.
12. Libidinous, lusty Larissa lays men like others lay linoleum.
13. Nasty news for Norbert – and expected by no-one.
14. Priggish Priscilla has always been privileged.
15. Ricarda was relishing the richly comic situation.
16. Sam is a socialist, but not so far off centre.
17. Theresa, a thorough-going Thatcherite, was Tory through and through.
18. Tom, a terrific talent, is still two years off twenty.
19. What Wilhelmina earned at weekends went unnoticed by the taxman.
20. Yusuf became a Yuppy, materialistic, even mercenary.

Options

A. the black economy / B. a bolt from the blue / C. till one is blue in the face / D. to be in a blue funk / E. true blue / F. a golden boy / G. to worship the golden calf / H. a golden handshake / I. the golden mean / J. a green old age / K. the grey matter / L. to be in the pink of condition / M. to be tickled pink / N. a pinko / O. to be raised to the purple / P. a scarlet woman / Q. to be born with a silver spoon in one's mouth / R. to be yellow / S. white heat / T. to take up the white man's burden

Field 3: Black and White Together

Your Task

In each of the sentences below, insert one (or more) of the phrases containing the word 'black' listed beneath to complete the idiom and the sense. The correct answers are to be found on page 147.

Sentences

1. 'Drama next door! The police have just come with a ___ and taken away both neighbours in it!'
2. 'For heaven's sake don't put it in your study! The room's a ___! Things go in there and never come out, lost irretrievably!'
3. 'Be careful with him: he's a troublemaker with a ___ in his past!'
4. He was one of the few ethical people in the Faculty, a real ___.
5. The pickets stood at the factory gates shouting 'scab' and '___' whenever a strike-breaker tried to pass.
6. 'I bet the bank doesn't allow me a mortgage: I must be on their ___ by now. I haven't been in the ___ for years.'
7. He was badly mugged and beaten up, waking up in hospital ___.
8. She really looked daggers at me yesterday. Oh boy, did she give me a ___! I must be in her ___!
9. 'Little Johnny's come home with a ___ after a nasty fist-fight.'
10. 'He always claims to be virtuous, but I suspect his ___ image.'
11. The power cut ___ parts of the town between 9 and 11.30 p.m.
12. 'Hell, chaps! We can't have him in the Club! Let's ___ him.'
13. 'No way, mate. Sorry. We're not unloading your ship. Your firm's been ___ by the union.'
14. The former German Chancellor's brief loss of memory, or ___, became, for a short time, one of his better-known political acts.
15. 'I won't believe it till I see it in writing, in ___.'
16. His aunt won't have anything to do with him. After his leaving the Catholic Church she regards him as the ___ of the family.
17. The ___ demanded £100,000 to keep silent on the politician's misdemeanours in the not-so-distant past.
18. Her incensed father called him a 'scoundrel' and a '___'.
19. ___ often formed at the exposed cross-roads in cold and wet weather, making the place a real accident ___.
20. 'He's going quietly mad. The ___ will soon take him away.'
21. The wind was getting up, making ___ on the surface of the sea.
22. What a coward he was! Always showing the ___! That was what made her despise him. He was now her ___ , her bugbear.

Options

A. *bête noire* / B. black (2x) / C. blackball / D. black books / E. black eye / F. blackguard / G. black hole / H. black ice / I. blackleg / J. black list / K. black look / L. blackmailer / M. Black Maria / N. black out / O. black-out / P. black sheep / Q. black spot / R. black and blue / S. black and white / T. white feather / U. white horses / V. white knight / W. whiter than white / X. men in white coats

Field 4: Sophisticated Shades

Your Task

Consider the idioms of colour below and decide which of the explanations beneath is likely to be the genuine meaning. The correct answers are to be found on page 147.

Idioms

1. **to cry blue murder**
   = to A. make unnecessary trouble B. make one hell of a noise C. attribute guilt to somebody else D. be a war-monger

2. **a golden parachute**
   = a A. large sum of money offered in the event of one's losing a job B. sensational rescue C. a yacht's spinnaker D. rich legacy

3. **the thin red line**
   = the A. line between life and death B. British army C. bottom line of a balance sheet D. sentence in a murder trial

4. **golden handcuffs**
   = A. favourable prison conditions for celebrities B. heavy jewellery C. cash incentives to top employees D. marriage to a wealthy person

5. **(to go) brown-bagging**
   = to A. wear military trousers B. eat a packed lunch in the open air C. travel light D. go hiking with a rucksack

6. **greener pastures**
   = A. biological farming areas B. Eire C. the clover belt in the U.S. Midwest D. happier hunting grounds to which someone goes

7. **a blueprint**
   = a A. plan for a project B. potato print C. official stamp D. workman's clothing

8. **the pink pound**
   = money spent by A. British tourists abroad B. foreign tourists in Britain. C. homosexuals D. British women on underwear

9. **into the blue wide yonder**
   = towards A. death B. the seven seas C. the distance D. heaven

10. **yellow journalism**
    = A. war propaganda B. government-inspired journalism C. reporting on China D. sensationalist gutter journalism

4

UNIT **Idioms of Weather**

Field 1: Idioms of the Wind

Your Task

Imagine you are involved in the mini-dialogues below. Which of the idioms of the wind listed beneath would best fit which situation? The correct answers are to be found on page 148.

Dialogues

1. – Uhuh. Look what's coming. Let's go down this side-street. I'm scared.
– Oh , they're just three cuddly Rottweilers. No need to ***.
2. – I spent half an hour in his *Sprechstunde*! But still no intelligent answer!
– That's always the way with him. You might as well ***.
3. – There is a lot of whispering in the Common Room. Suspicious.
– Yes, it is fishy. You know, ***.
4. – It's a marvellous idea. But where's our starting capital?
– Don't worry. We'll rattle some up somehow. Somehow we'll ***.
5. – You know, the first twelve kilometres are the worst.
– Yes, after that you can just run and run. You seem to ***.
6. – Look, Bert, do I tell 'er I love 'er or don't I?
– Yeah. ***, Sid. Nothing ventured, nothing gained. Faint 'eart never won a fair lady, yer know.
7. – Oh, no! What a scandal! How did the blasted press ***?
– Some rat must have told them. Some Judas.
8. – I think I should act immediately, Jeeves. No delay, what?
– No, Sir. No. Far better to be diplomatic, to wait and ***.
9. – You're not against the bill, then?
– On the contrary, I ***. I hope it is passed by a clear majority.
10. – Is this peasants' revolt to be taken seriously, Lord Chancellor?
– I'm afraid it must be, Your Majesty. It could be the proverbial ***, an unhappy presage of things to come.

Options

A. to get your second wind / B. to get wind of sth. / C. to get the wind up / D. to raise the wind / E. to see which way the wind blows / F. there is something in the wind / G. to be a straw in the wind / H. to throw caution to the winds / I. to whistle in the wind / J. to wish sth. a fair wind

> “*Two central features identify an idiom. The meaning of the idiomatic expression cannot be deduced by examining the meaning of the lexemes. And the expression is fixed, both grammatically and lexically.*”

DAVID CRYSTAL, *Cambridge Encyclopaedia of the English Language*

Field 2: Essential Weather

Your Task

Complete the crossword below, which is made up of twenty-seven basic idioms derived from basic weather conditions. The correct answers are to be found on page 148.

Crossword

Clues

Across

2. poltern, toben; prahlen (7)
8. 'mal so, mal so' reagieren (4,3,3,4)
9. unverhoffter Glücksfall (8)
10. Stopp (bei Löhnen, Preisen) (6)
13. stürmen, stürzen; wütend ausstoßen (5)
14. dreist; cool (4)
15. Eindruck machen (3,3)
16. auftauen (von Personen) (4)
17. Wind von etwas bekommen: *get ___ of sth.* (4)
18. Kugelhagel: ___ *of bullets* (4)
20. das Eis brechen: *to break the ___* (3)
23. Er kommt hereingeschneit: *he ___* (7,2)
24. Im Eifer des Gefechts: *in the ___ of the argument* (4)
25. vage (4)
26. verdunkeln, trüben (5)

Down

1. Milchglas: ___ *glass* (7)
3. Ruhe vor dem Sturm (4,6,3,5)
4. lawinenartig anwachsen (8)
5. Nicht den blassesten Schimmer haben: *to have not the ___* (8,4)
6. unpässlich (5,3,7)
7. ratlos sein: *to be in a ___* (3)
11. sich in eine gefährliche Lage begeben: *to skate on ___* (4,3)
12. jn. kaltstellen: *to leave s. o. in the ___* (4)
15. (sich) beruhigen ___ *down* (4)
19. an die Öffentlichkeit bringen (3)
21. brüllen, donnern (7)
22. Unklarheit; Verwirrtheit (4)

Field 3: Weather, Hot and Cold

Your Task

Read the text below on the English public school novel and then decide which of the idioms of temperature below best complete the idiom and sense. The correct answers are to be found on page 148.

Article

The public school novel (or drama or film) from Th. Hughes's *Tom Brown's Schooldays* (1857) to William Boyd's *School Ties* (1985) is one of the fascinating yet neglected sub-genres in English literature. Though they caused [1] ___ debate in their day, the works tend to be left out in the [2] ___ by the traditional canon.

The fascination of the genre is fourfold. Firstly, the novels are situated in the [3] ___ atmosphere of a 'total institution', each (of course) a [4] ___ of iniquity, vice and whatnot. From the outset, the trials and privations of school life make things [5] ___ for the protagonist. Inevitably, our hero or heroine gets into [6] ___ water: he or she may suffer injustices designed to make one's blood run [7] ___; may be given the [8] ___ shoulder and sent to Coventry; may be exposed, in the [9] ___ of the moment, to all types of temptation. Will the protagonist, – inevitably a [10] ___-blooded youngster, a young [11] ___ – manage to keep [12] ___, to maintain English [13] ___?

Secondly, the genre, especially in its trivial form, has a remarkably enduring quality. The same conflicts cause [14] ___ to rise. The same old-fashioned teachers talk [15] ___ air. The same new teachers, always [16] ___ favourites, pour [17] ___ water on traditional ideals.

Thirdly, as the above suggests, the genre does change markedly with time. Viewed historically, the genre blows [18] ___ and [19] ___ on the institution it portrays. Hot in Th. Hughes and Dean Farrar, cold from Alec Waugh's *Loom of Youth* (1917) on. The authors gradually get [20] ___ feet, and the schools begin to feel the [21] ___. Yesterday's vice becomes today's ideal. Yesterday's [22] ___ potato is today's truism. More and more the genre views the institution in the [23] ___ light of day and finds it wanting.

And finally, there is something very English (not Scottish or Welsh) about the genre. Of course there are major German novels parallel – from Hesse's *Unterm Rad* (1906) and Musil's *Törless* (1906) to Dittberner's *Das Internat* (1974). There is the great French school novel such as Alain Fournier's *Le grand Meaulnes* (1913). Each of them treats the school distinctly [24] ___. But they lack the tradition and intertextuality, lack the ongoing, urgent discussion of a major institution of the land. The English genre, in its shifts and developments, its changing ideas and ideals, is a [25] ___ to the state of the nation.

Options

cold (7x) / cool(ly) (2x) / heat (2x) / heated / hot (7x) / hotbed / hothead / hothouse / hot-line / sang-froid / temperature(s)

Field 4: More Extreme Weather

Your Task

Complete the crossword below, noting that the first letter of each word and the number of letters in each word are given. The correct answers are to be found on page 148.

Crossword

Clues

1. Happy?! She was deliriously happy! Over the moon, on (5,4)!
2. Just four days after the ad appeared, they were overwhelmed – (6,5) – with requests for their new product.
3. Her first appearance in the Scala was a triumph. She took Milan (2,5).
4. 'You will be careful, Sally, won't you?' – 'Yes, don't worry, I'll keep a (7,3,4).'

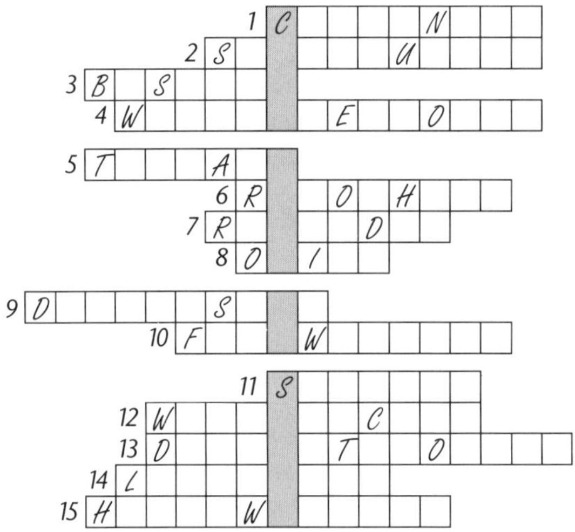

5. The perpetrator of the foul deed had disappeared – vanished into (4,3).
6. The situation was desperate, but there was still a (3,2,4) if they acted swiftly.
7. 'Don't let's spend all the money, dear. Let's put some aside for a (5,3).'
8. It was a bold project. Too bold, the directors decided. They put it (2,3) for a year or two.
9. 'Goodness, how young Amelia has changed! She used to be so innocent, as pure as the (6,4). But now look at her!'
10. 'Just like Barry to desert us in a crisis. I suspected he was just a (4,7) friend. Now we have the living proof.'
11. 'Uhuh. The boss in a foul mood again. Watch out for (7) again today, folks.'
12. 'Has she changed her mind again?! She changes like a (7,4)!'
13. It was a big donation. Generous. Noble-minded. But compared with the size of the problem it was just the proverbial (4,2,3,5).
14. The test was far easier than expected. She went through it as fast as (9)!
15. Or had she overlooked something? Why were the other candidates apparently making such (5,7) of it?

Key Phrase: They were together through thick and thin, (4,4,2,5).

5

UNIT

Idioms of the Natural World

Field 1: Basic Nature

Your Task

Read the text below and then decide which of the sixteen characters involved is best characterised by which of the basic idioms of Nature listed below. The correct answers are to be found on page 148.

Text

Wasn't life full of surprises! What an amazing, fascinating reunion! And all her classmates of ten years back had come! Well, not Hubert of course. So sad about his fatal accident two years ago .... Not everyone had changed. Look at Jeremy! Still randy, still into wine, women and song! And Charlotte certainly *looked* as if she was still taking the path of least resistance. Still 'Charlotte the harlot'! And trust Georgina to marry a moneybags! She must lead a life of luxury! Ingrid was still incorrigibly optimistic and blue-eyed, of course. Lew seemed not just crazy but fit for an asylum. Bashful Basil was as frail and spineless as ever. And Freddy was still a real pain in the ****. But hadn't Nigel done well, setting up his own business! And Margaret seemed to be rolling in it working at the Stock Exchange. Enid said she wanted to follow in her footsteps. And for Kay and Daniel the prospects were good, too. They'd married, and clever old Kay seemed to be a professor in the making. Olive? Hard to discover what she was up to. She gave such evasive answers! But fancy puritanical Patrick becoming a drop-out and bumming around all over the globe! Why had she herself changed so little? Shy, modest Annabelle. Always the bridesmaid, never the bride. Perhaps she should have a word with Jeremy... .

Cast

ANNABELLE – BASIL – CHARLOTTE – DANIEL – ENID – FREDDY – GEORGINA – HUBERT – INGRID – JEREMY – KAY – LEW – MARGARET – NIGEL – OLIVE – PATRICK

Options

A. to be a wilting lily / B. to push up daisies / C. to take the primrose path / D. to be a bed of roses / E. to be a weed / F. to be a wallflower / G. to have a rosy future / H. to look through rose-coloured spectacles / I. to be a thorn in the flesh/side / J. to sow one's wild oats / K. to be a rolling stone / L. to be off one's nut / M. to be a budding (...) / N. to beat about the bush / O. to be in clover / P. to branch out on one's own / Q. to take a leaf out of s.o.'s book / R. to bark up the wrong tree

> *I have laboured to refine our language to grammatical purity, and to clean it from colloquial barbarisms, licentious idioms, and irregular combinations.*

DR SAMUEL JOHNSON, *The Rambler*, 15 January, 1752

Field 2: Natural Dialogue

Your Task

Imagine you are involved in the mini-dialogues below. Which of the idioms of Nature listed beneath would best fit which situation? The correct answers are to be found on page 149.

Dialogues

1. – When you're up at university, don't spend all your time swotting!
– No, *carpe diem*, my dears! ***!
2. – Brilliant speech, old man! Cicero couldn't have done better! Worthy of Churchill in his prime! Olivier and Gielgud ...
– Thanks, but don't exaggerate, don't ***.
3. – What is your advice to the government at this critical time?
– They must ***. Draconian measures are the only way open to us.
4. – Venus will have to keep in peak form to ward off the youngsters!
– Yes, she'll have to fight, have to ***. But tennis will be the winner.
5. – Really, you know, we should dismiss him.
– True, but it *** to sack a man who has done so much for us.
6. – Isn't it difficult to have a long conversation with her?
– Yes, it always ends in confusion! She's always ***.
7. – What a career! Two years ago a humble student and now ***!
– Yes, but these new university courses do produce high-fliers.
8. – Oh, hell, we're really in the soup this time!
– Yes, we're sure ***. Oh what a tangled web we weave ..., eh?
9. – ***, Sally? A penny for your thoughts!
– Thanks. Yes, I've got an almighty problem to think over.
10. – My English has really gone downhill!
– Yes, appallingly! Shockingly! You've really ***.
11. – It would be bold, but we could sell our American subsidiary.
– What?! Our major source of revenue! No, that would be ***!
12. – You looking for your personal file too, Lothar?
– Yes, but in this labyrinthine *Stasi* place you might as well ***.
13. – Isn't it high time they had a change of government?
– Yes, let's hope they *** that lot at the next opportunity.
14. – What a day! Boy, am I fagged out! Exhausted!
– Me, too. It's these idioms. I'm off to get some sleep. I must ***.

Options

A. to be at the top of the tree / B. to be up a gum tree / C. to chew the cud / D. to eat the seed-corn / E. to gather rosebuds while ye may / F. to get hold of the wrong end of the stick / G. to gild the lily / H. to go against the grain / I. to go to seed / J. to grasp the nettle / K. to hit the hay / L. to look for a needle in a haystack / M. to look to one's laurels / N. to turf out

Field 3: The Gardening Life

Your Task

Read the headlines below, each of which contains one or more idioms derived from the field of gardening, and then select the German translation below which best conveys the meaning of the word or phrase underlined. The correct answers are to be found on page 149.

Headlines

1. **IRA grass reveals identity of killers**
2. CHANCELLOR POINTS TO 'GREEN SHOOTS' OF RECOVERY
3. **Millions lopped off Arts budget**
4. **NEW MANAGEMENT TO 'CUT OUT DEAD WOOD'**
5. ***Government led us up the garden path, protesters claim***
6. Killer Virus in Africa Cuts Them Down in Their Thousands
7. **EVIDENCE PLANTED, MAINTAIN SUSPECTS**
8. **'We Will Not Let the Grass Grow Under Our Feet', Pledges PM**
9. HEAVILY PRUNED *HAMLET* TEXT RILES PURISTS
10. **OFFICIAL: ROWDY PUPILS TO BE TURFED OUT**
11. PM GOES ON THE STUMP
12. **NEWCOMERS CHERRY-PICK IDEAS, CLAIM ICI**
13. **'Everything in Garden Lovely', Claims Local Party**
14. GOALIE IS 'PICK OF THE BUNCH', SAYS MANAGER
15. **NEW INDUSTRIES TAKE ROOT IN WELSH VALLEYS**
16. TURF NEWS

Options

A. andrehen, zustecken / B. erste Anzeichen / C. alles in Butter / D. dahinraffen / E. nicht lange fackeln, keine Zeit verschwenden / F. Fuß fassen / G. Informant / H. das Beste klauen, stehlen / I. gekürzt / J. Leistungstärkste(r) / K. an der Nase herumführen / L. Pferderennen / M. der Schule verwiesen / N. gestrichen / O. Gegend als Wahlredner bereisen / P. Veraltetes, Überholtes, Ballast entfernen

Field 4: Trees and Bushes

Your Task

Complete the crossword below, which is made up of twenty-five idioms derived from bushes and trees. The correct answers are to be found on page 149.

Crossword

Across

3. In einem Dilemma sein: *caught in a* ___ (5,5)
5. & 14. Gewaltdrohung: *policy of the* ___ (3,5)
7. neues Leben beginnen*: turn over a new* ___ (4)
8. erschöpfen: *to* ___ (3) *the strength of*
11. Jüngling, Grünschnabel (7)
13. um den heißen Brei herum gehen: *to beat about the* ___ (4)
14. see 5 across
15. Hauptverkehrsader: ___ (5) *road*
16. gertenschlank (7)
20. buschig (bei Augenbrauen) (5)
21. Fernverbindung: ___ (5) *call*
22. britisch-tapfere Männer: *hearts of* ___ (3)
23. stammen von: ___ (4) *from*
24. sich nicht festlegen (5)

Down

1. "berappen": ___ (5) *up*
2. Prügelstrafe wiedereinführen: *bring back the* ___ (5)
4. durchblättern: (4,7)
6. sanfte Geräuschkulisse des Cricket-Spiels: *the sound of leather on* ___ (6)
7. kinderleicht: *as easy as falling off a* ___ (3)
9. Stammbaum: (6,4)
10. leere Hülse (4)
12. eine harte Nuß: *a hard* ___ (3) *to crack*
17. die amerik. Elite-Unis: ___ (3) *league*
18. in die Wildnis gehen: (Aus/NZEng) *go* ___ (4)
19. durch und durch korrupt, kernfaul: *rotten to the* ___ (4)

6 UNIT Idiomatic Structures I

Field 1: Pairs of Adjectives or Adverbs

Your Task

Each of the twenty-two idioms below consists of a pair of adjectives or adverbs. Show that you grasp their meaning by fitting them into the sentence in which they best complete the sense. The correct answers are on page 149.

Sentences

1. In the ___ past, there was no such thing as artificial fertiliser.
2. She doesn't believe in doing anything fast. She's always ___ .
3. They looked for it ___, but it was nowhere to be found.
4. 'That was settled and decided last week. It's all ___.'
5. It was a one-day wonder. Like so many men he was just ___.
6. 'Oh, stand up for yourself a bit more. Don't be so ___.'
7. Sir Walter was an early riser, always ___ by six and normally ten or so foolscap pages written before breakfast.
8. Steffi had no excuses: Lindsay beat her clearly, ___.
9. Why does that professor always act so ___? Arrogant devil!
10. You won't meet many people so unselfish and charitable. Such people are ___ nowadays.
11. 'All the nice girls love a sailor: bright and breezy, ___.'
12. Boy, does he look middle-aged! All ___.
13. Because of the many protests, the game will be re-played. Yesterday's result is now ___.
14. 'Thank goodness she didn't lecture as long as last week! ___ this time by comparison.'
15. Those two have been through it all together, through ___.
16. 'The exact figures we don't have: here's a ___ guestimate.'
17. 'He was hoping to inherit from Grandma. But she's still ___ at 95!'
18. 'I don't want anything special. Just a ___ one.'
19. She's forever hoovering and polishing. Her flat is appallingly ___, all ___.
20. 'Putting it briefly, and without wanting to put too fine a point on it, ___ of it is: you've failed – you're out on your neck.'
21. 'Can I bring back anything from Malaysia, honey?' – 'Just come back ___, my sweetie pie.'

Options

A. alive and kicking / B. common or garden / C. cut and dried / D. dim and distant / E. fair and square / F. fat and forty / G. few and far between / H. free and easy / I. here today and gone tomorrow / J. high and low / K. high and mighty / L. the long and the short / M. meek and mild / N. neat and tidy / O. null and void / P. rough and ready / Q. safe and sound / R. short and sweet / S. slow but sure / T. spick and span / U. thick and thin / V. up and about

Field 2: The 'as ... as' Construction I

Your Task

Part A.
Each of the adjectives on the left below is commonly used with one of the nouns on the right in an 'as ... as' construction. Fit the idioms together and check your answers on page 150, before going on to Part B opposite.

Idioms

as		as	
1.	black	A.	a cucumber
2.	blind	B.	a bug in a rug
3.	bold	C.	old boots
4.	bright	D.	mustard
5.	brown	E.	gold
6.	busy	F.	tinder
7.	cool	G.	death (warmed up)
8.	dead [2]	H.	Job
9.	deaf	I.	life
10.	drunk	J.	a lark
11.	dry	K.	button
12.	fit	L.	nails
13.	fresh	M.	a cricket
14.	good	N.	a post
15.	happy [3]	O.	a picture
16.	hard	P.	mutton
17.	keen	Q.	a bat
18.	large	R.	a fiddle
19.	mad	S.	a berry
20.	merry	T.	a church mouse
21.	pale	U.	a judge
22.	patient	V.	a daisy
23.	poor	W.	Solomon
24.	pretty	X.	brass
25.	right	Y.	a doornail
26.	snug	Z.	toast
27.	steady	AA.	a monkey
28.	sober	BB.	the day is long
29.	tough	CC.	rain
30.	tricky	DD.	a sheet
31.	warm	EE.	a sandboy
32.	white	FF.	a lord
33.	wise	GG.	a rock
		HH.	a bee
		II.	a hatter
		JJ.	a cinder

Your Task

Part B.

In each of the sentences below, insert one (or more) of the 'as .. as' phrases opposite so as to complete the idiom and the sense. The correct answers are to be found on page 150.

Sentences

1. The entire centre of the old village had burned to the ground in one night. The charred remains were as ___ in the morning light. After the long, dry summer the old half-timbered houses had been as ___.
2. 'Pardon me, Sir. Have you been drinking and driving, Sir?' – 'Nonshense, Conshtable, can't you shee I'm ash ___.'
3. The children were a baby-sitter's dream – as ___.
4. I really slept well last night, as ___, and this morning I felt as ___.
5. Yes, she's a clever young lass – as ___.
6. She was really poorly last week: on Thursday, she looked as ___. But now she seems as ___.
7. After long days on the beaches at Nice, Antibes and St Tropez, they were both as ___.
8. She's a tower of strength in a crisis. She always keeps as ___.
9. You can tell these students will go a long way – they're as ___.
10. 'Old man Maddocks? He kicked the bucket years ago! He's as ___!' – 'Eh?! I could have sworn I saw him yesterday as ___.'

11. She's been round the bend for years. She's as ___.
12. I don't feel any ill-effects from my weekend marathon. I must be as ___.
13. He marched into the manager's office as ___ and demanded a thumping big wage increase.
14. 'Oh, what a beautiful baby, my dear – as ___.'
15. They rarely have two pennies to rub together. They're as ___.
16. It's difficult to negotiate with them. They're tough and more than tough, as ___.
17. No goals against for five weeks now! Our defence is as ___.
18. 'Can you read this to me? Without my specs I'm as ___.'
19. 'You really got sozzled last night. You were as ___.'
20. You have to shout to get through to grandma. She's as ___.

21. She always seems so engrossed, so contented. She's as ___.
22. 'How was the seminar? Lively?' – 'Far from it. As ___.'
23. To sit through his lecture you need to be as ___. To understand its obscurities you have to be as ___.
24. 'It's not the warmest of rooms. But with the windows shut, the heating turned up full blast and three pullovers on, I'm as ___.'

For further 'as ... as' idioms see page 100.

Field 3: The 'Verb + Like' Construction

Your Task

The twenty-five idioms below all follow the 'verb + like' pattern. Fit the two parts of each idiom together, noting that on the right two 'answers' are bluff. The correct answers are to be found on page 150.

Idioms

	like	
A. to avoid s.o./sth.		1. fighting cocks
B. be off		2. a chimney
C. come down on s.o.		3. a shot
D. drink		4. the plague
E. eat		5. hot cakes
F. fight		6. a Trojan
G. get on		7. the wind
H. go		8. wildfire
I. go		9. a trooper
J. go		10. a Brando
K. live		11. a log
L. run		12. a horse
M. run free/flee		13. a leaf
N. sell		14. the clappers
O. sing		15. a bat out of hell
P. shake/tremble/quiver		16. water
Q. sleep		17. a duck to water
R. smoke		18. a ton of bricks
S. spend money		19. a bomb
T. spread		20. a hare
		21. nightingale
U. stink		22. cat and dogs
V. swear		23. Persephone
W. swim		24. a fish [2]
X. take to sth. like		25. a house on fire
Y. work		26. polecat

For more verb + like constructions, see page 99.

Field 4: Eponyms I

Your Task

Study the figures on the left, each of whom has become an 'eponymist' by giving his or her name to a common object or common concept listed on the right. Who gave the name to what, and what is the object or concept thus called? The correct answers are to be found on page 150.

Eponymists

1. Sir Donald BAILEY, engineer
2. Ladislav BIRO, artist
3. Amelia BLOOMER, feminist
4. Thomas BOWDLER, physician
5. John BOWLER, hatter
6. Charles BOYCOTT, farmer
7. Louis BRAILLE, blind man
8. Lord CARDIGAN, soldier
9. Rudolf DIESEL, engineer
10. Giuseppe GARIBALDI, patriot
11. Hans GEIGER, nuclear physicist
12. Elbridge GERRY, US governor
13. Thomas HOBSON, innkeeper
14. Patrick HOOLIGAN, Irish father
15. Leslie HORE-BELISHA, transport minister
16. Ned LUDD, labourer
17. Thomas MALTHUS, economist
18. Charles MACKINTOSH, textile chemist
19. Samuel MAVERICK, rancher
20. Franz MESMER, hypnotist
21. Louis PASTEUR, chemist
22. Samuel PLIMSOLL, MP
23. PYHRRUS, king of Epirus
24. Vidkun QUISLING, soldier/politician
25. Lord SANDWICH, gambler
26. Rev. W. A. SPOONER, classicist
27. Duke of WELLINGTON, soldier

A. light, rubber-soled gym shoe
B. process of purifying (milk)
C. engine based on air compression ignition
D. illuminated beacon at pedestrian crossing
E. a victory which is no victory
F. destruction of machines
G. (often talented) outsider
H. embargo
I. traitor
J. ball-point pen
K. currant biscuit ('squashed fly')
L. light raincoat
M. light meat meal enclosed in bread
N. alphabet for the blind
O. women's knickerbockers
P. soft woollen jacket
Q. stiff, low-crowned felt hat
R. counter for radio-active disintegration
S. temporary military bridge
T. removal of 'indecent' passages from books
U. transposition of initial letters of words
V. limitation of population
W. no choice at all
X. to 'bewitch', induce sleep by animal magnetism
Y. rowdy behaviour
Z. long rubber boots
AA. cheating by playing with election boundaries

For more eponyms, see page 103.

Step 5: British Proverbs I

Your Task

Below are twenty-six British proverbs, each of which, however, has been cut in half, the halves then being jumbled up. Connect the beginning on the left with the correct ending on the right and state the proverb's meaning. The correct answers are to be found on page 152.

Proverbs

1. It's no use crying	A. until you come to them
2. Absence makes the	B. pound foolish
3. A bad workman always	C. has its/his day
4. Actions speak	D. wise after the event
5. Don't cross your bridges	E. where it is narrowest
6. All good things	F. lead to Rome
7. It's an ill wind that	G. hangs long
8. All's fair	H. has no turning
9. Cross the stream	I. over spilt milk
10. The early bird	J. is sweetest
11. It's easy to be	K. louder than words
12. All roads	L. blames his tools
13. A creaking gate	M. so you lie on it
14. Honesty	N. blows nobody any good
15. As you make your bed	O. heart grow fonder
16. Forbidden fruit	P. all wounds
17. Time heals	Q. be choosers
18. Those whom the gods love	R. is the best policy
19. Fine words	S. come to an end
20. Beggars can't/mustn't	T. butter no parsnips
21. All work and no play	U. where angels fear to tread
22. A fool and his	V. makes Jack a dull boy
23. Fools rush in	W. in love and war
24. Every dog	X. catches the worm
25. It's a long lane that	Y. money are soon parted
26. Penny wise	Z. die young

For more British proverbs see page 138.

Revision I

Exercise 1: Literary Lives

Your Task

In each of the sentences below, insert one of the phrases learned in the foregoing six units to complete the idiom and the sense. The correct answers are to be found on page 152.

Sentences

1. Keats, perhaps the most tragic of British poets, was ___ in his prime by tuberculosis when still only in his mid-twenties.
2. George Eliot's output is impressive for its broad ___: key translations, probing social novels, novellas, poetry and superb letters.
3. Working at a ___ under threat of terminal illness, Anthony Burgess completed *The Doctor is Sick* (1964) in fewer than six weeks.
4. Rose Macaulay's star was in the ___ in the 1920s, when her works were more widely read than those of, say, Virginia Woolf.
5. Of all British poets, Pope has perhaps the most intellectual, astringent, ___ wit.
6. Disraeli was surely the best novelist ever to become Conservative prime minister. Yet his novels are not just ___ in import.
7. Dylan Thomas and Brendan Behan were two of the great drinkers among British writers of the C 20th, each allegedly often as ___.
8. Byron's rise to fame was ___: with *Childe Harold's Pilgrimage* (1812), he almost overnight achieved dominance of the literary scene.
9. Galsworthy reached the ___ of his creativity with the first three volumes of the *Forsythe Saga*; the subsequent two trilogies are a ___.
10. What a ___ of gifted novelists lived and worked in the Glasgow of the 1980s and 1990s – Kelman, Gray, Banks, Spence, Torrington...
11. Dramatist, novelist, religious tract-writer, pioneer of the Sunday School movement and *habituée* of the London salons of the late eighteenth century, Hannah More was almost the archetypal ___.
12. Theodor Fontane was the late developer among European novelists. Has any British writer achieved so much in such a ___?
13. The meandering form of Kerouac's novel *On the Road* (1957), the bible of the beatnik generation, is the embodiment of the life of the roving hobo, the ___.
14. The longer the twentieth century went on, the more Huxley's scientific dystopia *Brave New World* (1932) seemed a ___ of things to come.
15. The rich, 'euphuistic' rhetoric of Lyly's verse can today seem overdone, often tending to ___ the ___.
16. The underground newspapers of the Radicals Cobbett, Hetherington and Wooler were a real ___ in the flesh of the government in the pre-Reform days of the 1810s and 1820s.

Exercise 2: Making Tracks

Your Task

Read the text below on the development of the British railway system and then decide which of the idioms learned in the foregoing six units best complete the idiom and sense. The correct answers are to be found on page 152.

Text

The railway was the third infrastructure of Britain's first Industrial Revolution, following the canal and the turnpike road.

Railway building began in the 1830s, especially in the years 1835-7, when many of the [1] ___ routes were established, but [2] ___ in the period of 'railway mania' in 1845-7. In those years, investors and constructors threw caution to the [3] ___ and built, built, built. There were relatively few regulations, little red [4] ___. It was easy to raise the [5] ___ with so much excess capital in the early Victorian economy. Thus the railways straddled the land with [6] ___-league boots, rival companies often building rival lines, sometimes higgledy-piggledy and [7] ___ and ready. By 1860 there were 9,069 miles of railway, the densest network in the world. One can imagine the [8] ___ caused by such construction work, the turmoil brought by the Irish 'navigators', the same rough and tough workforce which had created the canals. (If one can't, then one should study Dickens's contributions to *Household Words* and *All the Year Round*.)

The system, all but complete by 1890, reached its [9] ___ in 1920, only to fall away in the inter-war years, being nationalised in 1947. In the early 1960s, the now notorious Beeching Report portrayed the British network as being in the [10] ___ of its life. For good or for ill, this set the [11] ___ for the coming years. Management was now determined to cut out dead [12] ___. Thousands of miles of track were [13] ___. Many [14] ___ lines were [15] ___ off. Local communities moved [16] ___ and [17] ___ to save their local line. But to no avail. The government was not prepared to [18] ___ any more money in to what it saw as a dying system. The network shrank to only 55% of its 1914 extent. The much-loved side-line, the type depicted famously in Edith Nesbit's *The Railway Children* (1906), was no more.

A [19] ___ had been crossed. And another was crossed in the 1980s when the state-owned system was re-privatised. Of course today's trains are [20] ___ away from the 'puffing Billies' of [21] ___. But in other ways, it was back to [22] ___, back to the Victorian days of rival companies and criss-cross systems. Many held privatisation responsible for the sad spate of accidents in the 1980s and 1990s. Things had certainly come to an unhappy [23] ___.

Have the railways in Britain had their [24] ___? Have they reached the end of the [25] ___? It is an open question. The past, however, seems sadly to show that the country does not get the infrastructure it deserves: the infrastructure invents the country it requires.

7 UNIT Idioms of Insects, Birds and Fish

Field 1: The Birds of the Air

Your Task

In each of the sentences below, insert one (or more) of the bird names listed beneath to complete the idiom and the sense. The correct answers are to be found on page 152.

Sentences

1. 'The PM is adopting an ___ policy, hiding from reality. Instead of facing the issues, he just ___ off on official tours and suchlike.'
2. Though unfinished, the symphony is a magnificent ___-song, both for its composer and for the Romantic Age, which bows out in these rich, plangent, clamorous, yearnful chords.
3. 'She's a real ___: a sower of rebellion, revolution and riot.'
4. 'My present *Hausarbeit* is so gripping I've become a real ___, working into the early hours in the sheer exhilaration of thinking.'
5. 'Let's talk ___. I prefer to get down to business straightaway.'
6. His bigamy exposed, the candidate was finished, a dead ___, in the Bible Belt. The voters gave him the ___, hissing his speeches.
7. 'He's forever ___ about his damn family! He's besotted with them. When it comes to the Pratt-Slymes, all his ___ are ___!'
8. 'We must be careful in these days of futures and junk bonds: we cannot take risks and play ___ and ___ with our money.'
9. 'The kids have really blossomed! Two years ago they were ugly ___, but now they're lively, self-confident – and happy too!'
10. 'Watch out!! Phew! Another near miss! If you go on ___- walking across the road like that, your days'll soon be numbered!'
11. 'Yes, dreadful, isn't it! She's always talking! Even during lectures she chatters like a ___! And it's so embarrassing!'
12. 'How far is it?' – 'Well, it's seven miles as the ___ flies, but in reality, round the estuary, it's about twenty-five miles.'
13. 'I'm an early riser this fine weather! Up with the ___ each morning to enjoy every breath of life I can eagerly, greedily suck in!'
14. 'It's a terrible impasse. Our hands are tied. We've got an ___ round our necks.'

Options

albatross / bird / crow (2x) / drake(s) / duck(ling)(s) (3x) / goose (geese) / jay / lark / magpie / night bird / ostrich / stormy petrel / swan(s) (3x) / turkey

> *Jedermann weiß, dass man beim Englischlernen auf die zahlreichen idiomatischen Wendungen zu achten hat.*

ERNST LEISI, CHRISTIAN MAIR, *Das heutige Englisch* (1999)

Field 2: Insects

Your Task

Consider the idioms below and decide which of the explanations beneath is likely to be the genuine meaning. The correct answers are to be found on page 153.

Idioms

1. **to think one is the bee's knees**
   = to think one is A. insignificant B. all-important C. a maker and shaker D. rather more athletic than one in fact is

2. **a fly-on-the-wall report**
   = a report that is A. detailed B. wholly out of proportion C. liable to make some heads roll D. written as if by an insider

3. **We were badly stung**
   = we were A. 'ripped off' B. very surprised C. shocked D. ill-treated, even man-handled

4. **to have ants in the pants**
   = to be A. very active B. a money-bags C. long unwashed D. unable to keep still

5. **a fire-bug**
   = a(n) A. type of fire-work B. arsonist C. pistol D. armed schoolchild

6. **to drone on**
   = to A. work hard B. continue unruffled on one's way C. to talk and talk D. study late at night

7. **a nit-picker**
   = a A. school doctor B. pest-controller C. hair-splitting pedant D. manager who chooses bad staff

8. **to have a bee in one's bonnet**
   = to A. be totally crazy B. have an *idée fixe* C. be hyper-active D. be intellectually aware and a live-wire

9. **squashed flies**
   = A. currant biscuits B. enemies overcome C. past problems D. the snows of yesteryear *(les neiges d'antan)*

10. **a waspish person**
    = a person who is A. quick off the mark B. vindictive C. intellectually sharp and acute D. irritable

Field 3: Insects, Molluscs and Invertebrates

Your Task

Read the text below in its entirety and then decide, in each case, which of the insect or mollusc idioms listed beneath best completes the sense. The correct answers are to be found on page 153.

Text

Few sieges [1] ___ their way into the collective consciousness except the very spectacular, like Troy, or the very vindictive, like Carthage and Drogheda, or those where a relief force ultimately does come to the rescue – Londonderry, Lucknow, Mafeking. In such cases, however, the siege does not just enter history: it becomes myth.
Consider Lucknow in the great northern plain of India, besieged during the Sepoy Mutiny in the summer of 1857. Even the earliest diaries, ballads and histories tend to mythologise. Outside, in the plains, the callous insurgents swarming like [2] ___, rushing like [3] ___ to the candle as each assault is launched. Inside, the stalwart English commander – no [4] ___ on him! – capably mounting what defence he can. His stout-hearted men, as chirpy as [5] ___. All working like [6] ___. All making a [7] ___-line for the ramparts when an attack is imminent. All vigilantly preparing for the next assault long after the natives have [8] ___ off. And even the slender British womenfolk with their [9] ___ waists doing their bit.
It takes a post-imperial age, and perhaps different literary genres, to give a fuller, truer picture. Perhaps the first assaults were mere [10] ___-bites, the assailants dispatched as easily as swatting [11] ___. But not the later. The siege was nasty, and particularly nasty because it was slow. It proceeded at a [12] ___'s pace, even [13] ___. But, little by little, the deprivations increased, the ailments augmented, the diseases spread, hope flagged. And finally the besieged garrison and beleaguered inhabitants fell like [14] ___. In the heats of the Indian summer even the most minor of [15] ___ could soon be aggravated into an appalling infection.
Such is the image in J. G. Farrell's much-praised historical novel *The Siege of Krishnapur* (1973), but even that is rather male-dominated and eurocentric. Perhaps one should turn to an Indian novel, Manohar Malgonkar's *The Devil's Wind: Nana Saheb's Story* (1972) to gain a welcome glimpse of the other side of the picture. Certainly, even more than the risings in the Canadas in 1837, the Sepoy Mutiny showed that the British had stirred up a [16] ___ nest with their imperial ambitions. At the very time that the Second British Empire was taking shape, here was the writing on the wall.

Options

bee / beetle / bug(s) / crickets / drone / flea(s) / fly *or* flies (3x) / hornet(s) / moth(s) / slug(gish) / snail / termite(s) / wasp(s) / worm

Field 4: Fish, Shellfish and Fishing

Your Task

In each of the sentences in Parts 1 and 2 below, insert one (or more) of the fish or fishing idioms listed beneath to complete the idiom and the sense. The correct answers are to be found on page 153.

Sentences

Part 1

1. 'And now here she comes, the Princess herself, wearing a fetching ___-pink ensemble with matching hat and accessories.'
2. The plan will please no-one: it is neither one thing nor the other, neither ___, flesh, fowl nor good ___.
3. 'She's an unfeeling person, a real cold ___.'
4. The wretched slaves were packed like ___ into the hold of the ship.
5. 'Your play is highly creative, provocative and postmodern, Laetitia, but will it please the public? Is it not likely to be ___ to the general?'
6. 'Don't ask him to organise it! He couldn't run a ___ stall!'
7. He was a poor rower indeed, always catching ___.
8. 'Have no financial dealings with him – the man's a ___.'
9. 'It is a most encouraging and humane gesture, one which warms the very ___ of my heart.'
10. 'It is only a tiny investment and a risk well worth taking in light of the possible gains. Sometimes one must throw a ___ to catch a ___.'
11. 'The Girl Guides' Camp was super, Dad. We had a ___ of a time!'
12. They are unimportant people here, just ___, ___, ___ even.

Options

caviar / cockle(s) / crab(s) / fish (2x) / mackerel / minnow(s) / red herring / salmon / sardine(s) / shark / small fry / sprat / tiddlers / whale / whelk

Sentences

Part 2

1. This is utterly appalling. We must protest at this. We must ***.
2. She went to imperial India, the Raj, in the ***, out for a husband.
3. 'Did they respond to your incentive?' – 'Yes, they ***.'
4. 'Of course, I myself am a far from brilliant mind...' – '*** again?'
5. It was a compelling, far-ranging comparative essay with broad horizons. The author really ***.
6. He's a great Camus and Enzensberger fan, totally *** on them.
7. 'I'm suspicious. There's something very odd here. It's ***.'
8. 'What are you after? What are you ***, eh?'
9. Property speculation in and around Nice is not the cleanest of businesses, as Graham Greene showed. To invest there is to ***.
10. She got the job when the head-hunters came to the University *** talent. But sadly she was out of her element in the new job, a ***.

Options

A. to angle for sth. / B. to be a fish out of water / C. to cast one's nets wide(ly) / D. to cry 'stinking fish' / E. to fish for compliments / F. to fish in troubled (or murky) waters / G. the fishing fleet / H. to be fishy / I. to be hooked on / J. to rise to the bait / K. to trawl for

8 UNIT Idioms of Larger Animals

Field 1: The Basic Animal in Man

Your Task

Complete the crossword below, noting that the first letter of each word and the number of letters in each word are given. The correct answers are to be found on page 153.

Crossword

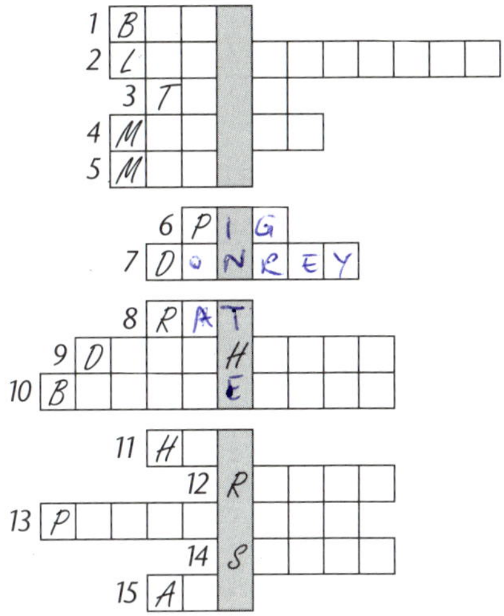

Clues

1. A somewhat crazy person is called (4).
2. A most courageous person is described as (4-7).
3. A sycophantic person is known as a (4).
4. A mischievous or playful child is a little (6).
5. A stubborn person is a (4).
6. A greedy person with an excessive appetite is a (3).
7. A foolish individual is a (6).
8. A person who deserts friends or a cause is a (3).
9. A person of as yet unknown abilities is a (4, 5).
10. A man with a thick neck can be described as (4-6).
11. A greedy person who wolfs his or her food is a (3).
12. A person who is illtempered or irritated is (5).
13. Another description of a stubborn person is (3-6)
14. A timid or stupid person is a (5).
15. A foolish individual can also be called an (3).

Key Phrase: A person who turns out to be a hidden or secret enemy is a (5,2,3,5).

> *Languages with a minimum of inflection are very likely to depend more than others on stereotyped expressions or idioms. [...] It is doubtful whether such idiomatic expressions are so much commoner in English than in other languages – for example French – as those learning our language believe, but they undoubtedly bulk large in the mind of foreigners.*

ALBERT C. BAUGH and THOMAS CABLE, *A History of the English Language* ([3]1978)

Field 2: Essential Animals

Your Task

In each of the phrases below in Part A, insert one of the animals listed beneath to complete the basic idiom and the sense. Then move on to Part B. The correct answers to both parts are to be found on page 153.

Idioms

Part A

A. as crafty as a ___
B. variable, inconstant person: a ___
C. a boat capsizes: it turns ___
D. to hunt out: to ___ out
E. an alleged culprit: a ___
F. male pre-wedding party: ___ party
G. spy, leaker of documents: ___
H. to shift responsibility: pass the ___
I. as prickly as a ___
J. to fight fiercely: fight like a ___
K. to imitate: to ___
L. with keen eye-sight: ___-eyed
M. major share: ___'s share
N. to keep on asking: to ___
O. to rush to collective disaster: rush like ___
P. walk two-by-two: in a ___
Q. false tears: ___ tears
R. start a rumour: start a ___
S. silly: ___-brained
T. to run fast: to ___
U. to eat fast: to ___ down
V. feel suspicious: smell a ___
W. big and clumsy: ___
X. celebrate, fête: ___
Y. selfish driver: road ___
Z. to pursue: to ___
AA. hard work: ___ work
BB. unofficial strike: ___ strike
CC. very antiquated type: a ___
DD. avoid in cowardly manner: ___ out of sth.

Options

ape / badger / buck / chameleon / chicken / crocodile (2x) / dinosaur / donkey / elephant(ine) / ferret / fox / hare (3x) / hedgehog / hog / hound / lemming(s) / lion(ize) (2x) / lynx / mole / rat / scapegoat / stag / tiger / turtle / wild-cat / wolf

Your Task

Part B

In the following sentences, insert both an animal and a substantive/adjective from among those listed beneath to complete the sense.

Sentences

1. Driving – no, crawling – into Manchester each morning, one knows one is in the unending modern struggle for a livelihood, the ___ ___.
2. They're ardent goers to exhibitions, poetry-readings, the theatre, talks, lectures and what-have-you – real ___ ___ and ___ ___.
3. It's a lovely veteran car, but it doesn't run – the archetypal ___ ___.
4. 'Clumsy, tactless, a real boor, an oaf! Talk about a ___ in a ___!'
5. 'He doesn't notice! Insensitive dullard! He's got a ___ like a ___!'
6. He was the bread-winner and slaved to keep the ___ from the ___.
7. Precisely the ___ ___ in the Far East have high growth rates.

Options

beaver / bull / elephant / rat / rhinoceros / tiger / vulture / wolf // china-shop / culture / door / eager / economy(ies) / hide / race / white

Field 3: Puzzling Animals

Your Task

Consider the idioms of animals below and decide which of the explanations beneath is likely to be the genuine meaning. The correct answers are to be found on page 154.

Idioms

1. **to make a dog's dinner of sth**
= to make (a) A. good meal B. good job C. quick work D. mess

2. **the rat pack**
= A. the human race B. tabloid journalists and paparazzi C. traitors, those who betray you D. get-rich-quick business-people

3. **a fat cat**
= a(n) A. mafia boss B. unduly self-satisfied person C. businessman who takes windfall profits D. obese person in the USA

4. **to see which way the cat jumps**
= to A. wait and then follow public opinion B. witness a burglary C. have foresight D. have keen eye-sight

5. **to swap horses in mid-stream**
= to A. change plan after the start B. change husband/wife C. mix one's drinks D. change the direction of one's journey

6. **to talk the hind-leg off a donkey**
= to talk A. rubbish B. persuasively C. endlessly D. viciously

7. **to twist the lion's tail**
= to A. taunt the police/ the authorities B. annoy or provoke Great Britain C. fight back against a bully D. take unnecessary risks

8. **weasel words**
= words that A. betray others B. irritate C. take the force out of what was said before D. sound well, but are vapid and vague

9. **to play possum**
= to A. put one's head, ostrich-like, in the sand B. collect odd items and knick-knacks C. be motherly D. pretend to be able to do sth.

10. **to be a rogue elephant**
= to A. be clumsy B. flout authority and run amok C. be randy D. be a perpetual joker

11. **to be a paper tiger**
= to be a(n) A. avid reader B. sham enemy C. journalist D. softy at heart

Field 4: Animals of the Farm

Your Task

Imagine you are engaged in the mini-dialogues below. Which of the animal idioms listed beneath would best suit which situation? The correct answers are to be found on page 154.

Dialogues

A. – No. I insist that the children are back by 7 o'clock at the latest.
– From a party! ***. Don't be such a spoilsport.
B. – Can you perhaps give us some clear guidelines here?
– No need. Do it your own way. ***.
C. – Oh, come on, Melanie. Tell us. Tell us. Come on.
– No. No. Not a word. My lips are sealed. ***.
D. – Well, off we go!
– Hey, ***! I'm not ready yet. Hang on a bit!
E. – I'm not happy with our translation. It's not great prose.
– Look at the original! That's not so great either. ***.
F. – He tells us one thing and the other side something quite different.
– Yes, I'm afraid he's trying to be all things to all men. He ***.
G. – Immediately after my *Diplom*, I'm going to open a computerised fast pasta chain in Western Samoa.
– Hmm. ***. You'll need a good bit of starting capital first.
H. – Who's the best person for this marketing job?
– Well, ***. Choose the person to suit the particular task. Try Birte. She's not so hot at accountancy but marketing is right up her street.
I. – Oh to be in Western Samoa, with a queue of customers waiting ...
– Come down to earth, my dear. ***. They don't eat pasta!
J. – At least the crash persuaded me to have the brakes checked.
– Hmm. Bit late, mate. ***.
K. – Can we go on avoiding the problem?
– No, we must ***. It's better in the long run.
L. – Just going out to mow the lawn, my dear.
– But Cecil, ***. The gardener can do that for us.
M. – It's a bit rusty, of course. And it needs a new chain.
– But it's still a bicycle for free. Be grateful. ***.
N. – Your daughter's coming home after a year away? Big party?
– Yes, you bet! We're ***.

Options

1. to take the bull by the horns / 2. to kill the fatted calf / 3. There's more than one way to skin a cat / 4. Don't be a dog in the manger / 5. Don't keep a dog and bark yourself / 6. First catch your hare then cook him / 7. to run with the hare and hunt with the hounds / 8. Horses for courses / 9. Don't look a gift horse in the mouth / 10. Hold your horses / 11. Don't lock the stable door after the horse has bolted / 12. Wild horses wouldn't drag it out of me / 13. If wishes were horses, beggars would ride / 14. You can't make a silk purse out of a sow's ear

Field 5: Farmyard, Pasture and Field

Your Task

In each of the sentences below, insert one (or more) of the animal idioms listed beneath to complete the idiom and the sense, taking care to use the appropriate form The correct answers are to be found on page 154.

Sentences

1. 'Never expect German professors to shift from that principle: it's one of their ___.'
2. It annoyed me intensely, really got my ___.
3. The living conditions in the Welsh iron towns of the 1850s were notorious: the workers ___ it in makeshift encampments.
4. That was one of the major questions of the Eighties in the West. Is it healthy for a country if the state is the ___ for ailing industries?
5. Talk about ___ love! Our youngest has just fallen for a classmate Romeo, and she positively dotes on him!
6. Simon, look at that used car very carefully before purchase. Don't buy a ___ in a poke, whatever you do!
7. The idea is pea-brained. It's a totally ___-eyed scheme.
8. No, he put up no resistance: he was as meek as a ___.
9. It seemed to be a marvellous find, but later turned out to be worthless, a terrible let-down – the proverbial ___'s nest.
10. 'Hmm. It's a tough job. Give it to old Rowlandson. He's been a party stalwart for years. He's a real old ___.'
11. It took a great deal of wheeling and dealing, general ___-trading, before the coalition pact was sealed.
12. At his funeral it emerged that no-one really knew him at all: he had lived and died a lone ___.
13. They are both very level-headed, feet-on-the-ground types with a good deal of ___ sense.
14. The manager was a real old ___, who had come through the bad times in the Seventies and Eighties battered but unbowed.
15. If men gave her the ___-whistle, she would double back and pinch their bums in return.
16. The question baffled all of them. They were all ___.
17. The President was ruthless. He didn't hesitate to sack his ministers, throwing them to the ___ to save his own neck.
18. 'Is that all they pay you?! That's miserly! It's just ___ feed!'
19. She's far too shy for the job. She wouldn't say boo to a ___.
20. 'Did you find the book you wanted in Hay?' – 'No, it was a fruitless exercise, chronicles of wasted time, a ___ chase.

Options

A. calf / B. chicken / C. cock / D. fox(ed) / E. goat / F. goose / G. horse (2x) / H. lamb / I. mare / J. milch cow / K. pig (2x) / L. sacred cow(s) / M. war horse / N. wild goose / O. wolf, wolves (3x) / P. workhorse

Field 6: Pets

Your Task

Read the sixteen headlines below, each of which contains an idiom derived from the field of household pets, and then select the German translation below which best conveys the meaning. The correct answers are to be found on page 154.

Headlines

1. **Marines 'Unwitting Guinea-Pigs in Scientific Experiments'**
2. SCHOOLCHILDREN PARROT FOREIGN LANGUAGES, STATES REPORT
3. **'1940 DOG-FIGHTS SECURED BRITAIN'S FREEDOM'**
4. **Anti-War Protesters: The Tail Wags the Dog**
5. **Teachers Have Hang-Dog Attitude, Say Inspectors**
6. I WAS AN OFFICE DOG'S-BODY
7. **Leader Tells Party to 'Stop Pussy-Footing'**
8. **Appointee: I'm Nobody's Poodle**
9. CAT-CALLS DISRUPT MP'S SPEECH
10. **NEW FILM IDOLIZES PUPPY LOVE**
11. **School Outrage Described as 'Copy-Cat Killing'**
12. **Damaged, Dog-Eared Volume Fetches Record Price at Auction**
13. TEACHERS' PETS STILL GET BETTER GRADES
14. **Gentleman Cat Burglar Confesses to 250 Offences**
15. **MONTE STARS 'THINK THEY ARE THE CAT'S WHISKERS'**
16. 'I HAD KITTENS BEFORE FINAL', CONFESSES MARTINA

Options

A. Armesündnermiene / B. mit Eselsohren / C. Fassadenkletterer / D. furchtbar nervös sein / E. leisetreten / F. Lieblinge / G. Luftkämpfe / H. Mädchen bzw. Arbeitskraft für alles / I. nachgemacht / J. nachplappern / K. Unwesentliches bestimmt eine wesentliche Entscheidung / L. Pfeifkonzert(e) / M. kein Vasall, kein Lakai / N. Teeny-Liebe / O. total toll / P. Versuchskaninchen

Field 7: Animals in Proverb and Saying

Your Task

Below are thirty proverbs and sayings, each of which concerns animals. Each saying, however, has been broken into two halves, and the halves have been muddled up. Fit the halves together again and then use them in context in Part B overleaf. The correct answers are on page 154.

Idioms

Part A

1. MANY A MICKLE	A. cows come home
2. IT'S WATER	B. before swine
3. WHAT'S SAUCE FOR THE GOOSE IS	C. one's high horse
4. THERE ISN'T ROOM	D. before the horse
5. TO KILL TWO BIRDS	E. before you find a prince
6. HE'S THE COCK	F. kettle of fish
7. TO PUT THE CART	G. to swing a cat in
8. WILD HORSES COULDN'T	H. fight
9. TO RISE LIKE A	I. the horse's mouth
10. GIVE A DOG A BAD	J. fish to fry
11. TO THROW (CAST) PEARLS	K. flock together
12. IT CAME STRAIGHT FROM	L. to the shorn lamb
13. YOU MUST KISS A LOT OF TOADS	M. off a duck's back
14. WHEN THE CAT'S AWAY	N. name (and hang him)
15. TO SEPARATE THE SHEEP	O. drag/tear me away
16. THAT'S A DIFFERENT	P. with one stone
17. TO HAVE OTHER	Q. than his bite
18. TO WAIT TILL THE	R. phoenix from the ashes
19. HEAVEN TEMPERS THE WINDS	S. from the goats
20. THAT COCK WON'T	T. changes its spots
21. HIS BARK'S WORSE	U. the mice will play
22. BIRDS OF A FEATHER	V. sauce for the gander
23. TO GET UP ON	W. among the pigeons
24. TO PUT THE CAT	X. of the walk
25. A LEOPARD NEVER	Y. makes a muckle
26. EVEN A WORM	Z. will turn
27. CURIOSITY	AA. to beat a dog with
28. AS WELL BE HANGED	BB. killed the cat
29. ANY STICK WILL SERVE	CC. strain at a goat
30. TO SWALLOW A CAMEL AND	DD. for a sheep as a lamb

Sentences

Part B

1. 'Your children had one hell of a party while you were abroad!' – 'Well, what do you expect? ***.'
2. 'I've decided to learn five new words each day. After all, ***.'
3. 'I wouldn't leave a university town and a *Studiengang* like this for anything. *** from it.'
4. 'Don't worry too much about his rude remarks. ***.'
5. No-one trusts him now, although the newspaper allegations were disproved. That's the way of the world. ***.
6. 'He's not the right man either? Well, just keep on trying, Christiane. Nowadays, with role models changing so much, ***.'

7. 'She's showing more courage and self-confidence at last? Hooray! It seemed hardly possible, but ***.'
8. He's the centre of attention, the limelight lad, the ***.
9. She's completely insensitive to criticism. It's like ***.
10. The professor spoke as if the audience were not worthy of his wisdom, as if he was ***.
11. 'Perhaps they'll make a good pair. They have the same interests, and ***, you know.'
12. 'Can't come this evening, I'm afraid. I'm booked. I ***.'

13. 'Despite the war, our town will be re-built. It will ***.'
14. My new flat is terribly cramped. 9 square metres! There ***!
15. He was very fortunate to inherit so much money and win on the National Lottery in just the week when he was unexpectedly made redundant. But then, of course, ***.
16. 'First things first. Don't run before you can walk. Don't ***.'
17. She invited both sets of grandparents to the same meal, thus ***.
18. 'At last you've turned up! I've ***.'

19. 'I think we should look into these strange goings on.' – 'Be careful, Paul. ***.'
20. Forget it, Jeremy, that's a poor plan. ***.
21. 'Petty crime doesn't pay, Boris. Try the big time. ***.'
22. 'The typical hypocrisy of the law. As Börne said: The small criminals are hounded, the biguns get away with anything. ***.'
23. He's always so arrogant, so hoity-toity, always ***.
24. The captain held three practice matches to weed out the less able players, to ***.

25. The information is certainly authentic: it ***.
26. That's a very different matter, different altogether, ***.
27. His remark certainly raised a real storm. It really ***.
28. It's the same for all concerned: ***.
29. It is so easy to find fault with almost anyone. ***
30. He'll never improve. Incorrigible, that's what he is. ***.

9 UNIT Idioms of the Human Body

Field 1: Body and Life

Your Task

Read the passage on the literary figure of the *picara* below and insert the most suitable body idiom among those listed beneath.

Text

Who has not read with pleasure Defoe's *Moll Flanders* (1722) or Grimmelshausen's *Courasche* (1669)? Each of the title figures is a characteristic *picara*: each goes through a multitude of roles and succeeds in almost everything she turns her [1] ___ to. Each suffers countless setbacks, but takes them on the [2] ___. Each, to put it over-bluntly, holds her [3] ___ high though life kicks her in the [4] ___. Dangers? The *picara* escapes with life and [5] ___. Authorities? She never [6] ___ under, or bends the [7] ___. Lovers? She twists them round her [8] ___. Troubles? She succeeds by the sweat of her [9] ___. Why do we revel in such figures? After all, the *picara* is not wholly admirable. She lies and doesn't bat an [10] ___. She always, self-centredly, has an [11] ___ on the main chance. She even profits from the [12] ___ of war.
First, one suspects, it is the *picara's* vitality which appeals to us. She is always ready to chance her [13] ___. She is not averse to the sins of the [14] ___. She is drawn to the proverbial [15] ___-pots of Egypt. Again and again, she lets her [16] ___ down. She leads the life we would if we could – or just might, if we didn't take fright.
Second, the world of the *picara* is a world we have lost. She had *wunderseltzame* adventures: we have adventure holidays and bungie-jumping. Only there do we live her life of [17] ___ or nothing.
In modern literature a *picara* is a rarity. True, Rita Mae Brown's *Rubyfruit Jungle* (1973) is in the same [18] ___; Irmtraud Morgner's Trobadora Beatriz is a woman of the same [19] ___. But in general, the *picara* has fallen foul of Schiller's *Entzauberung der Welt*, of Hegel's *Prosa der Verhältnisse*. And the farther she is from us, the more we furtively admire her. Who doesn't want to live [20] ___ loose and fancy free? Who doesn't want at times to show bare-[21] ___ insolence? Yes, we give the *picara* our collective [22] ___ up!

Options

arm / brow / chin / eye / eyelid / faced / flesh (2x) / foot / hair / hand / head / kidney / knee / knuckle / limb / little finger / neck / sinew(s) / teeth / thumbs / vein

> *We must use words as they are used or stand aside from life.*

IVY COMPTON BURNETT, *Mother and Son* (1955)

Field 2: The Basic Body I

Your Task

In each of the phrases below in Part A, insert one of the parts of the body listed beneath to complete the basic idiom and the sense. Then move on to Part B. The correct answers to both parts are to be found on page 155.

Phrases

Part A

A. within easy reach: at one's ___
B. mad: off one's ___
C. agree with: see ___ to ___
D. tense *tête-à-tête*: ___ to ___
E. to irritate: get up s.o.'s ___
F. depressed: down in the ___
G. pay attention: lend an ___
H. like sweetmeats: have a sweet ___
I. furious: foaming at the ___
J. suppress feelings: grit one's ___
K. be indiscreet: have a loose ___
L. threats, pressure: ___-twisting
M. applaud: give a good ___ to
N. to bribe: to grease s.o.'s ___
O. to help: give s.o. a ___-up
P. full of resentment: full of ___
Q. look foolish: cut a poor ___
R. courage: ___
S. cowardly: yellow-___
T. quick description: __ sketch
U. master key: ___ key
V. shabby: down at ___
W. get adjusted: find one's ___
X. get up fast: show a ___
Y. weak in principle: ___less
Z. unable to resist: weak-___
AA. betrayal: stab in the ___
BB. close friends: ___ friends
CC. Don't despair!: ___ up!
DD. daft: soft in the ___

Options

arm / back / bile / bosom / chin / ear / elbow / eye (2x) / eyeball (2x) / feet / figure / guts / hand / head (2x) / heel / knee(d) / leg (2x) / liver(ed) / mouth (2x) / nose / palm / skeleton / spine / teeth / thumbnail / tongue / tooth /

Your Task

Part B

In the following sentences, insert both an adjective and a substantive from among those listed beneath to complete the idiom and sense.

Sentences

1. From 1923 to 1967 a long, illusory 'peace' reigned: then the Northern Irish issue raised its ___ ___ again.
2. A superb novel! One would give one's ___ ___ to have written it.
3. If the allies send ground troops in, the risk is that they will meet with fierce guerrilla resistance and get a ___ ___
4. The voters were sick and tired of him, fed up to the ___ ___.
5. The murder was calculating, premeditated, done in ___ ___.
6.The election results were humiliating: the outgoing PM tried hard to put a ___ ___ on it.
7. 'Your unpaid bill is very conspicuous: it sticks out like a ___ ___.'

Options

back (adj.) / bloody / brave / cold / right / sore / ugly // arm / blood / face / head / nose / teeth / thumb

Field 3: The Basic Body II

Your Task

Complete the crossword below, noting that the first letter of each word and the number of letters in each word are given. The correct answers are to be found on page 155.

Crossword

Clues

1. Keep up the good work, Paul. More power to your (5)!
2. He hadn't meant it. It was just a slip of the (6).
3. They were humiliated, losing (4) completely.
4. I can't do this homework. I'll go and pick my friend's (6).

5. It was unbearable. They refused to (7) it any more.
6. The prices here are shocking! We're paying through the (4).
7. I'll gauge the mood, keep my (4) to the ground.
8. He decided to get it off his (5) and admit it.
9. He knocked me (4,4,5).
10. Enough is enough! I've had a (8) of this government.
11. Fortune showed no surprise. She didn't turn a (4).
12. Susan didn't understand. She couldn't make (4,2,4) of it.
13. It's a difficult job, but Liz is making a good (4) of it.
14. He's at death's door, one (4) in the grave.
15. The burglar was trying to (4) up the drainpipe.
16. Get working, put your (8) to the wheel!
17. She didn't help at all, didn't lift a (6).
18. What you did was unjustifiable. You haven't got a (3) to stand on.
19. Keep alert. Be on your (4).
20. And keep a sharp look-out. Keep your eyes (7).
21. I bet old Wibke's got a guilty secret, some (8) in the cupboard.
22. Karin's dying to go to Sicily. She's set her (5) on it.
23. He said it without hesitation: he made no (5) about it.
24. They're not religious: they just pay (3-7) to the Church.
25. I'm sacked! Out on my (4)!

Key Phrase: to show one's emotions (4,4,5,2,4,6)

Field 4: The Essential Body

Your Task

Read the text below and then decide which of the characters involved is best characterised by which of the basic idioms of the body listed below. The correct answers are to be found on page 155.

Text

Old Aunt Agatha had one foot in the grave. Yes, Agatha, the old Victorian matriarch and battle-axe, old never-say-die, old cleanliness-is-next-to-godliness Agatha. But to whom would she leave the family fortune? Basil had last year made the bold prediction that it would be Cecily. But her rash words to her aunt ten years back had probably ruined her chances. Derek had never had a chance since his marriage to a double divorcee: that had really annoyed the old matriarch. Erudite Eileen had little hope either: she was so intellectual that Agatha could never understand her. Freddy treated his aunt snobbishly, Gertrude treated her as an inferior and Hubert was far too casual. So much for the three of them. About Iris, Agatha had had an unvoiced complaint for years, and poor Julian she made nervous and tongue-tied. Kathy had been discouraged by some cutting remarks, Lionel had always been a comparative nonentity in the family, Matilda was inquisitive to the point of rudeness and Norbert kept quite the wrong company. Olivia had confessed her wrong-doing, but she'd still done wrong. Pete was obsessed with witchcraft – a very nasty and un-Agatha habit. And Queenie had only just avoided excommunication! Roger had done nothing wrong, but could never relax. Susan had the advantage that you could never tell what she was thinking. But it seemed that Tim could now triumph easily over the rest. And yet who could tell? Really, who could? They were all doing their best in these last crucial days. Everyone was closely observing everybody else. The will could still be a complete revelation!

The Cast

AGATHA / BASIL / CECILY / DEREK / EILEEN / FREDDY / GERTRUDE / HUBERT / IRIS / JULIAN / KATHY / LIONEL / MATILDA / NORBERT / OLIVIA / PETE / ROGER / SUSAN / TIM /ALL OF THEM / EVERYONE / THE WILL

Options

1. to take a back seat / 2. to get s.o.'s back up / 3. to have a bone to pick with / 4. to have sth. on the brain / 5. to make a clean breast of sth. / 6. to be an eye-opener / 7. to be poker-faced / 8. to burn one's fingers / 9. to put one's best foot forward / 10. to let one's hair down / 11. to win hands down / 12. to be off-hand / 13. to talk over s.o.'s head / 14. to lose heart / 15. to be on one's last legs / 16. to look down one's nose at / 17. to poke one's nose into / 18. to breathe down s.o.'s neck / 19. to rub shoulders with / 20. to lose one's tongue / 21. to stick one's neck out / 22. to turn up one's nose

Field 5: The Anglo-German Body

Your Task

Below are eighteen matching pairs of English and German idioms. Each idiom involves a part of the human body. But in no matching pair do the idioms involve the same part of the body. Which idiom matches which? The correct answers are to be found on page 155.

Idioms

1. to have sth. on one's back
2. to put one's back into sth.
3. to rack one's brains
4. to be up to one's eyes in sth.
5. to do s.o. in the eye
6. at one's elbow
7. to have a finger in every pie
8. to keep one's fingers crossed
9. to keep one's hair on
10. to have one's heart in one's mouth
11. to pull s.o.'s leg
12. to be neck and neck
13. to be a pain in the neck
14. to be all thumbs
15. to tread on s.o.'s toes
16. to hold one's tongue
17. to be tongue-in-cheek
18. to be fed up to one's back teeth

A. jdm die Daumen drücken
B. jdm auf die Hühneraugen treten
C. bei der Hand
D. zwei linke Hände haben
E. Herzklopfen haben
F. sich den Kopf zerbrechen
G. Kopf an Kopf
H. jdn 'verarschen'
I. den Mund halten
J. etwas auf dem Hals haben
K. es faustdick hinter den Ohren haben
L. sich in etwas hineinknien
M. die Nase (gestrichen) voll haben
N. jdn übers Ohr hauen
O. ruhig Blut!
P. die Finger überall drin haben
Q. eine Nervensäge sein
R. bis über die Ohren ... sein

Field 6: The Puzzling Body

Your Task

Consider the idioms of the body below and decide which of the explanations beneath is likely to be the genuine meaning. The correct answers are to be found on page 155.

Idioms

1. **to be light-fingered**
   = to be A. musical B. lazy C. likely to steal D. good with money
2. **to jaw (away)**
   = to A. be often eating B. snore C. talk incessantly D. ruminate
3. **to rubber-neck**
   = to A. to head a spectacular goal B. to read s.o. else's newspaper over his or her shoulder C. do gymnastics D. toss drinks down
4. **to toe the line**
   = to A. follow official policy B. be pedantic C. be ready D. be sly
5. **to stand with one's arms akimbo**
   = with one's arms A. on one's hips B. raised to the skies C. hanging D. outspread in welcome
6. **to be long in the tooth**
   = to be A. an ardent meat-eater B. wise C. aggressive D. ageing
7. **to keep one's nose to the grindstone**
   = to A. concentrate B. scrutinize C. kow-tow D. work hard
8. **to be mealy-mouthed**
   = to be A. an inelegant eater B. reluctant to call evil evil C. self-important when speaking D. bad with one's elocution
9. **to get it in the neck**
   = to A. be firmly punished B. get a sore throat C. take a firm grip on a problem/situation D. totally misunderstand sth.
10. **to press the flesh**
    = to A. seduce B. woo voters C. grow fat D. be a doctor/surgeon
11. **to cut off one's nose to spite one's face**
    = to A. be a masochist B. to work oneself into the grave C. to hurt oneself when trying to hurt others D. to sing excruciatingly badly
12. **to turn someone's head**
    = to make someone A. insane B. conceited C. baffled D. a dupe

10 UNIT Idioms of Clothing

Field 1: Basic Clothing

Your Task

In each of the sentences below, insert one (or more) of the idioms of clothing listed beneath to complete the idiom and the sense. The correct answers are to be found on page 155.

Sentences

1. 'How dull, how deadly dull! That lecture bored the ___ off me!'
2. Charles told a good joke, but Andrew told a better one to ___ it.
3. That was a nasty, unfair remark, really below the ___.
4. Some passers-by pursued the thief, finally managing to ___ him.
5. The ships slipped away at night, under the ___ of darkness [2].
6. 'You're talking rubbish, talking through your ___.'
7. What's better on a cold evening than a crisp ___ potato, eaten piping hot with melted butter and grated Cheddar cheese? Mmm!
8. Ever since Sam was elected to the students' union he's been arrogant and self-important, too big for his ___.
9. The professor's questions caught me completely unawares and unprepared – with my ___ down.
10. They're generous folk: they'd give you the ___ off their back.
11. 'Yes, the old so-and-so's dead: he popped his ___ years back.'
12. He made a humble apology, going to the boss ___ in hand.
13. Secretly she scorned him, laughing at him up her ___.
14. He wasn't at all talented, but, as a Public School product, he was helped by the old school ___.
15. The air by the marshes was full of mosquitoes and flies, but the car ___ did its protective job and kept them out of the engine.
16. 'Stop making such an infernal noise! Put a ___ in it will you?!'
17. 'No, we won't! Stuff that up your ___!'
18. Typical 'woffle': ___ condemnations and sweeping statements.
19. It was a blot on his ___, spoiling his otherwise good reputation.
20. The TUC, the ___ organisation of the British trade unions, was founded as long ago as 1868, long before the Labour Party.
21. It was a novel full of rabid sex, a real '___-ripper.'

Options

belt / blanket / bodice / boots / bra / cap (2x) / cloak / clogs / collar / escutcheon (*Wappenschild*) / hat / jacket / kilt / mantle / pants / shirt / sleeve / sock / tie / trousers / umbrella

> *Some slang survives and is given the idiomatic franchise. [...] The idiomatic writer differs from the slangy in using what was slang and is now idiom.*

FOWLER, *The King's English* (1930)

Field 2: Essential Clothing

Your Task

Complete the crossword below, noting that the first or last letter of each word and the number of letters in each word are given. The correct answers are to be found on page 156.

Crossword

Clues

1. Keep calm! Keep your (5) on!
2. They've been sacked, simply given the (4).
3. To hit s.o. on the head, the 'topnot', is to (5) him or her.
4. Mum's the word! Keep it top secret. Keep it under your (3).

5. She's in the soup: who'd want to be in her (5) now?
6. She's the dominant figure in their house. She wears the (8).
7. You'll have to do it wholly impromptu, off the (4).
8. Needing a word with the headmaster, he tried every opportunity to (10) him.
9. She was upset and angry: it all made her hot under the (6).
10. When she was nervous she got confused, getting her (8) in a twist.
11. She set her (3) at him. Yes, he was the man for her to wed.
12. 'You must improve. Pull your (5) up!'
13. Oh yes, they're wealthy, really well-(6).
14. I lost money over the car, and I'm afraid I'm still out of (6).
15. The good entertainer or teacher always has a surprise up his (6).
16. She hated him: she wanted his guts for (7).
17. 'Shut your face! (4) up! Or I'll give you a good (4).'
18. The road was planned to by-pass, to (5) the town.
19. How acutely embarrassing! When my parents came, neither of us had a (6) on!
20. There they were, wearing their finest clothes, their (6,4).
21. And there we were, stark naked, in the (10)!

Key Phrase: it was run on a very small budget (2,3,3,2,1,10)

Field 3: Literary Clothing and Fabric

Your Task

Read the passage below on the literary achievement and political stance of Sir Walter Scott and then complete the idiom and sense by inserting the most suitable clothing word chosen from those listed beneath. The correct answers are to be found on page 156.

Text

'There he is,' said the Glasgow guide, pointing to the Scott memorial in George Square, 'facing South – where his money came from!' Does Sir Walter Scott really deserve such treatment? Is his *oeuvre* a plea for the Union under the [1] ___ of literature? Was he really hand in [2] ___ with the English Hanoverians? Did he really line his [3] ___ at the expense of his country?

There are certain passages, in the novels and especially elsewhere, which could lead one to this conclusion. But the thrust of the novels is far more ambivalent. Take *Waverley* (1814) for instance. As his name suggests, Edward Waverley, the protagonist, is the archetypal turn[4] ___. An English captain on the Hanoverian side, but also a daydreaming [5] ___-gatherer, he travels, on the [6] ___ of the moment over the Highland line. He is even dragged by his [7] ___ into the 1745 Jacobite uprising and the Battle of Prestonpans. Yet the more he and we see of the Highland culture, the more the [8] ___ is on the other foot. Edward's cultural tolerance (contrasted with that of his colonel, Talbot) is the greatest [9] ___ in his [10] ___. And what is the most emotional moment in the work, when one's heart is really in one's [11] ___? Surely the execution of the Highland chieftain Fergus MacIvor.

There is no need to draw a [12] ___ over the book's political qualities, but these must not obscure its literary. It is a milestone in realism, giving a 'no [13] ___' picture of Scottish society in 1745. It is a major impulse to historiography. And it launches the historical novel as genre. Scott does not hang up his [14] ___ after this success: with *The Antiquary* (1816), *The Heart of Midlothian* (1818) and *Redgauntlet* (1824), he pushes the genre further forward. On his demise, before and after his death, great writers from Cooper and Balzac to Tieck and Pushkin try to step into this dead man's [15] ___. But major though they are, none, as historical novelist, is a [16] ___ on Scott at his best.

In the present political climate in Scotland Scott will inevitably run the [17] ___ of criticism and some will put the [18] ___ in. Yet, though Scott may have been a dyed-in-the-[19] ___ Tory, he was not simply in the Englishman's [20] ___. That is a mark of his quality and of the genre he inspired. Yes, even today, in devolved Scotland and in left-wing Glasgow, one can still take off one's [21] ___ to Scott.

Options

boot(s) (4x) / cap / cloak / coat / coat-tails / feather / frills / gauntlet / glove / hat / patch / pocket (2x) / shoes / spur / veil / wool (2x)

Field 4: Anglo-German Clothing

Your Task

Each of the eighteen clothing idioms on the left has a matching German idiom on the right. In nine matching pairs the same piece of clothing is involved, but in nine pairs, a different piece. Find the pairs. The correct answers are to be found on page 156.

Idioms

1. STRAIT-LACED
2. TO EARN ONE'S SPURS
3. TO TIGHTEN ONE'S BELT
4. WITH KID GLOVES
5. TO REACH INTO ONE'S POCKET
6. TO BUCKLE DOWN
7. TO THE SHIRT
8. WHERE DOES THE SHOE PINCH?
9. TIED TO HER APRON STRINGS
10. TO CUT ONE'S COAT ACCORDING TO ONE'S CLOTH
11. BIRTHDAY SUIT
12. TO DIE IN ONE'S BOOTS
13. IN ONE'S POCKET
14. UNDER ONE UMBRELLA
15. PULL O.S. UP BY ONE'S BOOTLACES
16. TO TAKE ONE'S HAT OFF TO
17. TO ROLL UP ONE'S SLEEVES
18. TO WARM S.O.'S PANTS

A. den Gürtel enger schnallen
B. sich nach der Decke strecken
C. jdm den Hosenboden stramm ziehen
D. in der Tasche
E. Adamskostüm
F. unter einem Hut
G. in den Sielen (od. Stiefeln) sterben
H. zugeknöpft
I. vor jdn. den Hut ziehen
J. tief in die Tasche greifen
K. die Hemdsärmel hoch krempeln
L. mit Glacéhandschuhen behandeln
M. wo drückt der Schuh?
N. sich die Sporen verdienen
O. sich auf den Hosenboden setzen
P. bis aufs Hemd
Q. am Rockzipfel hängen
R. sich am eigenen Zopf nach oben ziehen

11 UNIT Idioms of Food and Drink

Field 1: Cooking

Your Task

Add a word of cooking in order to make idiomatic sense of the sentences below, selecting your word from those listed beneath and taking care to use an appropriate form. The correct answers are to be found on page 156.

Sentences

1. 'Phew! 39 degrees in the shade!! And no air-conditioning! Another ___, another ___ hot day!'
2. The accountant defrauded the management by ___ the books.
3. 'Ugh, no. He's just the typical thick-skinned, culturally unaware, insensitive, ___ manager type.'
4. 'The professors ___ me terribly during the exam. Their questioning was merciless.'
5. 'It really angered me – I'm still ___ with annoyance two-and-a-half weeks later.'
6. They left the suspect to ___ in his own juice for a few hours before hauling him out for questioning.
7. She improved the language of her essay, ___ it with some purple passages.
8. 'No, not with the ozone hole growing larger by the day! Others can go to the lakes and ___ in the sun. I'm staying in my shady study.'
9. The impassioned demagogue succeeded in ___ the crowd.
10. After her injury she was no longer the great, all-conquering player she had once been, no longer in peak form, no longer on the ___.
11. 'No, skipper. We can't leave port this evening. Just look at those clouds on the horizon. There's a storm ___.'
12. The new minister always spoke plainly, never ___ her words and calling a spade a spade.
13. I'll get my own back on the b******s! I'll ___ their goose.
14. The problem with the *Studiengang* is that it's ___-___. The professors should have the courage to think it right through and draw the consequences.
15. 'Stop being so angry! Just ___ down!'

Options

(half-)bake (2x) / (hard-)boil (2x) / brew / broil / cook (2x) / grill / lard / mince / scorch / simmer (2x) / stew / stir up

> *Slang is a language that rolls up its sleeves, spits on its hands and goes to work.*

CARL SANDBURGH, *New York Times*, 13 February 1959

Field 2: Bread, Cake and Pastries

Your Task

Complete the crossword below, noting that the first letter of each word and the number of letters in each word are given. The correct answers are to be found on page 156.

Crossword

Clues

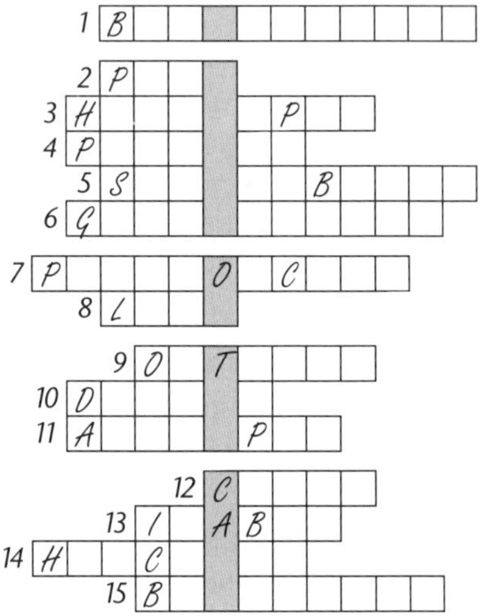

1. She was now the (11), earning the money to feed the growing family.
2. He was involved in all sorts of things, had his fingers in many (4).
3. They had to admit they were wrong and eat (6,3).
4. Experience is all. 'The proof of the (7) is in the eating.'
5. It's a marvellous invention – the best thing since (6,5)!
6. 'That makes a good day perfect, puts the icing on the (11).
7. 'Easy, easy! This is simplicity itself, a (5,2,4)!
8. 'Think, man, think! Use your (4)! What were you given a brain for?'
9. She had got them where she wanted them at last – at her mercy, over a barrel, (2,5)!
10. It was like that at the end of every month: broke, utterly broke in every sense – spirits low and no (5).
11. All neat and tidy, spick and span, all in (5,3) order! How awful!
12. They had nothing to eat, not a (5).
13. Virginia Woolf at times wore her hair fixed behind, done (2,1,3).
14. To say it sells well is an understatement. The book-shops can't order it fast enough. It sells like (3,5).
15. In the terrible years of the Depression, many found themselves through no fault of their own in dire poverty, on the (9), dependent on the demeaning charity of soup-kitchens and food-queues.

Key Phrase: She wanted her part, her share of the spoils, her 'cut' – (1,5,2,3,4)

Field 3: Fruit

Your Task

Add a fruit substantive in order to make idiomatic sense of the sentences below, selecting your word from those listed beneath and putting the word in an appropriate form. The correct answers are to be found on page 156.

Sentences

1. 'Things seemed to be perfect. But now they have gone terribly wrong. Everything's gone ___-shaped!'
2. 'And Beth?' – 'Oh, she got the best job of all of them, a really ___ job at a top university.'
3. 'I don't care. I don't care one jot. Not one little bit. Not a tinker's cuss. Not a ___.'
4. No matter where you work, no matter how good your colleagues, there is always one bad egg, one rotten ___ in the bunch.
5. There they were necking, seducing each other before her eyes. She was tired of playing ___ and simply went home, leaving them to it.
6. Whenever the speaker made a chauvinist remark, she made a slightly obscene noise, giving him the ___.
7. 'But when I heard that I just lost all control, I went ___, berserk.'
8. Her new, much-admired, highly-beloved Mac computer deserved its name: it was truly the ___ of her eye.
9. This new *Freischussregelung* is a clever idea: it allows you essentially two goes, two attempts, two bites of the ___.
10. And then, totally out of the blue, came the collapse of the Yen. That destroyed our markets and our plans: it really upset the ___ cart.
11. Klaus-Rüdiger, the inveterate *Englandfreak*, spent three terms at Oxford and came back with a gown, a boater and a really ___ accent.
12. What a dull bunch! How uninspired and uninspiring! Why don't they come up with a few fresh ideas? Why don't they *say something*? Instead of just sitting there like ___.
13. After the incoming government had suffered several mishaps, it prudently appointed a minister without portfolio to foresee and forewarn against future slips – a minister for ___-skins, as the press dubbed him.
14. 'Who told you?' – 'Who? Well, no-one in particular. I just came to hear of it, just heard it on the ___-vine.'
15. She said that she hated inline-skating. Skating was silly. But that was just jealousy, just ___ Secretly, she was a suppressed skater.

Options

apple (3x) / bananas / cherry / fig / gooseberry / grape / lemon(s) / pear / plum(my) (2x) / raspberry / sour grapes

Field 4: Vegetarian Foods

Your Task

Read the twenty alliterative biographies below and then decide which life is best characterised by which of the idioms of vegetarian food listed beneath. The correct answers are to be found on page 157.

Biographies

1. Anja is alert, intellectually alive and a live wire
2. Anja's pal Alec is all activity and alacrity
3. Carew has never come out of a coma after his cruel car crash
4. Eager Enid needs no inkling of encouragement
5. Flora is unfailingly, unflinchingly unflappable
6. Goofy Gale is forever gawking at the goggle-box
7. Inane Ian is addicted to the internet and e-mail
8. Penniless Penny is the pauper of the parish
9. Rash and reckless Roderick revealed the real story
10. Say sweet somethings to shy Sheila and she'll turn a shade of scarlet
11. Savvy and sagacious Stefanie is surely sure-footed in her subject
12. Tini and Tina are truly identical twins
13. Younis and Una are young, the youthful on whom youth is wasted

Options

A. to know how many beans make five
B. to spill the beans
C. to not have a bean
D. to be full of beans
E. to be as cool as a cucumber
F. to be as keen as mustard
G. to be as like as two peas in a pod
H. to be a couch potato
I. to go as red as a beetroot
J. to be a vegetable
K. to be in one's salad days
L. to be a mouse potato
M. to know one's onions

Field 5: Puzzling Foodstuffs

Your Task

Consider the idioms of foodstuffs below and decide which of the explanations beneath is likely to be the genuine meaning. The correct answers are to be found on page 157.

Idioms

1. **a lollipop lady**
   = a woman who A. has physical attractions but little more B. helps schoolchildren cross the road C. is a sweet-addict D. is of lax morals

2. **to quarrel with one's bread and butter**
   = to A. have digestive problems B. dislike and find fault with one's job C. need a change of life-style D. have marital problems

3. **to be ham-fisted**
   = to be A. clumsy B. no artist C. greasy-fingered D. tight with money, miserly

4. **Dead Sea fruit**
   = A. exotic foodstuffs B. utter nonsense C. a thing of promise which transpires to be worthless D. a treacherous and dangerous gift

5. **to know one's onions**
   = to be A. a good gardener B. a good cook C. an expert (in any field) D. a francophile

6. **to salami-slice sth.**
   = to A. make a mess of sth. B. to cut/divide sth. into manageable pieces C. destroy sth. by pettiness D. enjoy sth. exquisitely

7. **money for jam**
   = A. government subsidy B. money for achieving nothing C. a bribe D. money wasted on a senseless project

8. **toffee-nosed**
   = A. upper-class and snobbish D. with a badly broken nose, e.g. of a boxer C. unkempt and dirty, squalid D. ill-mannered

9. **to be above the salt**
   = A. too old to eat spiced food B. in high office C. sophisticated in taste D. seated at the (socially) 'right' end of the table

10. **a cauliflower ear**
    = A. Provençal or Southern European cooking B. ear smashed into ugliness by boxing, rugby etc. C. ear embarrassed by what it has heard D. the ear of an eavesdropper, spy etc.

Field 6: Drinking

Your Task

Read the family chronicle below and then decide which of the characters involved is best characterised by which of the basic idioms of drinks and drinking listed below. The correct answers are to be found on page 157.

Text

It all began with old grand-dad de Bere, old Alfred: he had always liked to celebrate events with a good drink. 'Have a Madeira, my dear', as he loved to say. His wife Beatrice tried to dampen his enthusiasm for celebration – but to no avail. Naturally, their first son, Charles, was soon addicted to alcohol – by the age of ten, some say. Their next child, Daphne – poor creature – died of liver failure induced by drinking before reaching twenty. Her brother Edward, lasting longer, almost ruined the family finances by the sheer quantities he tossed down. And sister Faith, despite her name, took to drinking out of grief.

Paradoxically, the only glimmer of hope was that Charles had taken Gertrude Boosie as his bride. She herself, of course – *nomen et omen* – tippled so much that she was perpetually half-drunk. And their son Harry, going one worse, frequently suffered from hallucinations. His sister Isabelle was an alcoholic pure and simple – my goodness, oh, my dear, she soaked it up! But brother Jason was so far gone so soon that the doctors forced him to dry out on a health farm and then stay teetotal for life.

Well, when Alfred and Beatrice, now ruby-faced, celebrated their Ruby Wedding almost everyone had soon had too much of the old liquids. Everyone, that is, except Jason. He went around, as fit as a fiddle and as fresh as a daisy, explaining how milk contained so much strength and goodness. The trouble with the de Beres, the Boosies and the de Bere-Boosies, he said – not a bad play on words, really – was that they thought life was all de Bere and skittles.

Cast

ALFRED / BEATRICE / CHARLES / DAPHNE / EDWARD / FAITH / GERTRUDE / HARRY / ISABELLE / JASON / THE RUBY WEDDING GUESTS (2X) / THE TWO FAMILIES / MILK

Options

1. to be only here for the beer / 2. to have a lot of bottle / 3. to be on the bottle / 4. to be in one's cups / 5. to have one over the eight / 6. to see pink elephants / 7. to drink oneself into the grave / 8. to drive s.o. or be driven to drink / 9. to be half seas-over / 10. to splice the main brace / 11. to be a sponge / 12. to be on the wagon / 13. to pour cold water on sth. / 14. to spend money like water

Field 7: Essential Drinks

Your Task

In each of the sentences in Parts 1 and 2 below, insert one (or more) of the drink or drinking words listed beneath to complete the idiom and the sense. The correct answers are to be found on page 158.

Sentences

1. 'You're going!? The day is still young! There's ___ in the jar!'
2. 'Poor Basil arrived back in College sopping wet! He went punting on the river, made the classic booboo and landed up in the ___!'
3. His career as a hooligan began with the British ___ louts rampaging on the Costa Brava.
4. 'Well, the mistake's made now. No use crying over spilt ___.'
5. He was so helpful and kind-hearted – the ___ of human kindness.
6. The bastards threw Molotov ___ in at the windows.
7. To open her evening poetry-reading she presented two short pieces as an ___.
8. After such a miserable period, the good news came as a real ___, a ___ lifting everyone's spirits.
9. 'No, I wouldn't do it, never, not for all the ___ in China.'
10. The launch of Felicity's novel was a real ___ occasion attended by some of the *crème de la crème* and by top nobs in the book trade.
11. The new task gave her a new *raison d'être* and new *élan*, proving a real ___ of life.
12. 'Glorious. Magnificent. Up here in Tyrol the air is like ___.'
13. They sat at the feet of the master and ___ in his every word.
14. 'Basil can count himself lucky. He might have met a ___ grave in the river. He should learn to punt!'
15. 'Where are going in the hols, Eustace?' – 'Oh, mater and pater are taking me to some continental ___ place on the Med, where those froggy painter johnnies used to work – L'Estaque, I think it's called.'
16. 'Oh, boy, am I tired! I'm all in! I feel sooooo ___!'
17. The poetry was heady, mind-spinning stuff, rich in language, metaphor, image and symbol, a real infusion, a potent ___.
18. 'Hmm. This is not as easy as it might seem. Quite tricky really.' – 'Yes, it's a really ___ exercise.'
19. 'I'm not happy with the final passage in the speech. It's a little over-stated. Can we perhaps ___ it down a bit?'
20. 'We're in a real pickle now! We're really in hot ___.'
21. 'Did you tell your friends about today's guest lecturer?' – 'No need, my dear, they knew already. Good ___ needs no bush!'
22. The Party was no longer the full-blooded Left, just a gathering of pinkos, '___ socialists', as the media dubbed them.

Options

apéritif / champagne / Chardonnay / cocktail / drink (2x) / elixir / groggy / juicy / lager / milk (2x) / pick-me-up / potion / tea / tonic / water (2x) / watery / watering / whiskey / wine (2x)

Field 8: Last Drinks

Your Task

Complete the crossword below, made up of types, quantities and states of drink, noting that the first or last letter of each word and the number of letters in each word are given. The correct answers are to be found on page 158.

Crossword

Clues

1. 'I don't enjoy this in the least. It's not my cup of (3).'
2. It was glorious walking by the coast: the air was like (9).
3. 'One has to work sometime. Life isn't all (4) and skittles.'
4. We could not make her out: she was odd – a (3) person.
5. A superficial reform will fail. You can't put new (4) in old bottles.

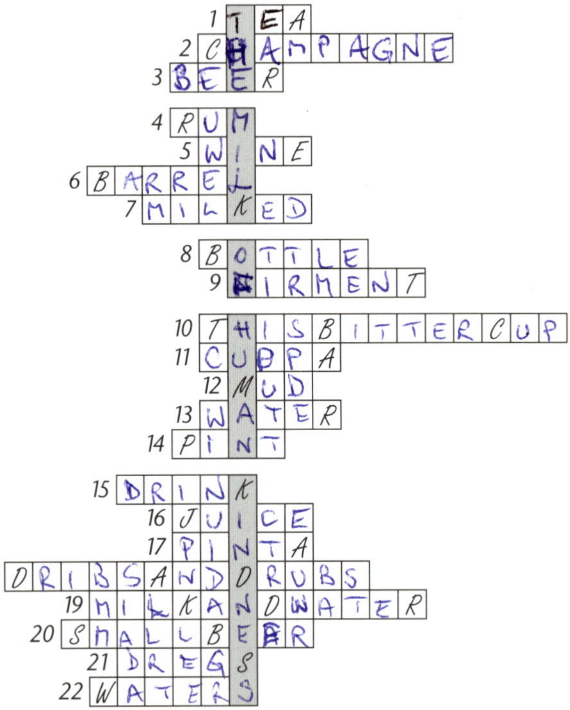

6. The prof. knew I knew nothing: he had me over a (6) and exploited it.
7. He (6) the club funds for years before being discovered.
8. Be more outgoing. Don't (6) everything up inside.
9. In the long, hot summer of riots the whole land was in (7).
10. 'I have no desire to do it. May (4,6,3) pass from my lips.'
11. 'Come and have a chat an' a (5) dear. The kettle's on.'
12. 'Cheers, Bert. Elbows up! Here's (3) in your eye!'
13. The theory is no good: it does not hold (5)
14. As the proverb says, you can't put a quart in a (4) pot.
15. Poor Paula fell overboard and spent a few cold minutes in the (5).
16. 'We must find a petrol station sharpish: we need more (5).'
17. Remember the famous sixties ad: 'Drinka (5) milka day'?
18. Almost no guest was on time: they came in (4,3,4) all evening.
19. It was a feeble sermon. No full-blooded sentiment. Just (4,3,5).
20. That's unimportant, just (5,4).
21. 'They mix with the lowest types, Bertrand, the real (5) of society.'
22. Each year the upper classes went to a spa to take the (6).

Key Phrase: She was cured not by the doctor but by her grandparents' love, not by medicine but by (3,4,2,5,8)

12

UNIT **Idiomatic Structures II**

Field 1: The 'To be + on' Construction

Your Task

Read the twenty alliterative biographies below and then decide which life is best characterised by which of the 'to be + on' idioms listed beneath. The correct answers are to be found on page 158.

Biographies

1. Alan is all awake and a-watching, ready to avert attack.
2. Artistic Antje is always advancing in her Arts and Crafts.
3. Bertha is botheringly and bewilderingly busy.
4. Colin the convict is provisionally out of clink.
5. Dorothy the doctor is ready to dash to aid the dying.

6. Eager Elizabeth is expecting her eighth.
7. Frank, now fat and forty, may never find a filly to wive.
8. Grace is geared up to expect great danger.
9. Horace is all honesty, all honour and even-handedness.
10. Iris is itchily irritable and inveterately jittery.

11. Jim is always jolly well genned up and in the picture.
12. Kate is climbing up and almost coining the cash.
13. Len and Laurel's love-life is loathesomely lousy.
14. Mandy is a magistrate meting out meet justice.
15. Never-late Neville is always in the nick of time.

16. Oliphant is omnipresently on the look-out for offenders.
17. Policeman Patrick is perpetually plodding the pavements.
18. Rob is recovering from rickets and rare raw rashes.
19. Sandy is certain to 'suss' your sense and significance.
20. Trevor is forever being told off or 'ticked off'.

Options

To be on the ... ([ ] denotes no definite article)

A. alert
B. ball
C. beat
D. bench
E. [ ] call
F. carpet
G. dot
H. [ ] edge
I. go
J. [ ] one's guard
K. level
L. make
M. mend
N. [ ] parole
O. prowl
P. rocks
Q. shelf
R. [ ] tenterhooks
S. up and up
T. (right) wave-length

Field 2: Idioms of Noun Pairs

Your Task

Each of the thirty-three nouns on the left below is commonly used with one of the nouns on the right in a noun pair construction. (The connecting word is 'and' except where indicated.) Fit the idioms together and check your answers on page 159, before going on to Part B opposite.

Noun Pairs

Part A

		AND		
A.	BAG		1.	TEAR
B.	BEER		2.	BLOOD
C.	BITS		3.	ENDS
D.	BLOOD		4.	ENGLISHMEN
E.	BODY		5.	NEEDLES
F.	CLOAK		6.	REASON
G.	EFFING		7.	CRANNY
H.	FLESH		8.	BY CROOK
I.	HAMMER		9.	TONGS
J.	HAND		10.	LIMB
K.	HEART		11.	JONES
L.	HELL OR		12.	VIGOUR
M.	UP HILL		13.	MAIN
N.	BY HOOK OR		14.	SKITTLES
O.	LIFE		15.	QUIET
P.	LIFE		16.	RUIN
Q.	LOVE OR		17.	BONE
R.	MAD DOGS		18.	PARCEL
S.	MIGHT		19.	MONEY
T.	NOOK		20.	SOUL
U.	ODDS		21.	TIDE
V.	PART		22.	BLINDING
W.	PEACE		23.	DOWN DALE
X.	PINS		24.	NAIL
Y.	RACK		25.	BAGGAGE
Z.	WITHOUT RHYME OR		26.	THUNDER
AA.	SKIN		27.	DAGGER
BB.	SMITH		28.	FOOT
CC.	SONG		29.	HIGH WATER
DD.	TIME		30.	PIECES
EE.	TOOTH		31.	SOUL
FF.	VIM		32.	SOUL
GG.	WEAR		33.	DANCE

Your Task

Part B

In each of the sentences below, insert one (or more) of the noun pair phrases opposite so as to complete the idiom and the sense. The correct answers are to be found on page 159.

Sentences

1. The midday heat in Cawnpore was appalling, strength-sapping, stultifying. Only ___ would have risked going out.
2. A real Presbyterian Bible-thumper, he always gave ___ sermons.
3. She'll stop at nothing. She'll do it ___, by fair means or foul.
4. He couldn't resist a gripping ___ spy novel. Preferably a Childers, a le Carré or a Bontly.
5. They smashed it down, going at it with all their strength, ___.
6. Most of the stuff at the flea market showed clear signs of ___.
7. Damn this traffic and building site noise. Oh, for some real ___!
8. Life at university is hard toil for most, 70% perspiration, 30% inspiration. It's not all ___ and *gaudeamus igitur*.
9. Revelling in singing in the choir, she put ___ into each anthem.
10. The government's education policies are ___, lacking all logic.
11. 'Immigrants,' said Margaret, 'are just not our ___.'
12. 'We won't miss an event like that. We'll be there come ___.'
13. When she's had a few stiff drinks she really livens up and glows like a glow-worm. She's the ___ of a party after midnight.
14. They traipsed for miles, ___, before reaching the next village.
15. The two things are not separate and should not be dealt with separately. The one is integral to the other, ___ of it.
16. A marvel of industry, the cleaning lady always worked with ___.
17. No, he wouldn't do it, not for anything, not for ___.
18. Many Irish 'great houses' have fallen into decay, going to ___.
19. He was bound totally, ___, to his domineering spouse.
20. 'That's what average, ___ people do. I'm different.'
21. The Secretary worked ___, with total commitment.
22. She fell asleep during the lecture and woke up with ___ – if only the lecture had been such a prickling sensation!
23. '___ wait for no man', Max Weber shows, was one of the central tenets of the early Protestant ethic in America.
24. The workmen swore. Father swore. Our neighbour swore. The new double-garage was not erected without a good deal of ___.
25. 'I am not attempting that climb! I don't want to risk ___.'
26. He stood forlornly on the platform, surrounded only by ___.
27. I haven't much to do this evening, just a few ___, a few ___.
28. The door was obstinate. They had to use all their strength, ___.
29. Stop making such a fuss, such a ___ about every tiny problem.
30. They looked for it everywhere, high and low, in every ___.
31. After the nerve-racking exam weeks they had both lost weight terribly and were just ___. Others they could name had put on kilos.
32. They would fight fiercely, ___, to prevent the building of a nuclear power plant, a new runway or an undesirable by-pass.

Field 3: Idioms Involving Internal (Half-) Rhymes

Your Task

In each of the sentences below, insert one (or more) of the internal rhymes or half-rhymes beneath so as to complete the idiom and the sense. The correct answers are to be found on page 159.

Sentences

1. The lecture was appallingly disorganised: the information in it came ___.
2. The exercise was simplicity itself, just ___.
3. How refreshing to feel the ___ of gentle rain-drops after such a parched drought.
4. She came rushing in to my room ___ with the news.
5. The two of them are forever cuddling and kissing, all ___.
6. Our neighbours are arrogant and conceited, really ___.
7. Oh, marvellous! Fantastic! ___.
8. The cabinet must now take a decision. It can't ___ any longer.
9. It's glorious to live in a sleepy village, away from the ___ of the throbbing city.
10. They are a little over-aesthetic, even affected, rather ___ people.
11. 'Get down to it! Roll up your sleeves! Don't be so ___!'
12. This cupboard's full of more or less useless things, all old ___.
13. The ideas in this paper are vagueness itself, deplorably ___.
14. In the 'silly season' of high summer, the journalists thirsted for any ___ of information.
15. On the way home he would often ___ in this pub or that.
16. The negotiations became difficult when they came to the details, the ___.
17. She loved the sound of the barrel-organ played by the ___ man.
18. 'I'm sick of our relationship. It's all in-fighting and ___.'
19. I'm afraid they both seem to be complete fools, utter ___.
20. 'Oh, my goodness! My room is all ___. It'll take donkey's years to tidy it!'
21. The conspirators met secretly, all ___at dead of night.
22. 'Wow, you've got a daring bikini! It's the most ___bikini I've ever seen!'
23. 'No, we'll have to grasp the nettle. We may not want to. But we've got to go, ___.'
24. 'How stupid of me! What a ___ I am!'

Options

A. argy-bargy / B. arty-farty / C. dilly-dally / D. helter-skelter / E. easy-peasy / F. higgledy-piggledy / G. hoity-toity / H. hurdy-gurdy / I. hurly-burly / J. hugger-mugger / K. knick-knack / L. lovey-dovey / M. mamsy-pamsy / N. nitty-gritty / O. nitwit / P. pitter-patter / Q. shilly-shally / R. silly billy / S. super-duper / T. teeny-weeny / U. tit-bit / V. topsy-turvy / W. wishy-washy / X. willy-nilly

Field 4: The Pejorative

Your Task

Study the twenty-eight expressions on the left below and then decide which is likely to be the habitual pejorative (depreciatory) form for the persons, objects or institutions on the right. Note that this exercise contains some offensive (*) words. The correct answers are to be found on page 159.

Pejoratives

1. the anorak
2. the Beeb
3. the bimbo
4. the binge
5. the blurb
6. *bog-standard
7. the bumph/bumf
8. the cake-hole
9. *crap
10. *the frog/froggy
11. funk-hole
12. the geek
13. to gripe
14. gunge
15. the hack
16. *the kraut
17. the plonk
18. the pong
19. pseud
20. the rag
21. the shrink
22. *the sleazebag
23. the smoothie
24. the spiel
25. the stiff
26. the toff
27. the tree-hugger
28. to veg out
29. the weepie
30. the wimp

A. mediocre, low quality
B. rubbish, nonsense
C. low quality journalist
D. sentimental film
E. newspaper
F. ardent follower of one hobby
G. bore, socially inept person
H. the BBC
I. psychiatrist
J. German
K. orgy of eating/shopping
L. to do nothing creative
M. to complain, complaint
N. refuge for a coward
O. woman of low IQ, high sex appeal
P. description of book on jacket
Q. Frenchman
R. bureaucratic information
S. mouth
T. pretentious person
U. corpse
V. sordid, despicable person
W. environmental activist
X. stink, malodorous smell
Y. dull, uninteresting person
Z. greasy dirt
AA. prolonged blah-blah
BB. low-quality wine
CC. show-off aristocrat
DD. person of (insincerely?) polite manners.

Field 5: The 'Verb + Adverb' Construction

Your Task

Nouns made up of verb + adverb - such as 'set-back', 'drop-out' and 'take-off' – are becoming increasingly common in modern English. Which of those idiomatic nouns listed beneath would best suit which of the sentences below? The correct answers are to be found on page 159.

Sentences

1. They decided to miss the early lecture, preferring a ___.
2. The imported strawberries were way too expensive, a real ___.
3. Few even bothered to vote: the ___ was a miserable 19%.
4. It was a terrible crash: his beloved 2CV was a complete ___.
5. Who would give her the best ___? She needed a good reference.
6. It was acutely disappointing, a real anti-climax, a ___.
7. The early 1980s saw a menacing ___ of nuclear arms.
8. They reported the *bizarre* ___ next door to the authorities. Such occurrences were at the best suspicious, at the worst quite unpalatable.
9. It was a disappointing translation with some bad ___.
10. That's a marvellous photograph. Let's have a large ___ made.
11. There had been so many ___ recently. They locked all doors.
12. After the ___ of their marriage they lived wild lives for a time.
13. They were caught in a traffic ___ – a long ___ from the motorway interchange – and were badly delayed.
14. The first tasks were tricky, but the next just the reverse, a ___.
15. Direct taxes were indeed reduced, but the average citizen was actually *worse off* owing to a ___ through indirect taxation.
16. The headmaster gave the culprits a twenty-minute ___.
17. 'Wow! Yessir! This new group sure is a ___!' – 'Well, one thing's for sure, their latest concert was a total ___.'
18. 'Row?! Oh, boy! I'd say so! Yes, it was a real ___.'
19. After the ___ our firm will just be part of a large conglomerate. Let's organise a management ___ instead.
20. That TV presenter's a ___. Always ego-tripping.
21. We don't fully understand your invoice. Could you please send us a detailed ___?
22. The firm is strangely run. It's a really odd ___.
23. The spring floods were severe. ___ is still going on.
24. In the ___ to the election, both major parties threw as much mud as they could in the hope that some of it would stick.

Options

A. blow-up / B. break-down / C. break-in / D. break-up / E. build-up / F. bust-up / G. buy-out / H. claw-back / I. dressing-down / J. give-away / K. goings-on / L. hold-up / M. let-down / N. lie-in / O. mopping-up / P. rip-off / Q. run-up / R. sell-out / S. set-up / T. show-off / U. slip-up / V. tail-back / W. take-over / X. turn-on / Y. turn-out / Z. write-off / AA. write-up

Revision II

Exercise 1: Historical Moments

Your Task

In each of the sentences below, insert one of the phrases learned in the foregoing six units to complete the idiom and the sense. The correct answers are to be found on page 159.

Sentences

1. Henry VIII's Reformation policies really put up the ___ of religious traditionalists in the North of England: the series of rebellions known as the 'Pilgrimage of Grace' (1536) was their response.
2. The Suez fiasco of 1956 was the greatest foreign policy *débâcle* in recent British history: the British really lost ___ there.
3. 'Robinocracy', the name given to the governmental system of Sir Robert Walpole, effectively meant government based on bribes and favours, where everybody greased everybody else's ___.
4. A recent study of Britain's far-flung Second Empire appropriately bore the title *The ___ Share*.
5. Bernadette Devlin, the youngest MP at Westminster when elected in 1969, soon gained a reputation for being a ___ on account of her firebrand speeches and tempestuous interventions.
6. In the years from 1956 to 1970 Britain ___ fatefully long over membership of the then Common Market. Successive governments failed to take the ___ by the ___.
7. The recall of Churchill to the premiership in 1940 was a risk, but one which paid off handsomely. The old ___, who had experienced the Boer campaigns of 1899–1902, really proved his worth.
8. The hated new tax of Ship Money, the 'eleven years' tyranny' with no parliament, the growing Puritan mood in the land – when the Short Parliament was finally called in 1640 there was a real storm ___.
9. The queen of the Counter-Reformation, 'Bloody Mary', in whose five-year reign some 280 Protestant martyrs were burned at the stake, was the most ___ Catholic ever to sit on the throne of England.
10. 'The English are slow to move, like a stomach.' George Eliot's phrase still holds true. Notably, some British institutions have shown a ___ development. Even in the 1990s several ___ remained.
11. In the years of C 19th and C 20th British hegemony based on the two-power standard, all other nations' fleets were mere ___ or ___ compared with the dominant and domineering British navy.
12. The brief reign of Richard III ended at the Battle of Bosworth Field (1485): he died in his ___.
13. The image of 'Bad King John' (1199–1216) is in part due to biased chroniclers. In fact, John made quite a good ___ of government.

Exercise 2: In the Family

Your Task

Read the text below on the development of the genre of the family chronicle and then decide which of the idioms learned in the foregoing six units best complete the idiom and sense. Correct answers are to be found on page 160.

Text

Many people have a quite wrong image of the genre of the family chronicle. They see it as a genre which treats the family as a sacred [1] ___, handling it with kid [2] ___.

Yet if one reads the European genre, from Maria Edgeworth's *Castle Rackrent* (1800) through John Galt's *The Entail* (1822) to Émile Zola, Samuel Butler, Th. Mann, John Galsworthy, Roger Martin du Gard, Joyce Cary and on to Graham Swift and Salman Rushdie, one sees that here the family runs the [3] ___. Many of the novels are semi-autobiographical: their authors have a [4] ___ to pick, and they do not [5] ___ their words. They take the [6] ___ by the horns. Their [7] ___ are not portrayed as [8] ___. Often, indeed, they dip their pen in [9] ___. Butler's acidulous *The Way of All Flesh* (posth. 1903) is a case in point. Or M. E. Saltykov-Shchedrin, for example, writes that his *The Golovlevs* (1880) was written to 'attack the family principle'.

This function is made possible by the genre's form. The family chronicle is the opposite of the far-ranging picaresque novel. It is a stay-at-home genre, offering a [10] ___-on-the-wall account of all the [11] ___-on in the family. This is a genre which [12] ___ out the direst secrets of the family, a genre which discovers the [13] ___ in the cupboard, a genre which spills the [14] ___.

Why does the genre have such a false image? Perhaps because some chronicles do tend to [15] ___ on, from long volume to long volume. Perhaps because the genre can easily be confused with the [16] ___-ripper or soap-opera.

For those who take the time to study it, however, the genre is a real [17] ___-opener. The attitude of the genre seems to be that you cannot, or should not, make a [18] ___ out of a [19] ___. It sees the family as an [20] ___ around society's neck. Or as an antiquated [21] ___.

In short, in the family chronicle, the family is on the [22] ___ and literature is on the [23] ___, sitting in judgement on an institution it here calls into question as nowhere else. And the more society moves towards the much-prophesied 'death of the nuclear family', the more the genre of the family chronicle – from Zoë Fairbairns to Kate Atkinson – searches for alternatives. Only time will tell if this is a [24] ___ ___ chase.

13 UNIT Idioms of Travel and Transport

Field 1: Essential Paths

Your Task

In each of the sentences below, insert one (or more) of the words listed beneath to complete the idiom and the sense. The correct answers are to be found on page 160.

Sentences

1. 'Time for you to go, Joe. I'm going to make ___ for bed.' – 'Okay, I guess I'll hit the ___.'
2. It was a seminar for high-fliers, people in the fast ___ to the top.
3. I must get a new job. I'm getting in a monotonous ___ here.
4. 'A critic,' Kenneth Tynan once said, 'is someone who knows the ___ but can't drive the car.'
5. Her position had no chance of promotion. It was a totally ___ job.
6. Her pioneering work blazed the ___ in immunology.
7. 'Damn! I've lost ___ of that marvellous quotation. Where on earth can it be? Was it Frye, Booth, Said, Heath?'
8. 'No, it's the end, it's good-bye, Jake. This is the final farewell, the parting of the ___. Once and for all'
9. It was a complete red herring, leading us up the proverbial ___.
10. The new compact PC was far in advance of its rivals, ___ ahead.
11. 'The prices at motorway stops are exorbitant. It's ___ robbery.'
12. 'She's pregnant?' – 'Yes, been in the family ___ for months.'
13. Eventually, the two sides compromised, meeting each other ___.
14. 'Don't you ever think of anything else? You've got a ___ mind.'
15. The detective left no stone unturned, exploring every conceivable ___ of inquiry.
16. It was an agonising decision, a real ___ in her life. She sat down and re-read Frost's superb poem 'The Road Not Taken'.
17. They loved to put the golden oldies on the turntable and take a trip down memory ___ to the halcyon days of youth.
18. This is the type of exercise a person of my highly-developed language skills has no problems with. It's right up my ___.

Options

avenue / cross-roads / dead-end / garden path / half-way / highway / lane / one-track / road / rut / street / streets / track(s) (3x) / trail / way(s) (3x)

> *Idioms have very often been overlooked by dictionary compilers, for they are hard to 'alphabetize' and are too frequently judged to be slang or transitory. However, they often play a major role in the process of communication.*

EUGENE A. NIDA, *Language Structure and Translation* (1975)

Field 2: Further Ways

Your Task

In each of the sentences below, insert one (or more) of the words listed beneath to complete the idiom and the sense. The correct answers are to be found on page 160.

Sentences

1. The day was done. His battle was lost. His boats were burning. Wearily he wended his ___ homewards.
2. In Leipzig and then gradually all across the land, the citizens took to the ___ with increasing boldness to protest against the régime.
3. Remember *Éducation Sentimentale*. One of the main characters fails on account of *le défaut de ligne droite*. Don't allow yourself to be ___ too much in life.
4. Have the courage of your convictions. Stop being a mere stooge. Go your own ___.
5. 'Can I drop in and see you over the weekend? I'll be down your ___ and it'd be good to meet up again after so long a time.'
6. The government started yet another campaign against drinking and driving, against the proverbial 'One for the ___'.
7. His innovative and seminal research paved the ___ for many subsequent discoveries and refinements to the theory of genre.
8. She had risen in the world, had really come a long ___ since last I saw her.
9. No, we are not going to invest in this. It is clearly an inferior product, not in the same ___ as the others.
10. This craze will not last much longer: it is already on the ___ out down in London.
11. 'His health's improving. Intensive care has worked wonders. He seems well on the ___ to recovery.'
12. It is high time we began to market our products and to really get the show on the ___.
13. This is becoming frustrating! I still cannot ___ down that damn quotation.
14. You are barking up the wrong tree, mate. You are on the wrong ___ completely.
15. The changing demographic structure of the population and the demands it made on health and pension resources made great ___ into the state reserves.
16. 'I told you some time ago, Jake, it's curtains: this really is the end of the ___.' (Frankly, I wish to goodness I'd never met him. I wish he'd never crossed my ___.)

Options

line / inroads / path(s) (1x) / road(s) (3x) / side-track / street(s) (2x) / track(s) (2x) / way(s) (7x)

Field 3: Means of Human Transport

Your Task

Complete the crossword below, made up of idioms based on a means of transport, ancient or modern, noting that the first letter of each word and the number of letters in each word are given. The correct answers are to be found on page 160.

Crossword

Clues

1. 'First things first. Don't put the (4) before the horse.'
2. 'I guess they're stolen. They look as if they fell off a (5).'
3. 'Boss suit, lap-top, Porsche. He's trying to enter the (3)-set.'
4. 'Handsome?! His face looks like the back of a (3).'
5. Though both individualists, they work well in (6) as a team.

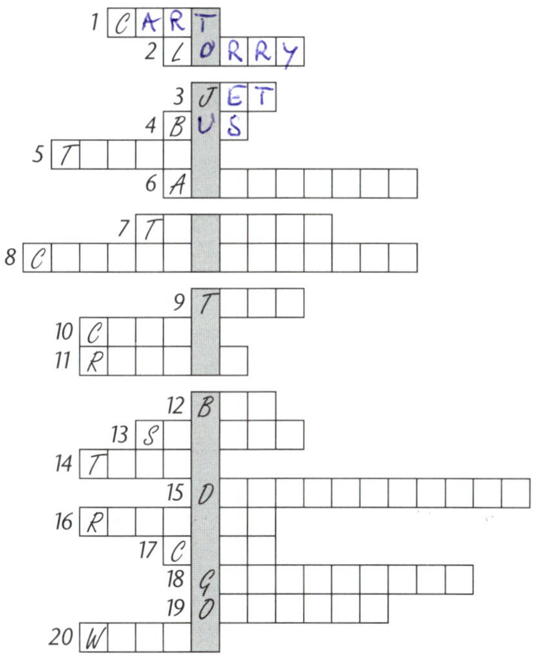

6. The party's prospects were ruined by the scandal. It really upset the (5-4)!
7. Was the PM going quietly insane? Some maintained he had been off his (7) for years.
8. 'Your argument is wholly lacking in logic. One could drive a (5,3,6) through it.'
9. She loved to (4) down the motorway at fifty m.p.h. over the limit.
10. 'Come on, slow (5)! Hurry!'
11. 'Strewth! Your motorbike goes like a (6), like a bat out of hell!'
12. 'You've missed the (3), pal, and you won't be getting another opportunity like that this side of eternity.'
13. 'You'll have to move fast. Get your (6) on, mate!'
14. From the off, the winner, Red Rum, went like a (5).
15. She was the power behind the firm's success, the real (7,5).
16. Management?! Utter chaos, more like it! What a way to run a (7)!
17. 'Can I leave these books at your place? I don't want to (4) them around all day.'
18. 'Yes, they're rich. Got on the (5,5) back in '79.'
19. But what will Mr Average say, the man on the Clapham (7)?
20. 'Still teetotal, Basil?' – 'Yes, old man, been on the (5) since I picked up that nasty virus in the Congo.'

Key Phrase: to support a cause once it seems certain to win (2,4,2,3,9)

Field 4: Ships, Boats and Navigation

Your Task

Read the fifteen headlines below, each of which contains an idiom derived from the field of navigation, and then select the German translation below which best conveys the meaning. The correct answers are to be found on page 160.

Headlines

1. Leader tells Party to 'Batten Down the Hatches'
2. MANAGEMENT CLEARS THE DECKS FOR NEW VENTURE
3. Party Ideologues See 'Clear Blue Water'
4. 'PADDLE YOUR OWN CANOE' IS BEST ADVICE FOR SELF-DOUBTERS
5. University Equipment 'Went Out with the Ark', Say Students
6. Former Prime Minister Told to Stop Rocking the Boat
7. Manager Resolves to Take Fans' Criticism on Board
8. STUDENTS SHOWN THE ROPES IN FRIENDLY FRESHERS' WEEK
9. Give Escaped Prisoner a Wide Berth, Police Urge
10. CRITICS 'ON THE WRONG TACK' ARGUES MINISTER
11. Foreign Minister Gives Argentina a Shot Across the Bows
12. SEA CHANGE IN AUSTRIAN POLITICS
13. TOWN THEATRE GIVEN LIFE-LINE
14. REPORT: EUROPEAN UNIVERSITIES HAVE 'MUCH LEEWAY TO MAKE UP'
15. Wreckers Again at Work

Options

A. beherzigen, ernst nehmen / B. einen Bogen machen um / C. in Deckung gehen (die Luken schalken) / D. eingeweiht / E. auf falscher Fährte / F. deutliche ideologische Unterschiede / G. klar Schiff machen / H. Rettungsring, -linie / I. Rückstand aufholen, Versäumtes nachholen / J. Saboteure / K. die Sache gefährden / L. Trendwende / M. vorsintflutlich / N. Warnschuß / O. werde selbständig(er)

14 UNIT Idioms of Buildings

Field 1: Doors, Floors, Fences

Your Task

Read the fifteen alliterative biographies below and then decide which life is best characterised by which of the idioms listed beneath. The correct answers are to be found on page 161.

Biographies

1. Alan is adviser to the P.M.
2. Bernard is the bread-winner
3. Cathy comes home to find her parents still out at work
4. Dave is easily defeated in a discussion
5. Ethel is often easily embarrassed

6. Felicity takes life too fast
7. Irene is in positions of great influence
8. Kate got the job through connections
9. Lay-about Lawrence is often asked to leave
10. Mark cannot make up his mind

11. Nevil is notoriously nervous
12. Patrick goes uninvited to private parties
13. Ruth is a great repairer of ruined relations
14. Sam is a secret receiver of stolen goods
15. William is a worthy member of society

Options

A. to get in through the back door / B. to walk the corridors of power / C. to be shown the door / D. to keep the wolf from the door / E. to be a fence / F. to rush one's fences / G. to sit on the fence / H. to go on a fence-mending expedition / I. to sink through the floor / J. to be floored / K. to be a gate-crasher / L. to be all keyed up / M. the kitchen cabinet / N. to be a latch-key child / O. to be a pillar of society

> *Throughout the 1980s and 1990s, there has been a quickening of interest among theoretical linguists, and among specialists in lexicography, discourse analysis, language acquisition, and foreign language teaching, in what were traditionally known as 'idioms', and are variously called 'word-combinations', 'fixed expressions' and 'phrasal lexemes'. The interest reflects a keener awareness than before of the pervasiveness of ready-made combinations in written and spoken language.*

R. E. ASHER and J. M. Y. SIMPSON, eds,
The Encyclopaedia of Language and Linguistics (1978)

Field 2: Basic Buildings

Your Task

Complete the crossword below, made up of idioms based on types of building – for human or animal habitation and use – noting that the first letter of each word and the number of letters in each word are given. The correct answers are to be found on page 161.

Crossword

Clues

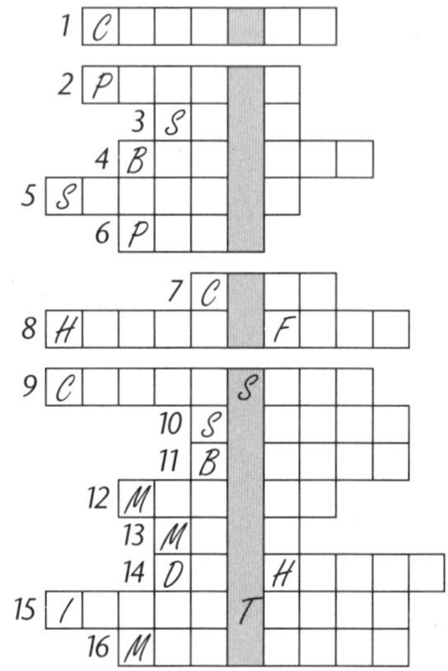

1. The simplest of relationships: little money but plenty of passion – just love in a (7).
2. 'Disgustingly untidy! Don't expect me to live in this (6)!'
3. 'The worst thing about an office party is the conversation: everyone talks (4).'
4. 'Him an administrator!?! He couldn't even organise a piss-up in a (7)!'
5. 'They're living together?' – 'Oh, yes. They've been (7) up together for a year now.'
6. 'To hell with him. Why doesn't he take a long walk off a short (4)?'
7. 'The prisoner's gone! He's flown the (4) during the night!'
8. Destined to be a world-wide celebrity, she had her place reserved in the (4,2,4).
9. 'Totally tactless. And clumsy. Like a bull in a (5,4).'
10. As so often, they reacted after the event and not in anticipation of it. They simply closed the (6) door after the horse had gone.
11. The government gave an extra sum to (6) the financial gap.
12. 'The professor's a (6) piece. He should have retired years ago. Some of his attitudes went out with the Ark.'
13. 'They're stinking rich. They've got a (4) of money, you know.'
14. He was in disgrace. No doubt about it. His name was mud now. This time he was really in the (3-5).
15. The professor seemed to live in and for another sphere, rarely descending from his (5,5) to the mean, terrestrial world of mortals.
16. 'Everyone here seems to be stark, staring bonkers. Sometimes you think you're living in a (8).'

Key Phrase: She was a person one could always rely on for help and support, (1,5,2,8)

Field 3: Parts of Buildings

Your Task

Consider the idioms of parts of buildings below and decide which of the explanations beneath is likely to be the genuine meaning. The correct answers are to be found on page 161.

Idioms

1. **to spend a night on the tiles**
   = to A. be homeless B. be drunk C. have wild sex D. be broke
2. **to put up the shutters**
   = to A. die B. defend o.s. C. pretend not to hear D. close shop
3. **to get in on the ground floor**
   = to A. break in B. hit below the belt C. tell lies D. be involved from the start
4. **to have a good cellar**
   = to A. have good wine B. be strong C. be principled D. inherit money
5. **to go down the drain**
   = to A. be wasted B. be lost C. go to America D. fail
6. **to be up the spout**
   = to be A. spoiled B. pregnant C. wasted D. filthy dirty
7. **to have a tile loose**
   = to be A. dilapidated B. divorced C. crazy, 'bonkers' D. half drunk
8. **window-dressing**
   = A. fine clothes B. flowery language C. camouflage D. a feast
9. **it's the pits**
   = it's A. the worst B. difficult C. low-class D. repairs time
10. **parlour tricks**
    = A. lies B. gossip C. kissing D. mischief
11. **to go from pillar to post**
    = to go from A. A to B directly B. the frying pan to the fire C. place to place aimlessly D. up the promotion ladder
12. **to indulge in backstairs intrigue**
    = to indulge in intrigue A. in secret B. which is underhand C. among servants against the master D. outside the (pol.) cabinet

Field 4: Buildings in Headlines

Your Task

Read the headlines below, each of which contains one idiom derived from the field of house and home, and then select the German translation below which best conveys the meaning of the word or phrase underlined. The correct answers are to be found on page 161.

Headlines

1. **Labour home and dry at 2.30 a.m.**
2. **RSC record: full house at every performance bar two**
3. CLUB MEETING DESCENDS INTO ROUGH HOUSE – FIVE ARRESTS
4. **Product now a household name, records boss with pride**
5. VILLAGERS PROTEST AT 'HOUSE OF ILL-FAME'
6. **Home Truths from Abroad**
7. **Black candidate romps home**
8. RESULTS 'NOTHING TO WRITE HOME ABOUT'
9. **NATO homes in on ethnic cleansers**
10. **'Coming Home' brings war home to Americans**
11. **It's 'home from home' declares delighted star**
12. SPEECH BRINGS HOUSE DOWN
13. PM GOES ALL ROUND THE HOUSES, CLAIMS INTERVIEWER
14. CANDIDATE'S WAYWARD PAST COMES HOME TO ROOST
15. **Children from broken homes 'more prone to underachievement'**

Options

A. nichts Aufsehenerregendes / B. ausverkauft / C. Bordell, Freudenhaus / D. um den heißen Brei herum reden / E. haushoch gewinnen / F. heimsuchen / G. Keilerei / H. aufs Korn nehmen / I. landesweit bekannt / J. nachvollziehbar machen / K. Ovationen bzw. tobendes Gelächter auslösen / L. unangenehme Wahrheiten / M. aus zerrütteten Familienverhältnissen / N. am Ziel angekommen / O. zweites Zuhause

15

UNIT Idioms of the Household

Field 1: Furniture

Your Task

Read the twenty alliterative biographies below and then decide which life is best characterised by which of the idioms of furniture listed beneath. The correct answers are to be found on page 161.

Biographies

1. Boris can booze more bottles of beer than anybody
2. Chrissy was in a quandary but is now in the clear
3. Derek couldn't decide between the Defence Ministry and dentistry
4. Dilly is in dire difficulties demanding decisions in a dilemma

5. Guy has a ghoulishly ghastly and guilty secret
6. Harold is an habitué of this high society hotel
7. Ina initiated government intervention for this industry
8. Lew was not re-elected in his Lothian constituency

9. Martha and Martin were made to exchange ministries
10. Oliver? It's all over! Over and out!
11. Prue became professor at a prodigiously precocious age
12. Roberta took revenge on her rivals

13. Sam played second fiddle in his relationship with Samantha
14. Sweeney had a liking for sweeping statements
15. Theo is thrilled by tourism but only on TV
16. Tracy is there transitionally till the true candidate turns up

Options

A. to be an armchair traveller B. to give blanket condemnations C. to gain a chair D. to play musical chairs E. to have a skeleton in the cupboard F. it's curtains for G. to featherbed H. to be part of the furniture I. to be off the hook J. to lose one's seat K. to take a back seat L. to be in the hot seat M. to keep a seat warm for s.o. N. to fall between two stools O. to drink (s.o) under the table P. to turn the tables

> *Hush little bright line,*
> *Don't you cry,*
> *You'll be a cliché*
> *By and by.*
> FRED ALLEN

> *Jede Redensart ist die Fratze*
> *eigener Gedanken, ein*
> *"Mitesser" im Zellengewebe*
> *des Denkers.*
> CHRISTIAN MORGENSTERN

Field 2: Household Goods

Your Task

Complete the crossword below, made up of idioms of household goods, noting that the first letter of each word and the number of letters in each word are given. The correct answers are to be found on page 161.

Crossword

Clues

1. Another idiom forgotten! My memory's getting like a (5)!
2. I've gone badly downhill. I really must (5) up my idioms.
3. 'Joe's dead?' – 'Yes, kicked the (6) two years back.
4. No interview! The tennis star was (7) off to the airport.
5. 'Sorry. Got to stay in and (3) up vocab. for a test'
6. 'She can talk! She's as bad as the person she's criticising. It's a case of the (3) ...
7. ... calling the (6) black.'

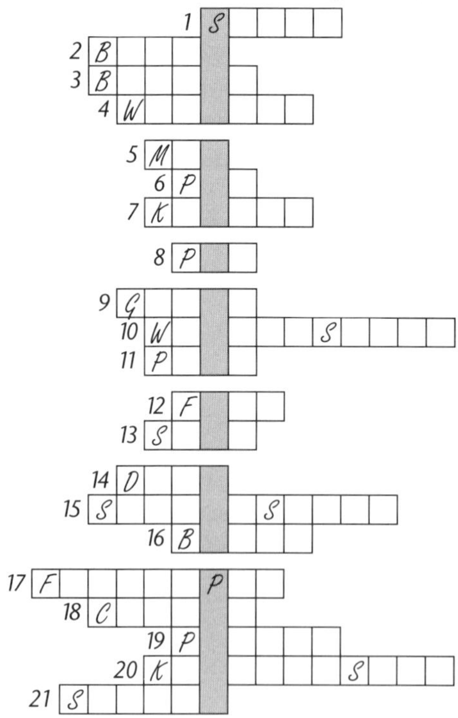

8. It proved to be a rare, lucky success, just a flash in the (3).
9. The police continued to (5) the detainee into the early hours: question upon question.
10. 'Come on, folks. We must win this one or we'll be bottom of the league and get the (6,5).'
11. 'Rich? They're stinking rich! They've got (4) of money.'
12. 'Did you have a successful day with the collecting box?' – 'Yes, people are normally willing to (4) out when Christmas is coming.'
13. Witchcraft in the parish! Satanic masses! The village was becoming a (4) of iniquity! The vicar preached sternly to his flock.
14. After every General Election, the prime minister is allowed to (4) out honours to his or her favourites – often in the form of peerages.
15. Always privileged, she had been born with a (6,5) in her mouth.
16. A new (5) sweeps clean.
17. 'We'd be as badly placed as before. Out of the (6,3) into the fire.'
18. 'He's not good enough for her. He can't hold the (6) to her.'
19. His first book was savaged by the critics – really (6).
20. 'Your car looks well-loaded for a two-week holiday, Bert.' – 'Yes, I get the feeling we're taking everything but the (7,4).'
21. 'One last effort! We're not going to throw in the (6) now!'

Key Phrase: She's overburdened with work/worry (4,3,1,3,2,3,5)

Field 3: Utensils and Furnishings

Your Task

Consider the idioms of utensils and furnishings below and decide which of the explanations beneath is likely to be the genuine meaning. The correct answers are to be found on page 162.

Idioms

1. **to peg out**
   = to A. collapse drunk B. die C. give long speech D. knock down
2. **to be tarred with the same brush**
   = to be A. from same family B. of same education C. suspected of same deeds D. have same shoddy opinions
3. **to be a pot-hunter**
   = to be after A. women B. drink C. sporting trophies D. antiques
4. **a mug shot**
   = a A. police photograph B. bad photo C. bad shot D. dead hit
5. **you could cut the air with a knife**
   = the air was A. smelly B. tense C. foggy D. full of jollity
6. **to put the knife in**
   = to A. operate on B. give fatal blow C. wound D. insult
7. **to burn the candle at both ends**
   = to A. overspend B. overcook C. be a miser D. overwork
8. **a square peg in a round hole**
   = a A. misfit B. unhappy person C. awkward person D. corpse
9. **to be on the wrong side of the blanket**
   = to be A. in the cold B. unloved C. unmarried D. illegitimate
10. **to bite the carpet**
    = to be A. a bad actor B. angry C. bad-tempered D. dead
11. **to be on the carpet**
    = to be A. discussed B. disciplined C. half drunk D. furious
12. **a wet blanket**
    = a A. bore B. incompetent lover C. spoilsport D. bad worker
13. **to suffer a curtain lecture**
    = to be A. scolded in bed B. given the last rites C. be bored out of one's mind D. to speak long-windedly

Field 4: Containers

Your Task

In each of the sentences below, insert one (or more) of the containers listed beneath to complete the idiom and the sense. The correct answers are to be found on page 162.

Sentences

1. 'We can't go yet. It's raining, pouring – ___ down!'
2. 'Oh, this exam's going to be a disaster. I can't control myself. I'm at the end of my tether. I can't face it. I'm just a ___ of nerves.'
3. The pound sterling was buoyant, reaching a ten-year high against a whole ___ of other currencies.
4. 'This plan is full of complications and contradictions. It's not been thought through. It'll never work. It's a ___ of worms!'
5. She was a very quick-witted girl guide, and to prove it she could ___ the compass backwards and forwards in a matter of seconds – a remarkable feat of memory (but perhaps not so useful really).
6. Some participants in the negotiations disliked this or that clause. Others recognised that it was a ___ deal: they had to 'lump it or leave it' – take it as a whole or get nothing.
7. 'The *Land* really must fund its universities better.' – 'But of course, they say it can't. The ___ are allegedly empty. Same old story.'
8. His book was a devastating attack on post-modern literary criticism. It was the last nail in the ___ of Yale deconstruction, Parisian post-structuralism and whatnot.
9. The contributions to the symposium were of very varying quality and even content orientation. All in all it was a very mixed ___.
10. She was a real live wire, full of verve, a real ___ of energy.
11. Don't risk everything on one venture: don't put all your eggs in one ___.
12. 'Hey! What a lap-top you've got! 904,4 MB RAM!! And three simultaneous CD-ROM drives! It must have cost a ___!'
13. 'Yes, it did. It would have broken the bank if I hadn't had money stored away in my savings book, in the bottom ___, so to speak.'
14. One must expect such things. There are all part and ___ of life in our society.
15. After the strike yesterday and the snow last night, the train timetable is all in confusion, all to ___.
16. She just closed her eyes and crossed any six numbers on the lottery ticket, taking ___ luck. And that method didn't work either.
17. 'Did they reach an agreement?' – 'Yes, it took them until the early hours, and it was a typical bit of Euro-fudge. But now, it's in the ___.'
18. 'Isn't Emily thin these days!' – 'Yes, she's just a ___ of bones, poor dear.'

Options

bag (3x) – basket (2x) – box – bucket – bundle (2x) – can – coffers – coffin – drawer – package – packet – parcel – pot (2x)

16

UNIT **Family and Proper Names**

Field 1: The Essential Family

Your Task

In each of the sentences below, insert a family word, or family words (at times preceded by an adjective), to complete the idiom and the sense, noting that the first letter of and number of letters in each word are given. The correct answers are to be found on page 162.

Sentences

1. Poor Sue has an acute headache – a (M & F, 6,3,6) of a migraine.
2. 'Brother Joshua is dead?' – 'Yes, he was, alas, gathered to his (F, 7) in late autumn.'
3. 'Rats! Quit when things got tough and left me holding the (B,4)!'
4. What! Humble Gießen is (T,7) with Versailles and Winchester?!
5. 'You've got nothing to teach them. They've far more experience and nous. You can't teach your (G,11) to suck eggs, you know.'
6. 'I think the class teacher gave him a few words of plain and firm advice, talking to him like a Dutch (U,5).'
7. 'Marvellous news! Betty's in the (F,6) way! Isn't that lovely!'
8. Her husband's death gave her a new lease of life and she lived on for thirty years as a (M,W 5,5)
9. 'They're very simple folk – just (C,C 7,7) so to speak.'
10. 'I love it. Nothing I like doing more. It's (M,M 7,4) to me.'
11. 'This is simple! Like a hot knife through butter! It's (C,P 6,4)!'
12. Stephenson's 'Rocket' is reputed the first ever steam locomotive – the (D,5) of them all – although some now shed doubt on this.
13. She was quite beyond reproach or blame – like Caesar's (W,4).
14. Stephenson gained the fame, but was it really his (B-C,5-5)?
15. The newspapers pilloried the project. The minister became an (A,S 4,5) for their attacks.
16. 'Stop blubbering! Don't be a (C-B, 3-4)!'
17. 'A chip off the old block! Like (F,6) like (S,3).'
18. 'Yes, such behaviour does seem to run in the (F,6).'
19. 'Her husband's always at the links, my dear. She's a (G,W 4,5).'
20. Generous with his money, the uncle proved to be a real (S,D 5,5).
21. They liked to have a bit of slap and tickle, a bit of kiss and cuddle, a bit of (H,Y,F 4,4,6) in the back of the car.
22. Don't be too rash. Don't throw out the (B,4) with the bath water.

> *The language of familiar dialogue and colloquial pleasantry [...] is always in a high degree idiomatic, both in the terms and phrases employed, and in construction.*

H. ROGERS, *Essays*, II, iii (1839)

Field 2: Puzzling Names

Your Task

Consider the idioms of proper names below and decide which of the explanations beneath is likely to be the genuine meaning. The correct answers are to be found on page 162.

Idioms

1. **it's Buggins' turn**
   = A. my B. your C. anyone's turn D. the turn of the next in line
2. **Lord and Lady Muck**
   = people A. of importance B. of no importance C. of imagined importance D. who are impostors
3. **on Shanks's pony**
   = on A. foot B. the dole C. one's last legs D. parole
4. **to keep up with the Joneses**
   = to A. hate your neighbours B. imitate them C. argue with them D. be friendly with them
5. **to do sweet Fanny Adams**
   = to A. make love B. play music C. sing D. do 'fuck all' (i.e. nothing at all)
6. **the real Mackoy/McCoy**
   = A. a true Scot B. the culprit C. the real thing D. Mr Right
7. **a Tommy Atkins**
   = a A. bore B. a World War I soldier C. a gentleman D. sailor
8. **a tail-end Charlie**
   = A. stuck in a traffic jam B. unemployed long-term C. the last and lowest D. the last and (therefore) luckiest
9. **Jack Frost**
   = A. frost B. a cool customer C. a cold person D. a bad lover
10. **to go to Davy Jones's locker**
    = to A. steal B. mine for coal C. drown D. be a sailor
11. **a simple Simon**
    = a A. genius B. victim C. dupe D. simpleton
12. **a Girl Friday**
    = a A. career woman B. woman office dogsbody C. weekend lover D. an all-round talented woman
13. **to be a Paul Pry**
    = to be A. nosey B. a spy C. a researcher D. a detective
14. **to be a smart Alec**
    = to be A. clever-clever B. a know-all C. intelligent D. brilliant
15. **a Peeping Tom**
    = A. the last drink B. an C 18th Irish rebel C. a very early riser D. a voyeur
16. **to give a Roland for an Oliver**
    = A. to swindle, cheat B. to re-marry a better man C. to share what little one has D. to give as good as one gets

Field 3: Names in Dialogue

Your Task

Study the situations listed below and then decide which of the colloquial idioms of personal names listed beneath would best express your message. The correct answers are to be found on page 163.

Situations

You You You You You You You You You You You You You You You You You

1. wish to go to the toilet in a friend's house
2. have failed to recognise someone
3. shout out in annoyance, anger or frustration
4. want to tell someone that he/she has no alternative
5. see that your friend's petticoat is showing beneath her dress

6. think that something is utter rubbish
7. have received and understood a message
8. inform someone that you don't give a damn about their problems because you're in the clear
9. tell someone that you have no intention of doing what they wish you to do
10. have heard a piece of news before

11. want an acquaintance to share a ciggy or similar product
12. consider that something is evenly balanced
13. wish to say that something will happen in next to no time
14. tell someone that if they follow a course of action they will get what they want

Options

You Say You Say You Say You Say You Say You Say You Say You Say You

A. I didn't know him from Adam
B. It's all my eye and Betty Martin
C. Then it's Bob's your uncle
D. Don't bogart that joint
E. Charlie's dead
F. Hobson's choice
G. Blow you, Jack
H. before you can say Jack Robinson
I. Where's the John/john?
J. Not on your Nelly
K. Oh, for Pete's sake!
L. Yes, and Queen Anne is dead
M. Roger
N. It's even Stevens

Field 4: The Name 'Jack'

Your Task

Consider the 'Jack' idioms listed below and then decide which of the explanations beneath is the correct one in each case. The correct answers are to be found on page 164.

Idioms

1. a jack-in-office
2. a Jack of all trades
3. to jack up
4. a Jack-in-the-box
5. to climb like a steeplejack
6. Jack is as good as his master
7. a cheapjack
8. to be on one's Jack Jones
9. Every Jack has his Jill
10. a Jack Tar
11. to jack in
12. every man jack
13. to hit the jackpot
14. Jack Sprat
15. I'm all right, Jack!

Options

A. all the foolish / B. to be alone / C. to sit on one's backside / D. bad boss, bad workers / E. damn you, mate / F. a bureaucrat / G. a cheap labourer / H. to climb well / I. to destroy something precious / J. equal rights for workers / K. everybody / L. to give sth. up / M. a handyman in many fields / N. to increase / O. a know-all / P. a person always leaping to his or her feet / Q. a nuisance / R. an officious official / S. there's a partner for everyone somewhere / T. a pompous person / U. a road-repairer / V. a sailor / W. every screw has a nut / X. a skinny person / Y. to be a social climber / Z. a street vendor / AA. to support / BB. to win on the pools / CC. you're the one that's mad

17

UNIT **Idioms of Professions, Tools and Money**

Field 1: Craftsmanship

Your Task

Read the passage below on the nature of satire inserting the most suitable word from the language of craftsmen and mechanics beneath to complete the sense.

Text

It is great satirists such as Swift, Voltaire, Kraus and Tucholsky who lay down the [1] ___ of their chosen mode. And one [2] ___ of their writing is that they [3] ___ their colours to the mast. They hold their target in a [4] ___-like grip and they give it a [5] ___. To read their works is to see the difference between the ironist, such as Th. Mann, and the satirist, such as Pope: as N. Frye put it, satire is militant irony.

Why is the satirist a relatively unacknowledged figure? Precisely, one feels, because he goes at his subject [6] ___ and [7] ___. Of course, the satirist writes literature. He does not just call a [8] ___ a [9] ___. But he has a clear [10] ___ to grind. There is a directness to satire different from the obliquities literary critics habitually delight in. The satirist doesn't beat about the bush. He gets down to [11] ___. And he doesn't give [12] ___ for parties, conventions or reputations.

The historical novelist [13] ___ over the ashes of the past. The satirist stokes the fires of the present. Of all the literary genres satire is perhaps closest to politics. The aim of the satirist must be to throw a [14] ___ in the works.

But does he bring the machines to a standstill? Were Swift's renowned *Drapier's Letters* (1724-35) the last [15] ___ in the coffin of British colonialism in Ireland? No. Did Kraus or Horváth lay the spectre of German and Austrian militarism? No. Did Evelyn Waugh's *Decline and Fall* (1928) herald the end of the British public school? Of course not. But the greatness of satire [16] ___ precisely on the significance, even obduracy of its target. Only the lesser satirist tilts at easily toppled targets. The reward of the great satirist is different: he has [17] ___ the problem, he has [18] ___ the lie. His motto could be the lines of Matthew Arnold:

'When the forts of folly fall,/They'll find thy body by the wall.'

Options

axe / benchmark / brass tacks / hallmark / hammer (2x) / hammering / hinge / nail (3x) / rake / spade (2x) / spanner / tongs / two pins / vice

> *idiom* A sequence of words that is a unit of meaning; also called a 'fixed' or 'frozen' expression.

DAVID CRYSTAL, *Cambridge Encyclopaedia of the English Language* (1995)

Field 2: Puzzling Tools

Your Task

Consider the idioms of tools below and decide which of the explanations beneath is likely to be the genuine meaning. The correct answers are to be found on page 164.

Idioms

1. **to talk nuts and bolts**
   = to talk A. tough B. basics C. nonsense D. business
2. **to do the spadework**
   = to do the A. investigations B. excavations C. easier bit D. hard work
3. **to play with edged tools**
   = to A. interfere B. act dangerously C. be delicate D. make passionate love
4. **to come under the hammer**
   = to be A. auctioned B. heavily defeated C. criticised D. flunked
5. **to screw one's eyes down**
   = to A. sleep deeply B. be really drunk C. read D. concentrate
6. **to be axed**
   = to be A. killed B. punished C. sacked D. cut
7. **a screwdriver factory**
   = a/an A. brothel B. bar C. assembly factory D. parliament
8. **to take a sledgehammer to crack a nut**
   = to be A. thorough B. violent C. using unnecessary force(s) D. liable to exaggerate
9. **to lay (it/sth.) on with a trowel**
   = to A. be gentle B. be generous C. hurt deliberately D. flatter grossly
10. **to be caught between hammer and anvil**
    = to be A. heavily defeated B. killed in an accident C. beaten up D. in a dilemma
11. **to down tools**
    = to A. end work for the day B. strike C. retire D. take a lunch/tea/coffee break
12. **the thin end of the wedge**
    = a(n) A. small portion B. small concession leading to a larger one C. last (and feebler) child D. dangerous (and perhaps final) illness

Field 3: Key Professions

Your Task

Complete the crossword below, made up of further idioms of professions, taking care to use the correct form.

Crossword

Clues

1. 'You're as mad as a (6)!'
2. Steffi did not just defeat opponents, she (9) them.
3. He was not in good form, having to (5) an injury.
4. 'Let's run the scheme as a kind of trial, a (5) project.'
5. The candidate stood as a 'Mr Clean' as an honest (6).
6. She's the perfect applicant – (6)-made for the post.
7. It was a dubious language school run by a (6) operator.
8. 'Vulgar?! She swears like a (8)!'
9. He loved to (6) around, doing unnecessary necessities.
10. From an early age she loved to (6) with mechanical things.
11. They were the closest of bosom friends, as thick as (7).
12. In vain did he protest that he was as sober as a (5).
13. The crooked manager had (8) the accounts for years.
14. He gambled away her money on an aptly-named 'one-armed (6)'.
15. The teacher had to (8) her class of 35 around the capital.
16. 'Are you going to retire next year, old boy?' – 'No, I'll (7) on.'
17. 'Let's have a (10) lunch in the next pub. Cheese, bread, pickles.'
18. 'He's forever arguing, that man – a real barrack-room (6).'
19. 'What am I, a teacher, doing organising a summer school? It's not a break at all – just a (7) holiday.'
20. 'Blimey! Their language! Each of 'em swears like a (7)!'
21. The drivers spent the first few laps (9) for position.
22. 'Oh, I'm just a simple chap, just a (5) of wood ... (see clue 23)
23. ... and (7) of water.'
24. 'Let's send someone ahead to (3) out the land.'
25. 'Paper due in tomorrow! Aargh! I'll have to (6) it up overnight.'
26. '26 questions – that's exactly two (6) dozen, and I've got 'em all!'

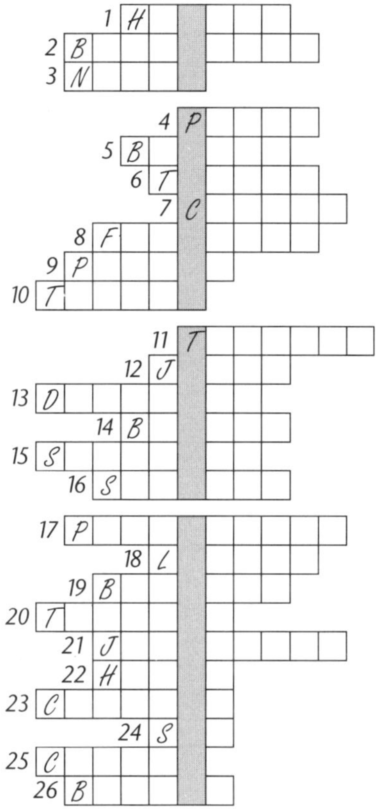

Key Phrase: The wolf set to guard the geese.

Field 4: Profession and Class

Your Task

In each of the sentences below, insert one or more of the professions listed below, to complete the idiom and the sense, taking care to use an appropriate form. The correct answers are to be found on page 164.

Sentences

1. 'Ooh, what a nice big one you've got, as the ___ said to the ___.'
2. As long as the two remained leaders of their respective parties, there was an unwritten, ___ agreement between them that certain topics would be left undiscussed, certain stones left unturned.
3. She was reading the later Barthes, Foucault and Eco, three of the ___ of European cultural criticism in the seventies and eighties.
4. The firm was in trouble. There was nothing for it but to call in a skilled professional consultant, a 'company ___' to put things straight.
5. 'Never try that restaurant, my dear! The food is unutterably, *indescribably* awful – it just ___ description!'
6. Of course the university Vice-Chancellor is not really to blame. The real culprit, the real ___ of the piece is the government.
7. 'And may I in conclusion call for a warm round of applause for the stalwart Mrs Stallsworthy, a woman who, as our trusty secretary for over twenty-five years, has done such ___ service.'
8. 'Broke! Bust! My last penny gone! Ruin staring me mockingly in the face! All gambled away! The cheats! They took me to the ___!'
9. 'Surely you don't believe that tall story! That's a real ___'s yarn if ever I heard one!'
10. 'I could eat a horse! I'm as hungry as a ___!'
11. 'What's wrong with Rainer? What a decidedly poor presentation! Not up to his usual standard.' – 'No, since re-reading *Global 2000*, he's given up all hope: he doesn't give a ___'s cuss for anything now!'
12. 'Your advice is unwanted, pal. Don't try to come the old ___ with us. We've been in this business far longer, okay?'
13. The country seemed to be yearning for a heroic rescuer, a noble-spirited ___ in shining armour to rid it of all its evils and woes.
14. 'But what would be the motive for her committing so cold-blooded and dastardly a crime?' – 'Well, Inspector, the villagers tell me that she had ___ a grievance against the victim from early youth.'
15. 'Oh, go and tell that to the ___! I'm not so easily fooled! I wasn't born yesterday, you know!'
16. 'Do you really think they'll try to elect a new leader?' – 'No – or at least they'd be very foolish to drop the ___ at this stage.'

Options

actress / bishop / cleaner / doctor / fisherman / gentleman / high priest / hunter / knight / marine / nurse / pilot / soldier / tinker / villain / yeoman

Field 5: Essential Money

Your Task

In each of the sentences below, insert one or more of the money-based phrases listed beneath, to complete the idiom and the sense, taking care to use an appropriate form. The correct answers are to be found on page 165.

Sentences

1. 'I do wish our Eustace had chosen a more eligible, *marriageable* young woman! She hasn't got ___ to rub together, you know!'
2. 'Let each give what he or she can – give the proverbial ___.'
3. Being a real estate agent in the post-1989 East was not the cleanest of jobs, but one certainly earned pots of money, a lot of the ___.
4. 'Only the 5th of the month, and broke already! I haven't got a ___.'
5. In the store one could spend pounds and pounds, but there was no salubrious public convenience where one could quietly spend a ___.
6. Strange to think that the humble ___ was the prototype of the modern 36-gear orienteering mountain-bike.
7. 'Her help is invaluable. She's worth her ___!'
8. 'Well, let's go the whole hog! If we're going to take tea in London, let's do it at the 'Ritz'! In for a penny, in for a ___!'
9. 'It was a *good* Ritz cucumber sandwich. But it cost a ___!'
10. 'I don't give a damn. Not a tinker's cuss. I don't give (a) ___!'
11. 'What tour operators! We found ourselves booked into cheapo hotels, and flying on a rickety, ___ plane. Never again!'
12. 'I'm convinced of it. Totally convinced. I'd bet my bottom ___.'
13. They were just get-rich-quick types, just out to earn a fast ___.
14. 'It's no use making false economies now and paying far more for repairs later. Don't spoil the ship for a ___ of tar!
15. 'Where are you working these days? Who pays you your ___?'
16. The poorer young men accepted the offer of the ___ and signed up for the army.
17. 'No, you just can't get rid of Cecily. She keeps turning up, never-wanted, but ever-present – like a ___.
18. 'Hear, hear! We have all come to appreciate Mrs Stallworthy's splendid, ever-reliable, indeed ___ qualities.'
19. In difficult times, the village cobbler went far and wide for work, toiling long hours to make an ___ and keep the wolf from the door.
20. The Faculty Board had almost come to a decision, but then Prof. Zankerzoff decided to have his ___ and the debate flared up again.

Options

A. bad penny / B. brass farthing / C. buck / D. dollar / E. filthy lucre / F. ha'p'orth / G. honest penny / H. king's shilling / I. penny / J. penny-farthing / K. pound / L. pretty penny / M. shekels / N. sou / O. sterling / P. two pennies / Q. tuppence / R. twopenny-ha'penny / S. two-penny worth / T. weight in gold / U. widow's mite

Field 6: Money, Money

Your Task

In each of the dialogues below, insert one or more of the 'money' phrases listed below, to complete the idiom and the sense, taking care to use an appropriate form. The correct answers are to be found on page 165.

Dialogues

1. –'What! All he does is teach once a week and do some admin.!!'
– 'Yes, what a cushy job, eh! ***!'
2. – 'Who do you reckon will win the coming election?'
– 'It'll be close, but *** I'd say Senator Sockem'll come through.'
3. – 'No need to worry about the cost, my dear. The firm's paying!'
– 'And the firm is rolling in it. So ***.'
4. – 'Do they pay you well as a waitress?'
– 'No! Peanuts! It's just ***, a bit of ready cash.'
5. – 'Will Sockem or Charmain win?'
– 'It's impossible to say. Too close to call. It's ***.'
6. – 'The judge was influenced by the wealth of the defendant!?'
– 'I'm afraid so. ***.'
7. – 'The mafia paid him to keep his trap shut?'
– 'Of course. ***.'
8. – 'Is the company a deserving object for investment?'
– 'That penny-farthing organisation? No. It would be ***.'
9. – 'If you're so much in favour of Republican ideas, you must support Sockem and contribute to his campaign fund.'
– 'You mean I must ***?'
10. – 'I offer you $1,500,000 down and no questions asked.'
– 'Okay, mister. You're on. But let's *** first.'
11. – 'She's not the best economiser?'
– 'The Duchess!? Economise!? She ***!!'
12. – 'How did they become so rich?'
– 'East End crime. Betrayal. Paid killing, maybe. It's ***.'
13. – 'The government thinks money solves all problems.'
– 'Yes, a problem crops up and they just ***.'
14. – 'How can she pay for her new furs and *accessoires*?'
– 'Her old man's rolling in it. He's a real ***.'
15. – 'Darling, let's go to the Seychelles, to Easter Island, to Sylt and to Baden-Baden this year.'
– 'My sweet, we can't afford to. We're ***!'

Options

A. for my money / B. a moneybags / C. pin money / D. money talks / E. it's money for old rope / F. money is no object / G. even money / H. to put one's money where one's mouth is / I. to spend money like water / J. to throw money at / K. blood money / L. hush money / M. not to be made of money / N. to throw good money after bad / O. to see the colour of s.o.'s money

18

UNIT **Idiomatic Structures III**

Field 1: The 'Verb + like' Construction II

Your Task

Fit the two parts of each idiom together, noting that on the right two 'answers' are bluff. Then insert the idioms into the appropriate sentence in Part B below.

Idioms

A. to fit like
B. to get on like
C. to go like (to 'work')
D. to go like (to submit)
E. to go through like
F. to grin like
G. to laugh like
H. to leak like
I. to look like
J. to look like
K. to need sth. like (ironic)
L. to smell like
M. to swarm like
N. to work like

1. a sieve
2. a Cheshire cat
3. lambs to the slaughter
4. a drain
5. nobody's business
6. something the cat brought in
7. a charm
8. a worm in winter
9. a pint of porter
10. a dream
11. a dose of salts
12. nothing on earth
13. a glove
14. a ghost
15. locusts
16. a hole in the head

Sentences

1. 'Information is always escaping from that ministry. It ___.'
2. 'From the first meeting they ___. A match made in heaven!'
3. 'I'm afraid she has not the slightest taste in clothing! My dear! A scarecrow has more style! She ___!'
4. After the long trip by camel through the Sahara – after long weeks of maximum heat and minimum hygiene – they both ___.
5. The jeans were exactly the right size – they ___.
6. 'Oh, no! Another urgent order! I ___ more work today ___!'
7. Afterwards, the reporters besieged Monica, ___ round her ___.
8. She still hasn't recovered. She was at the party, but she ___.
9. When the police caught me driving the wrong way down a one-way street, I said I was hurrying to my dying grandmother and it ___.
10. We thought we'd bought enough food for the weekend. But our guests and their beloved kids ___ it all ___ on Saturday.
11. The Swedes fell easy prey to belligerent Boris. They ___.
12. 'The exam was a total cinch. I was brilliantly prepared. It ___.'
13. It was embarrassing sitting next to her: she found the most unfunny things funny, ___ at the most inappropriate moments.
14. She was as pleased as Punch, going round the whole day ___.

Field 2: The 'as ... as' Construction II

Your Task

Part A
Each of the thirty adjectives on the left below is commonly used with one of the nouns on the right in an 'as ... as' construction. Fit the idioms together and check your answers on page 165, before going on to Part B opposite

Idioms

as		as	
1.	bald	A.	pitch
2.	black	B.	a pikestaff
3.	calm	C.	eggs is eggs
4.	cheap	D.	a hunter
5.	chirpy	E.	a new-born babe
6.	cold	F.	Croesus
7.	daft	G.	a pig with two tails
8.	dead	H.	a new pin
9.	dull	I.	a cricket
10.	flat	J.	Larry
11.	free	K.	Punch
12.	good	L.	a coot
13.	happy	M.	a bird
14.	hungry	N.	a board
15.	innocent	O.	charity
16.	mad	P.	dirt
17.	near	Q.	dammit
18.	neat	R.	a brush
19.	nutty	S.	a mule
20.	plain (clear to perceive)	T.	a beetroot
21.	pleased	U.	a dodo
22.	pleased	V.	sin
23.	rich	W.	ditch-water
24.	red	X.	houses
25.	safe	Y.	a fruitcake
26.	skinny	Z.	one's word
27.	stiff	AA.	a flounder
28.	stubborn	BB.	a rake
29.	sure	CC.	a/the March Hare
30.	ugly	DD.	a millpond

Your Task

Part B

In each of the sentences below, insert one (or more) of the 'as .. as' phrases opposite so as to complete the idiom and the sense. The correct answers are to be found on page 165.

Sentences

1. The landscape of East Anglia, reclaimed from the sea over the centuries, is as ___, the only hills being former islands.
2. 'Let's get some big firms as sponsors. After all, they're as ___.'
3. 'Some of those nondescript buildings erected in the Sixties really do disfigure the townscape. Frankly, some are as ___. The architects must be as ___, thoroughly ashamed at their work.'
4. It was a hot, hot day in August. And not a breath of breeze. The sea stretched shimmering into the distance, well-nigh motionless, as ___.
5. 'I just couldn't stand it. I had to leave the lecture. I had to. It was boring the pants off me! I tell you: it was as ___.'
6. 'Something's bound to go wrong. As ___. You know Sod's Law, don't you? If something can go wrong, it will!'
7. 'Food! And fast! I'm famished! Starving! As ___.'
8. 'She may look as ___, but she's got a long record of shop-lifting, drug-peddling and extortion behind her.'
9. 'You should have seen old Ricarda when she heard she'd passed the *Klausur*! She was as ___!'
10. 'We tried washing the table-cloth in starch, but now it's as ___!'
11. 'The final exam over! Life stretches before me like an unending adventure! No more constraints! I'm as ___.'
12. 'She seems to have recovered. She was at the ceilidh last night dancing and chatting as ___.' – 'Yes, but how thin she is, as ___!'
13. 'It's the rich that give the least: they're as ___.'
14. Some of the things at the street market must have fallen off a lorry. How else could they have been sold as ___?
15. 'You paid £2,000 for *that* old banger!? You must be as ___!'
16. 'We can just leave the kids in the garden. They're as ___ just playing there all day long. Thank goodness.'
17. 'You should see Bert! His old girl's just given birth to a bouncy baby. He's as ___. Drinks on him tonight!'
18. 'I hoovered, dusted, cleaned and polished before her parents came. You wouldn't have recognised my flat! As ___!'
19. 'He must be round the twist! Lunatic! As ___ and as ___!'
20. 'What a dull party! No life! No zip! As ___!'
21. 'Poor Joe. As ___ now. And he had such a fine head of hair!'
22. He was as ___. He kept his promise. 'Lafayette, we are here!'
23. 'She's obdurate, inflexible, as ___.'
24. 'Heavens, that was close! That bullet almost hit us, as ___! You said we were as ___ here, but we must be clearly visible as ___.'
25. The night was as ___ as the ships slipped silently out of the sound and headed seawards, bound who knew where?

Field 3: Common Abbreviations

Your Task

Each of the sentences below contains one or more common single-letter abbreviations. Establish their meaning by choosing the appropriate words from those listed beneath. The correct answers are to be found on page 166.

Sentences

1. The memo on her desk was indeed short and snappy. It read: 'Get the facts – asap, in fact pdq.'
2. 'What did you think of that candidate, Toni?' – 'Oh, NBG! Send in the next one!'
3. Grischa, tired of fighting, went AWOL and spent much of the War hiding with others in dense woodlands, living the life of the pre-historic hunters.
4. 'We're looking for b & b, but it would be nice to have h & c in the room as well.'
5. 'Something to wet your whistle, old man? A g and t, perhaps?'
6. The minister was ushered into the VIP lounge to await the press conference.
7. 'Another hopeless candidate! WPB the application and – send in the next one!'
8. 'What a week! Insufferable! It'd draw tears from a stone! TGIF!'
9. 'Hey, look at the invitation again. It says RSVP and BAB. Have we got any plonk left?'
10. 'You sometimes wonder what these university geezers get paid for! They do a couple of hours teaching each week and spend the rest of the time doing sweet FA – or so it seems!'
11. 'Don't forget to put the usual f.y.i. at the top of the page and p.t.o. at the bottom.'
12. 'Some party! Some disco! Some DJ!'
13. With the N plant to be sited only 2 miles from the village even the most apolitical and pro-atomic energy residents began to show signs of unease. The idea of a GM 'pharm' nearby did not please either.
14. With so much work being done at weekends on the QT, the tax authorities must be losing millions.
15. 'The clumsy fool rushed into the office without looking and nearly sent me A over T with the staff coffee!'
16. 'Of course I understand the implications. I may be young and naive, but I'm not a BF, you know.'

Options

a / absent / all / apex / arse / as (2x) / basket / bed / bloody [2] / bottle / breakfast / bring / cold / damn / disc / fool / for / Friday / fuck / genetically / gin / God / good / hot / important / information / it / jockey / leave /modified / no / nuclear / over / paper / person / *plaît* / please / possible / pretty / quick / quiet / *répondez* / *s'il* / soon / thank / tip / tonic / turn / very / *vous* / waste / without / your

Field 4: Eponyms II

Your Task

Study the figures on the left, each of whom has become an 'eponymist' by giving his or her name to a common object or common concept listed on the right. Who gave the name to what, and what is the object or concept thus called? The correct answers are to be found on page 166.

Eponymists

1. Karl BAEDEKER, publisher
2. Edmund Clerihew BENTLEY, writer
3. George BOOLE, mathematician
4. James BOWIE, soldier and adventurer
5. Dr Richard BUSBY, headmaster
6. Julius CAESAR, emperor
7. St CATHERINE, Christian martyr
8. Marcus Tullius CICERO, orator
9. George CUSTER, general
10. 12th Earl of DERBY, horse-racing fan
11. DERRICK, convicted rapist; hangman
12. DOYLEY, London draper
13. Quintus Fabius MAXIMUS, general
14. George FERRIS, engineer
15. MICKEY FINN, Chicago saloon keeper
16. Sigmund FREUD, psychiatrist
17. George GALLUP, statistician
18. Luigi GALVANI, Italian physician
19. Sir William GAGE, botanist
20. Luke HANSARD, London printer
21. William HOOVER, businessman
22. Thomas 'Stonewall' JACKSON, general
23. Capt. William LYNCH, vigilante
24. John MacADAM, engineer
25. Queen MARY I of England
26. Matthew PARKER, Archbishop
27. Sir Robert PEEL, PM
28. César RITZ, Swiss hotellier
29. Henry SHRAPNEL, artillery officer
30. Levi STRAUSS, clothing merchant
31. Sir Edward VERNON, 'Old Grog', admiral
32. King WILLIAM IV of England

A. fool
B. rotating fire-work
C. type of crane
D. eloquent guide
E. drugged drink
F. greenish plum
G. vacuum cleaner
H. printed parl. record
I. policeman
J. rough justice
K. inquisitive person
L. luxurious(ness)
M. soldier's fur hat
N. road-surfacing
O. jeans
P. diluted spirits
Q. paper undermat
R. vodka and tomato
S. opinion poll
T. form of algebra
U. slip of the tongue
V. fair ground wheel
W. witty four-line poem
X. guidebook
Y. stimulate to action
Z. stout hunting knife
AA. heroic last stand
BB. match between local clubs
CC. British socialist
DD. to obstruct
EE. delivery of baby through walls of abdomen
FF. metal fragments in shell

Field 5: Idiomatic Threesomes

Your Task Fit the threesomes together – one word from each box – and insert them into the appropriate sentence in Part B below.

Idioms

Part A

	(and)	(and)
A. lock	skip	the tall
B. cool	gone	jump
C. stuff	noon	got the T-shirt
D. high	tag	handsome
E. dead	the short	barrel
F. Tom	book	buried
G. hook	Dick	candle
H. morning	calm	Harry
I. rag	stock	collected
J. bell	seen/done that	the gatepost
K. the long	me	sinker
L. hop	line	rubbish
M. been there	wide	night
N. (between) you	nonsense	bobtail

Sentences

Part B

1. 'It's a secret, of course, but, ___, did you know that ...?' – 'Really?'
2. At the end of the millennium, a Briton and a German were the world-leaders in the demanding field athletics event of ___.
3. Like so many well-travelled, globe-trotting New Zealanders, his reaction to most places and sights was a blasé, world-weary '___'.
4. He was at his best in a crisis – always ___, whatever occurred.
5. Swift's Gulliver and Voltaire's Candide are the aptly-named archetypal dupes of world literature: they swallow everything ___.
6. 'Bullshit! Or, as my grandad would have said, ___!'
7. We don't want the hoi-polloi and riff-raff to come, not any ___.
8. 'In comes Lillee to bowl. It's short, Botham swivels, hooks – it's a glorious shot! It's gone ___ into the grandstand. A magnificent six!'
9. 'If I should die, think only this of me ...'. Rupert Brooke, author of these famous lines, was the most reflective of the poets to welcome World War I. But like the others he was ___ before the War's end.
10. She's a total workaholic, works ___.
11. I condemn it totally and utterly, ___.
12. The annual fair attracted into town the lower classes from miles around, every '___' as the anxious mayor disapprovingly put it.
13. All able-bodied men were conscripted to fight, ___.
14. It was mysterious, a case of witchcraft perhaps, of ___?

Revision III

Exercise 1: Literary Lives

Your Task

In each of the sentences below, insert one of the phrases learned in the foregoing six units to complete the idiom and the sense. The correct answers are to be found on page 168.

Sentences

1. Siegfried Sassoon was the most savagely satirical of the First World War poets, his work telling the unwelcome ___ from the front.
2. The naturalist novelist George Gissing was one of the most obsessively hard-working of British writers, often burning the ___.
3. Wordsworth's and Coleridge's *Lyrical Ballads* (1798), virtually ushering in British Romanticism, mark a ___ in English literature.
4. British literature contains few transgenerational literary families, where the parents have shown the children the ___, so to speak.
5. The major features, the ___, of Christina Rossetti's poetry are its verbal inventiveness, its metrical experiments, its marked pictorial imagery and its appeal to an unnamed lover or suitor.
6. Wyndham Lewis's *The Apes of God* (1930) is in part a cutting, disenchanted satire of the Bloomsbury Group: it really puts the ___ in.
7. The bizarre imagery of Craig Raine's 'Martian poetry' ___ on the world's being seen as if through the eyes of an alien from space.
8. Henry James's *The Ambassadors* (1903) and Conrad's *Nostromo* (1904) are often said to blaze the ___ and pave the ___ for the new, modernist novel.
9. Perhaps more than any other writer, Kate Millett really opened up the new ___ of inquiry now known as 'Feminist Literary Criticism'.
10. Langland's *Piers Plowman* (1360-87), with its intense criticism of Church corruption, is, like the works of Wycliff and the Lollards, one of the early ___ of a deviant British religious tradition.
11. Scott Fitzgerald was one of the rare spendthrift writers. For him, in the early 1920s at least, money was no ___: he spent it like ___.
12. Boswell was to Dr Johnson what Eckermann and Riemer were to Goethe. Such an amanuensis is, of course, worth his ___ in ___: he markedly increases your output.
13. Swift's Gulliver, Voltaire's Candide and Hasek's Schweik are three of the great innocents, *ingénus* and ___ ___ of world literature.
14. From Scrooge to Micawber, Dickens had the Balzacian talent of creating memorable characters, who then became ___ names.
15. On being asked in 1986 on what he would spend the Booker Prize money, Kingsley Amis is said to have replied: 'Booze, of course, then ___.'

Exercise 2: Idiomatic Gossip

Your Task

Read the passage of *médisant* gossip below from the *Fachschaft* common room and then decide which of the phrases learned in the foregoing six units best complete the idiom and sense. The correct answers are to be found on page 168.

Text

– I don't want to spread gossip, Stefanie, but between [1] ___, ___ and the ___ there's a new affair in the *Fachbereich* ...
– I know what you mean, Bianca. I saw them having a bit of [2] ___ after the ceilidh last night. What does she see in him? He's as ugly as [3]___ – and his taste in clothes! He looks like something [4] ___ .
– Yes, and [5] ___ is dead! That's yesterday's news, Stefanie! I don't mean Patrick and Anja. I don't see what she sees in him either – after all he'll soon be as bald as a [6] ___, but, well, every [7] ___ has his ___. Perhaps it's better than being left on the [8] ___. No, I mean –
– And our Anja's far too intelligent. So it's true, Antje and ... ?
– No, she's still [9] ___ up with that exchange student. Of course, they're both broke, so it's just love in a [10] ___. And frankly, he's nothing to [11] ___. Not what one would call the real [12] ___. No –
– I know, you mean Wibke and whatshisname! Well, go and tell that to the [13] ___! She's not serious about him. They spent a night on the [14] ___ together, but he proved a bit of a wet [15] ___, so I'm reliably informed. I don't want to put the [16] ___ in, but their neighbour told me it ended before you could say [17] ___ ...
– Oh, for [18] ___'s sake, Steffi! It's not that type of affair I'm on about. No, the new *affaire* in Faculty politics! Haven't you heard?
– Another political scandal! We need a new scandal like a [19] ___ in the ___! What is it this time? Did the *FBR* meeting descend into a [20] ___? You could cut the air with a [21] ___ when I left at 7.30.
– No, try again. It's not so much a political scandal as a cultural one.
– Ah, so another lector's position [22] ___?
– Of course, but that's nothing new. As they say in Israel, Telaviv. No, it's worse, Steffi. I have it on reliable information, my dear, that Mürbehaupt is to teach British cultural studies. And don't say 'All my [23] ___ and ___'. It seems to be true.
– Mürbehaupt?! He doesn't know Asquith and Attlee from [24] ___! That means that British Studies are down the [25] ___ and up the ___. It's just [26] ___-dressing! Don't they care what students need?
– You can always drive a [27] ___ and ___ through their arguments. We're just the [28] ___ of ___ and ___ of ___! It's Zankerzoff's brain-[29] ___, his revenge on Mürbehaupt for being so sub-literary.
– We must do something. And we'll have to get our [30] ___ on. Or else, as Gorbachev said, we'll have missed the proverbial [31] ___.
– Precisely, either we rock the [32] ___ now, or later we'll have to [33] ___ our own ___. It's action now or autodidacticism later.

19 UNIT Idioms of the Law

Field 1: The Basic Law

Your Task

Read the alliterative biographies below and decide which person's situation is best described by which of the idioms of law listed beneath. The correct answers are to be found on page 168.

Biographies

1. With her annals of a-legal action, Anna must always fear arrest.
2. Crooked Colin has a criminal and court record.
3. Dave does it. It may not be decent, but it don't break any law, do it?
4. Fiona thinks the laws are thoroughly foolish.
5. George claims it's not gentlemanly, doesn't fit the established code.
6. Ian indicates that strictly speaking it's not illegal in itself.
7. Ina is incomparable – just 'inique' as her friends say.
8. Julian decides to administer justice as he pleases.
9. Kate is taking the completely corrupt company to court.
10. Lorna believes loyally in law and order.
11. Martin says it must be done – right or wrong, it must.
12. Fraught Phil is frantically phoning the police.
13. Righteous and upright Rupert would never do anything 'wrong'.
14. Sally says they should be careful and not step into 'shady areas'.
15. Sonny says he'll summon in his solicitor to sue Susan.
16. Tricky-dicky Tracy thinks she knows a back-door around the law.
17. Virginia is a victim of the vicious ways of the world.
18. William will forever tell us what we should and shouldn't do.

Options

A. to be law-abiding / B. the law is an ass / C. to be a law unto oneself / D. to be on the wrong side of the law / E. to believe in the rule of law / F. to call in the law / G. in the eyes of the law / H. to find a loophole in the law / I. to go to law / J. to have the law onto s.o. / K. the law of the jungle / L. to keep within the letter of the law / M. to keep on the right side of the law / N. to lay down the law / O. the long arm of the law / P. necessity knows no law / Q. to take the law into one's own hands / R. the unwritten law

> *The average colloquial speech of any age is at best a compromise between a variety of different jargons, each evolved in and current among the members of a particular section of the community, and each, within certain social limits, affects and is affected by the others.*

HENRY WYLD, *A History of Modern Colloquial English* (1980)

Field 2: The Law Courts

Your Task

In each of the sentences below, insert one or more of the law-associated words listed beneath, to complete the idiom and the sense, taking care to use an appropriate form. The correct answers are to be found on page 169.

Sentences

1. The IRA dealt with informers summarily in swift 'trials' in so-termed ___.
2. Exhausted, ill-prepared and therefore nervy, the candidate failed to do himself full ___ in the exacting exam.
3. The debate on the bill is liable to be a real ___ of strength between the government minister and the up-and-coming opposition spokesman.
4. 'It's difficult! You have to ___ your brains for every answer. But, of course, that's what I came to university for: I knew it wouldn't be a holiday camp.'
5. Despairing of ever seeing an end to the debate, the government artificially limited the time available with the ___.
6. He had lied. He had deceived the electorate. Would they allow him to remain in office? He couldn't tell. One thing was clear: the ___ was out on both him and his government.
7. She always keeps her innermost thoughts to herself – always keeps her own ___.
8. Tormented by conscience and ___ by guilt, the culprit eventually gave himself up.
9. The prototype goes out for its first ___ run tomorrow.
10. Their interpretation of the contract is unfair – just special ___.
11. 'I hold no ___ for the government – far be it from me to defend them – but I do think that they have a point here.'
12. The marriage proved ill-fated, a grim, seemingly unending life ___ for both partners.
13. 'Your action weakens your chances – in fact, it puts you completely out of ___.'
14. The charity employed a TV star to ___ its cause to the public.
15. 'What do you advise?' – 'Well, frankly, I ___ prudence. Take great care with such people.'
16. 'Your position is strong. Very strong. Indeed, I would – and will – argue that you have a cast-iron ___.'

Options

brief / case / counsel 2x / court / guillotine / jury / justice / kangaroo court / plead(ing) 2x / rack(ed) 2x / sentence / trial 2x

Field 3: Crime and Punishment

Your Task

Complete the crossword below, made up of further idioms of law, noting that the first letter and the number of letters in each word are given. The correct answers are to be found on page 169.

Crossword

Clues

1. A friend made a moving (4) on behalf of the kidnapped lad.
2. With some of these questions I haven't got the foggiest (4)!'
3. 'Judge we not, brothers. Let his Maker judge him when he comes before a higher (8).'

4. Innocent cyclists paid the heavy (7) for his drunken drive.
5. Called to the (3) at last, he took up his career as a barrister.
6. At Summerhill a pupils' council sits in (9) on its peers and deals out punishments.
7. 'I wish to (8) a different course of action.'
8. The sentence is arbitrary, just the roughest form of (5,7).
9. 'He's a judge?' – 'Oh, yes, he's been on the (5) for years.'
10. The ship-yard was due for closure, but the government granted a three-month (4,2,9) for alternatives to be sought.
11. Ravenously hungry, she was able to do full (7) to the meal.
12. The case of the Tolpuddle Martyrs became a (Fr 5,7) in the 1830s: such was the public outcry that they were eventually pardoned.
13. 'The evidence is unambiguous. It's an open and shut (4).'
14. 'What's your considered opinion? What's your (7)?'
15. '(6,7)! Rocky, the roughest tackler in the team, has himself been fouled by an opponent and hospitalised for three weeks!'
16. Michael Collins predicted that his signing of the 1921 Treaty would be his death (6). Two years later he was indeed gunned down.
17. 'It's not my duty, not my remit, not my (5) at all.'
18. 'I've done nothing wrong. And yet I feel as if I were in the (4).'
19. 'The film idolises violence. The film censor is bound to be severely attacked – (9) even – for leaving this one almost uncut.'
20. The Royal Court Theatre was due to be shut down, but money from a private sponsor gave it a most welcome (8).

Key Phrase: support the opposing cause without believing in it (4,9,7)

Field 4: British and American History

Your Task

In each of the sentences below, insert one or more of the phrases derived from British and American history listed beneath, to complete the idiom and the sense, taking care to use an appropriate form. The correct answers are to be found on page 169.

Sentences

1. 'What is your new room like Silke?' – 'Oh terrible – tiny, cramped and gloomy, almost a ___.'
2. So there we were, back from the holiday with nothing in the fridge or cupboard to eat: we had to ___.
3. The new leader promised a new moral ___ to awaken the communitarian spirit of the nation.
4. Even after 1989, the Communist bloc was reluctant to follow the ___ and let its former satellites go their own way.
5. Take your chances, go to where the openings are, where the world's your oyster, ___!
6. 'Okay! This is it! Now is the moment! Off we go! ___!'
7. They were very active, can-do people, frankly, a little ___.
8. How would the new Chancellor of the Exchequer act? Would he be a ___, re-distributing wealth, or would he be another prudence-lover?
9. Appalled at their behaviour, the hostel warden ___.
10. There is no virtue in attempting to resist the inevitable, no virtue in playing ___.
11. We should ___. If we refuse to speak to him for a few days, that should make him realize how strongly we feel about it.
12. He's a very odd type, as ___.
13. In adversity such as this we must display our true British mettle, show the ___.
14. 'I don't consider that funny at all. To coin a phrase, '___'.'
15. That is a trivial response to a deep-rooted problem. It's tantamount to fiddling while Rome burns, to ___.
16. 'It would be foolish to go at things too fast. Gradualism is what is required here. We should adopt ___ tactics.'
17. He was compelled to admit his error and to ___.
18. Our student-assistant office is appallingly untidy: we must have a ___ on it before the semester starts or we'll never find anything when it's needed.

Options

A. 'We are not amused' / B. the Black Hole of Calcutta / C. blitz / D. King Cnut / E. to send s.o. to Coventry / F. a crusade / G. as queer as Dick's hat-band / H. Dunkirk spirit / I. Fabian / J. Geronimo! / K. gung-ho / L. to eat humble pie / M. to dine with Duke Humphrey / N. to read the Riot Act / O. Robin Hood / P. the Sinatra Doctrine / Q. to re-arrange the deck-chairs on the Titanic / R. Go West, young man!

20 UNIT War, Weapons and Peace

Field 1: War in Dialogue

Your Task

Study the situations listed below and then decide which of the colloquial idioms of war and weaponry beneath would best express your message. The correct answers are to be found on page 170.

Situations

You You You You You You You You You You You You You You You You You

1. are prepared to take care of the house while others go out.
2. think something is unlikely, but possible.
3. are worried about those in ultimate charge of nuclear weaponry.
4. think someone is not invulnerable
5. are prepared to listen to what a person has to say
6. think someone is a VIP
7. think someone is of considerable quality
8. support someone totally
9. are indulging in speculation
10. consider something goes a long way to guaranteeing success
11. think there is quite a good chance of success
12. want to tell someone to be more self-reliant
13. are prepared to have a try
14. are pleased with the performance of your new motorbike/car etc.
15. believe that you are not going to win this one

Options

You Say You Say You Say You Say You Say You Say You Say You Say You

A. There's a chink in his/her armour / B. It's a long shot / C. He/She is of great calibre / D. Fire away, old girl/old man / E. I'm with you up to the hilt / F. I can't fight your battles for you / G. It's half the battle / H. It's a shot in the dark / I. Whose finger's on the trigger? / J. He/She is a big shot / K. It goes like a bomb / L. I'll have a shot / M. There's a fighting chance / N. We're fighting a losing battle / O. I'll hold the fort

> *For semantic reasons, an idiom requires its own lexical entry in the lexicon, but many idioms participate in syntactic processes, as illustrated by the example 'The cat has been let out of the bag', in which the idiom has undergone passivication like any transitive structure.*

R. L. Trask, *A Dictionary of Grammatical Terms in Linguistics* (1993)

Field 2: Puzzling Weaponry

Your Text

Consider the idioms of weaponry below and decide which of the explanations beneath is likely to be the genuine meaning. The correct answers are to be found on page 170.

Idioms

1. **to bomb (AmE)**
   = to A. ball B. be a flop C. defeat heavily D. fart

2. **to bite the bullet**
   = to A. fight B. die C. do food-tasting D. do an unpleasant task

3. **to take a lot of flak**
   = to be A. a big drinker B. a worker with great stamina C. a big eater D. an object of criticism

4. **to call the shots**
   = to A. summon the police B. take the decisions C. summon the doctor D. be addicted to telephoning

5. **to go great guns**
   = to be A. in top form B. of aggressive nature C. have many children D. sing at the top of one's voice

6. **to be a trouble-shooter**
   = to be a(n) A. arguer B. Don Juan C. problem-maker D. problem-solver

7. **to be up in arms**
   = to A. be very active B. protest C. be off to war D. called up (to join the army)

8. **a hatchet job**
   = a(n) A. difficult task B. easy task C. violent attack on s.o. or sth. D. a sudden and totally unexpected death

9. **to hang fire**
   = to A. be delayed B. attack savagely C. spit on D. cook slowly

10. **to spike s.o.'s guns**
    = to A. support B. thwart C. betray D. capture

11. **to be quick on the draw**
    = to be A. sexually uninhibited B. swift to answer C. good at self-defence D. fast on the attack

Field 3: Doing Battle

Your Task

Read the alliterative biographies below and decide which person's situation is best described by which of the idioms of war listed beneath. The correct answers are to be found on page 170.

Biographies

1. Archibald has no arguments left
2. Buddy has been bluntly told he's got the boot
3. Charlotte has just issued a challenge
4. Choicely-named Chuck just chucks everything into the corner or the cupboard.

5. David is in dire difficulty, in double trouble
6. Evelyn eventually chooses the easiest option
7. Fair-haired, fair-faced Fifties film-starlet Fée was fitted out with a fabulously full-curved figure

8. Modernist Manuela means to keep in the forefront of the modern movement
9. Noel has put his name in for the new job
10. Olive has secretly outwitted her opponents

11. Paul is a perpetually pacific peace-maker
12. Quick-witted, quick-silver Queenie is quick and slick in her responses
13. Roger is in a right-royal rage

14. Sylvia has several strong points still up her sleeve
15. Uschi was ushered into the new job utterly unprepared
16. Weak-willed William will always withdraw

Options

A. to be a blonde bombshell / B. to be catapulted into / C. fight on two fronts / D. to throw down the gauntlet / E. to shoot from the hip / F. to enter the lists / G. to receive one's marching orders / H. to hold out the olive branch / I. to keep one's powder dry / J. to take the line of least resistance / K. to beat a retreat / L. to have no more shots in the locker / M. to sling (away) / N. to steal a march on / O. to be in the van / P. to be on the war-path

Field 4: Weapons II

Your Task

In each of the sentences below, insert one or more of the war-associated words listed beneath to complete the idiom and the sense, taking care to use an appropriate form. The correct answers are to be found on page 170.

Sentences

1. She looked ___ at her rival. Her flashing eyes, her savagely drawn-back lips, her bared teeth – everything spoke the unutterable truth: 'I wish her dead, roasting in hottest hell'.
2. They had had differences of opinion before: in fact, they crossed ___ every time they met at a conference.
3. 'These threats are not to be taken so seriously – much of the time they are mere ___-rattling.'
4. 'No. No, I'm not going to retract my statement or modify my position. On the contrary, I'm sticking to my ___.'
5. As an MP and later as a minister she had been tough, rough, argumentative and ne'er-say-die – a real old ___.
6. At last it seemed that the two sides were going to put their differences and quarrels behind them and bury the ___.
7. 'Just look at her sleek, new Alfa Romeo with built-in microwave oven for the quick snack *en route*! It must have cost a ___!'
8. 'They're such good people to have a tough discussion with. I just love going down to the pub to break a ___ with them again.'
9. He thought he had won the argument, but then the professor brought up the heavy ___, quoted Hegel, Max Weber, Adorno, Benjamin, Sloterdijk and himself and shot him down in flames.
10. 'Now in the tenth round the world champion is reeling! He's got no strength left! The punches aren't there any more! He's shot his ___! He's on his way out! What a sensation here tonight in Las Vegas!'
11. Her high ___ heels murdered any linoleum she walked over.
12. The professor put his knowledge at the disposal of the Ecology Party and took up the ___ in support of the endangered species.
13. The news hit Whitehall like a bolt from the blue, a total ___.
14. If a politician gets into difficulties, you can bet that the gutter press will ___ for him or her till they've drawn blood – or worse.
15. '21 lbs! There's no fish that size in our river! Old Sam's drawing the ___ again. He always was prone to exaggerate, the old windbag.'
16. It was all over. The former champion lay, as if ___, on the mat.

Options

artillery / battle-axe / bolt / bomb / bombshell / cudgel(s) / dagger(s) / gun(s) (2x) / hatchet / lance / long bow / pole-axe / sabre / stiletto / sword(s)

21 UNIT

Idioms of Books and Literature

Field 1: Words

Your Task

Study the situations listed below and then decide which of the colloquial idioms of words listed beneath would best express your message. The correct answers are to be found on page 171.

Situations

You You You You You You You You You You You You You You You You You

1. are surprised, flabbergasted even
2. ask someone to trust you on slender grounds
3. state that sth. was not said explicitly
4. are more than annoyed
5. are lost for words
6. promise to take a statement back if proved wrong
7. have a bone to pick with s.o.
8. think s.o. else is liable to be soon proved wrong
9. want sth. to be kept secret or hushed up
10. find that s.o. has said just what you intended to say
11. promise to use your influence on s.o.'s behalf
12. wish to stress a particular word or part of a message
13. find it unpleasant to say sth.
14. promise to speak personally to s.o.
15. issue a warning, emphasising a solemn prediction

Options

You Say You Say You Say You Say You Say You Say You Say You Say You

A. Famous last words!
B. My word!
C. I'll put in a good word for you.
D. If not, I'll eat my words!
E. I'll have a word in his/her ear.
F. Mark my words!
G. The words stick in my throat.
H. Mum's the word.
I. I'll have words with him/her.
J. Not in so many words.
K. 'Annoyed' isn't the word for it!
L. ... the operative word being ...
M. Words fail me!
N. You take the words out of my mouth.
O. You'll have to take me at my word.

> *For the idiom of words very little she heeded,*
> *Provided the matter she drove at succeeded,*
> *She took and gave languages just as she needed.*

MATTHEW PRIOR, *Jinny the Just* (1715)

Field 2: Books and Their Parts

Your Task

Complete the crossword below, made up of further idioms of books and their component parts, noting that the first letter of each word and the number of letters in each word are given. The correct answers are to be found on page 171.

Crossword

Clues

1. 'They were not very explicit. But reading between the (5), I would say we have a chance.'
2. Their skiing holiday in Davos was an almost complete disaster, a (7) of accidents.
3. 'Alchemy is a total mystery to me – a (4,4,5,5).'
4. 'Change I must: I'm going to turn over a new (4).'
5. 'No technology' is an (7) of faith with the Amish People.

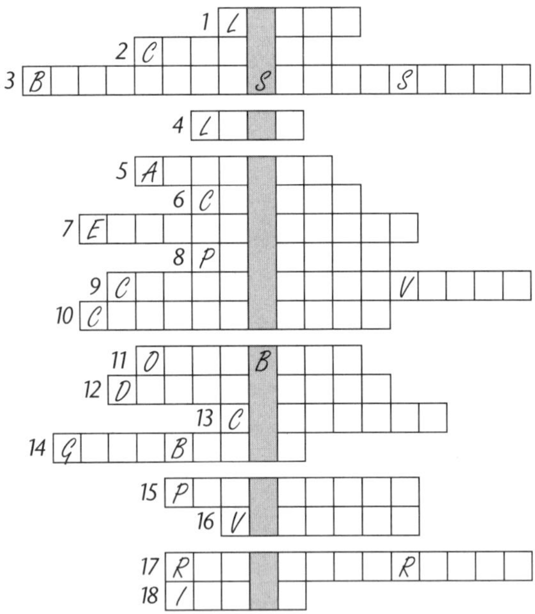

6. She specialised in other people's problems, writing an 'agony (6)' for a tabloid.
7. The winner of the title 'Brain of Britain' seemed to have (12) knowledge.
8. An inspired essay! One purple (7) after another!
9. She knew the regulations and could always cite (7,3,5).
10. Her knowledge was vast, well-nigh all-embracing, (11).
11. The candidate declared he had no secrets: his life was an (4,4).
12. 'If you can't think of the *mot juste*, just ask her: she's a walking (10) in several languages.'
13. 'I'm afraid the prof. overheard my less than flattering description of his didactic skills – so I must have really blotted my (8) with him.'
14. 'I think I'm still in favour with him, still in his (4,5).'
15. As minister without (9) he had a cabinet seat, but no ministry.
16. 'She's one of the quiet ones. But her actions speak (7).'
17. 'Oh, dear! My essay is only a miserable 307 words long and all the other candidates seem to have written vast tracts, (5,3,5)!'
18. The wage settlement was all the better in that it was (5)-linked and so could not be eaten away by inflation.

Key Phrase: I haven't the foggiest clue about it – (3,1,6,4,2,2).

Field 3: Puzzling Books and Words

Your Task

Consider the idioms of books and words below and decide which of the explanations beneath is likely to be the genuine meaning. The correct answers are to be found on page 171.

Idioms

1. **to say the word**
   = to A. set going B. say what you want C. agree to marriage D. propose marriage

2. **to drop a line**
   = to A. forget what to say B. give a hint C. write poetry D. write a note/letter &c

3. **to draw the line**
   = to A. say 'No' B. leave abruptly C. set limits D. be pedantic

4. **to bring to book**
   = to A. write down B. arrest and try C. ponder D. confess/admit

5. **that's one for the book!**
   = a A. noteworthy surprise B. win at horse-racing C. legal offence D. event worth writing home about

6. **to throw the book at s.o.**
   = to A. insult B. hurt C. swear at D. accuse of many misdeeds

7. **to suit s.o.'s book**
   = to A. fit in with life-style of B. kow-tow to C. be a good partner for D. obey rules laid down by s.o.

8. **a turn up for the book**
   = a A. a miracle B. surprise C. big betting win D. bad review

9. **the Book of Books**
   = the A. Bible B. Law C. dictionary D. old-style library catalogue

10. **to go by the book**
    = to A. die B. be pedantic C. be a book-worm D. be illiterate

11. **to cook the books**
    = to A. cheat B. swindle C. swot D. study law

12. **in my book**
    = A. to my mind B. in my memory/recollection C. according to the habits of my nation D. according to the habits of my family

Field 4: Literature

Your Task

Imagine you are involved in the mini-dialogues below. Which of the idioms of literature listed beneath would best fit which situation? The correct answers are to be found on page 171.

Dialogues

1. – Is he still an incurable optimist?
– Oh, yes. Still the eternal ***, still waiting for something to turn up.
2. – Does your Dad still refuse to pay for a holiday in the Seychelles?
– 'Fraid so. The old ***! A miser, that's what he is!
3. – And is she still pursuing her fanciful, totally unattainable ideals?
– She is! *** as ever!
4. – What was it like at the DHSS?
– Spine-chilling. ***. Miles and miles of corridors and queues.
5. – What a pity the star speaker didn't turn up.
– Absolutely. It was a non-event, ***.
6. – Twenty-two dead! Terrible. Who was the gunman this time?
– Another totally inconspicuous, clean living Mr Normal. A ***.
7. – What a ding-dong match! I've never seen a longer five-setter.
– Yes, a great game. Tennis history in the making. An ***.
8. – I didn't know he had such bad tempers! I was really taken aback.
– That's how he is. One day a *charmeur*, the next ... . He's a real ***.
9. – This is past a joke. The *Sprechstunde*'s being going on three hours now, and still no chance to get a mere signature!
– Yes, like ***. Except that that's more interesting.
10. – She's still head of her Civil Service department?
– Yes. Whichever party's in power! No difference! She's like the ***.
11. – Look at Emily! The picture of melancholy and lugubriousness!
– Yes, she likes to look ***, a bit 'Oh-death-where-is-thy-sting?'
12. – These forms are ridiculously pettifogging.
– Yup. ***. But what do you expect from modern bureaucracy?
13. – He's a larger than life character, isn't he?
– Oh, gosh yes – ***.
14. – I don't trust this biological cloning, do you?
– Of course not. ***, that's all it'll produce.
15. – He's a real *** figure.
– Too true. Amazing energy and scope. But – dangerous life style.
16. – Such a jolly chap, don't you think?
– Most genial company. ***. A bit of Olde, pre-Puritan Englande.

Options

dickensian / epic / faustian / Frankenstein's monster / like Hamlet without the Prince / hamletesque / Jekyll and Hyde/ kafkaesque / Lilliputian / Micawber / pickwickian / quixotic / Scrooge / the Vicar of Bray / Waiting for Godot / Walter Mitty

22

UNIT **Theatre and Music**

Field 1: Essential Instruments

Your Task

In each of the sentences below, insert one or more of the musical instruments listed beneath to complete the idiom and the sense, taking care to use an appropriate form. The correct answers are to be found on page 172.

Sentences

1. 'How on earth did their son get in to that school? He's not clever enough to pass the butter, let alone their entrance exam!' – 'Oh, his parents ___ it with the head. Two grand to the Appeal Fund.'
2. 'The real economic prospects are very bleak. The Chancellor was just ___ in the dark when he promised the recession would bottom out by the end of the year.'
3. 'Of course I'm fit! I'm as sound as a ___, as fit as a ___! It doesn't matter that my paunch is occasionally as tight as a ___!'
4. When abroad, the Prime Minister's favourite occupations seemed to be complaining about human rights in the host country and beating the ___ for the industry of the home country.
5. '"Neither a borrower nor a lender be!" And especially not to Sarah! Money to her is money lost beyond recall. You can ___ for it as far as she is concerned!'
6. '___ down, young man! Children should be seen and not heard!'
7. He only nipped in to the pub to wet his ___, but somehow he was still there at closing time.
8. 'Stop ___ with your pencil, Amanda! Pay attention!'
9. 'It's amazing they've still got jobs with the firm! With their record of non-achievement they should've been ___ out years ago!'
10. At the press conference launching the new manifesto, each minister seemed to feel it his or her duty to ___ forth the achievements of the government in its past term in office.
11. The circular saw had cut his finger off as clean as a ___.That was that. Four fingers from now on.
12. Desperately they tried to ___ the idioms into their already tired and strained minds before the nemesis of the final *Klausur*.

Options

bell / drum (4x) / fiddle (3x) / pipe / trumpet / whistle (4x)

> *There are two main kinds of lexical items involving two or more roots: 'compounds' like* horse-manure *and 'idioms' like* throw in the towel.

ELIZABETH TRAUGOTT and MARY PRATT, *Linguistics for Students of Literature* (1980)

Field 2: Musical Instruments II

Your Task

Complete the crossword below, made up of idioms of musical instruments and their component parts, noting that the first letter of each word and the number of letters in each word are given. The correct answers are to be found on page 172.

Crossword

Clues

1. The civil servant was aghast. She decided to blow the (7) on the ministry's manipulation of the facts and tell all to the press.
2. 'Always blowing your own (7)! Always boasting!'
3. He was a sensitive child, not just nervous but highly-(6).
4. 'I did my best for you, Harry. I pulled out all the (5). But – no use. They are adamant.'
5. He left her. He was fed up with just playing (6,7) to her first-choice lover.

6. 'Clever, this picnic table. It's so built that it can (10) into the smallest space.'
7. 'He's not a bad old cove. But he will (4) on about what he did at Dunkirk. If I've heard it once I've heard it a thousand times!'
8. Her voice rang out with a pure, almost ethereal tone, as clear as a (4), as if it pealed from the spheres of the farthest Beyond.
9. 'No, Minister. This won't be popular with the voters. Mention it as little as possible – just (4-5) on the whole issue. All right, Sir?'
10. "Stuff and nonsense!' my grandad would have said to that. 'Stuff and nonsense! (12)!"
11. 'Hello, miseryguts! Why have you got a face like a (6)? What have you got to be woesome about this time?'
12. She spent a long time talking to committee members, trying desperately to (4) up support for her scheme.
13. The leader's final speech to the conference was a rallying cry, a powerful, ringing (7) call to the party faithful and the undecided.
14. 'If only he hadn't spoken! Why did he all of a sudden (4) up and persuade them I was wrong?'

Key Phrase: 'He's doing something dishonest to get all that money! (3,2,3,6)! Probably defrauding the tax office!'

Field 3: The Stage

Your Task

Read the headlines below, each of which contains one idiom derived from the field of the theatre and acting, and then select the English paraphrase below which best conveys the meaning of the word or phrase underlined. The correct answers are to be found on page 172.

Headlines

1. **Labour <u>upstaged</u> by Conservative visit**
2. UNKNOWN MEMBER <u>STEALS THE SHOW</u>
3. MINISTER <u>PLAYS TO THE GALLERY</u>, UNION CLAIMS
4. **<u>Get in on the act</u>, speaker urges**
5. **Conference <u>stage-managed</u>, opposition claims**
6. **CHANCELLOR <u>WALKS THE TIGHTROPE</u>**
7. MINISTER <u>PUT THROUGH THE HOOP</u> ON DÉBUT
8. **BACKBENCHERS CALL FOR <u>SHOW-DOWN</u> WITH UNIONS**
9. RANK AND FILE NOW <u>RUN THE SHOW</u>, CHAIRMAN CLAIMS
10. **STOP <u>PLAYING TO THE CAMERAS</u>, SPEAKERS URGED**
11. **PM to party faithful: <u>get your act together</u>**
12. OPPOSITION <u>STAGES A RECOVERY</u>

Options

A. attention diverted from / B. capitulation / C. captures all the attention / D. copy winning policy / E. curry favour / F. defeated / G. dominate / H. faints / I. final show of strength / J. get organised / K. get moving / L. get out / M. given baptism by fire / N. hurry up / O. improves its position / P. inform self / Q. introduced to all / R. leaves dramatically / S. made a fool of / T. negotiation / U. plans recovery / V. pretends success / W. seeks easy applause / X. shows off / Y. speaks frankly / Z. get organised / AA. organised / BB. badly organised / CC. organised for maximum media effectiveness / DD. out-argued / EE. outrages / FF. performs elegantly / GG. performs difficult task / HH. seeking media attention

Field 4: The Stage II

Your Task

Read the text below and then decide which of the phrases underlined would be better expressed by which of the theatrical phrases listed beneath. The correct answers are to be found on page 172.

Text

When the Orthodox Party suffered an election defeat in the early Seventies – its third defeat at the polls in its last four attempts – there was much discussion (1:) in private as to whether the Party should elect a new leader and, if so, whom.

Of course, the ageing Lord Sleetham would have (2:)accepted without hesitation. And the donnish Sir Ralph Benjamin would have (3:)devoted all his energies to the job.

But what was needed was a figure who could (4:)set the Party moving again. A figure who had no (5:)fear of publicity. A figure who indeed revelled in the (6:)glare of attention.

But there seemed to be no crown prince, no clear candidate(7:) awaiting a summons. And the incumbent leader was clearly reluctant to stand down.

In the circumstances, the imminent Party Conference was seen as an (8:)appetiser for the coming leadership struggle. Some even viewed it – with some justification – as a (9:)trial run for the election itself.

In the event, one candidate and one only (10:)captured the attention.

The conference took place (11:)in a climate of mounting unease at decline – decline in national prestige, in the rate of the pound, in educational standards, in moral standards, in well-nigh everything under the British sun and moon.

In such a situation, Victoria Weaver was (12:) emerging at precisely the right moment. Steely-eyed, upright in bearing and unflinching in mien, she (13:)seemed ideally cast for the role of dragon-killer. She did not need to (14:) pretend – or if she was pretending, then she'd (15:)mastered her lines with total command. (16:)Following the lead given by the gurus of the right, its prophets, press and pamphleteers, she assailed the dual enemy of defeatism and decline.

The conference was hers, and the leadership – and the decade to come.

Options

A. to put on an act / B. against a backdrop of / C. to enter right on cue / D. to take one's cue from / E. a curtain-raiser / F. a dress rehearsal / G. the limelight / H. to learn one's part well / I. to look the part / J. to throw oneself into a/the part / K. to need no prompting / L. behind the scenes / M. to get the show on the road / N. to hold the stage / O. stage-fright / P. to wait in the wings

23 UNIT Idioms of Sport and Games

Field 1: The Game of Cards

Your Task

Complete the crossword below, made up of idioms derived from card games, noting that the number of letters in each word is given. The correct answers are to be found on page 172.

Crossword

Clues

1. He was a celebrated airman, a flying (3).
2. 'We're in a strong position: we've got a (4,4).'
3. Now! It's now or never. Now I must risk everything. Now I must (4) my ... *(see clue 14)*
4. Bloody annoying! Every time you tell a decent joke or story he manages to (5) it!
5. Society and fate treated her unkindly. She got a (3,4) in life.
6. The whole project is built on the sands: It's a (5,2,5).
7. After this govt scandal there is sure to be a cabinet (9).
8. She's been highly successful – she's really come up (6).
9. He's terribly secretive – keeps his (5) close to his chest.
10. Let's hope the tax reforms really give a (6,4) to the less well-off.
11. Amanda spent Christmas on the Seychelles. And now Cynthia is following (4) and flying down there over Easter.
12. It could happen. It's possible. It's well within the realm of possibility. It's (2,3,5).

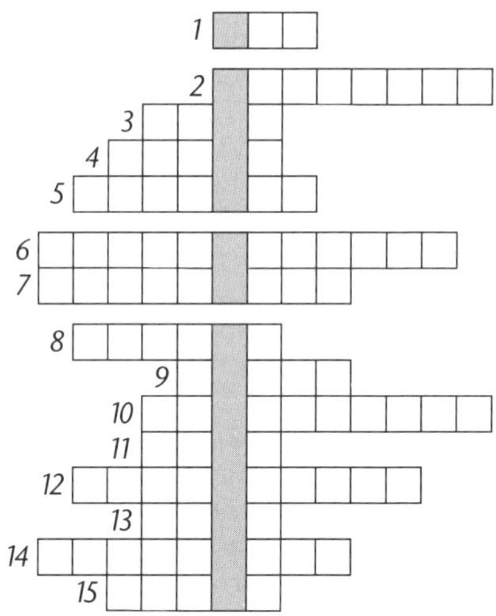

13. He decided to give up and just threw in his (4).
14. Yes! Now! Here it is – my (5,4)
15. She's an unknown, surprise quantity – the (5) in the pack.

Key phrase: It demands time, trouble care and attention: it's (1,4,2,8)

> *Obviously you must take idioms as separate linguistic units and learn them as distinct entities. It is useful to regard them as part of your receptive equipment for listening and reading, not absolutely necessary for your expressive activities in speaking and writing.*

SIMEON POTTER, *Language and the Modern World* (1960)

Field 2: Boxing

Your Task

In each of the sentences below, insert one or more of the words listed beneath, to complete the idiom and the sense, taking care to use an appropriate form. The correct answers are to be found on page 172.

Sentences

1. Of course Mrs Thatcher wanted the then Labour Party to survive. She needed a weak opposition as a kind of tame ___.
2. 'Wow! This is some vodka! Powerful stuff! It really ___.'
3 At first, Prime Minister's Question Time was a relatively gentle affair. But after the series of leaks and scandals it became progressively more savage. And by the end of the session, ___.
4. 'Are you going to apply for the post?' – 'Why not? It can't do any harm. I may have little chance, but I think I'll ___.'
5. 'An easy victory! A walk-over! We ___!'
6. A hard-hitting article; it called a spade a spade and didn't ___.
7. After three vain attempts to get his 'O'-Levels he simply gave up, ___, and became a committed and able road-sweeper.
8. 'And if he misbehaves, Jesabel, stand for no nonsense! ___ and send him to his room on a diet of bread and water. That'll learn him!'
9. She was dog-tired. Flaked out. So she slowly drank two glasses of her favourite Burgundy, hurled herself onto her pillow, pulled the continental quilt up to her eyes and was ___ next morning.
10. 'Does Wimbledon operate on the league or group principle?' – 'No it's a ___ pure and simple.'
11. 'The Labour party political broadcasts have been much better in the early days of the campaign.' – 'Yes, so far they're clearly in the lead there. It's definitely ___ Labour.'
12. It was a mean, callous and thoroughly unfair thing to do. Straight out of the Dirty Tricks Department, really ___.
13. The first scandal had severely shaken her career. The second had all but ended it. This third brouhaha was surely ___.
14. Failure stared her in the face. Could she do it? Could she? One last effort. No. No. That was it. The proverbial *finis*. She had to ___.
15. Three pints she could usually manage on a good day, but after the fourth she was really ___ any day of the week.
16. Sometimes she just used him as a ___ for her aggression, other times as a springboard for her flights of wild fantasy.

Options

A. a knock-out punch / B. below the belt / C. to throw in the towel / D. to put one's hat in the ring / E. to be out for the count / F. to throw up the sponge / G. to be fighting fit / H. to pack a punch / I. a punch-bag / J. first round to / K. to win hands down / L. to box s.o.'s ears / M. the gloves are off / N. to pull one's punches / O. a knock-out / P. a sparring partner

Field 3: This Sporting Life

Your Task

In each of the sentences below, insert a word or words from the world of sport to complete the idiom and the sense, noting that the first letter of and number of letters in each word are given, as is the individual sport from which the idiom is drawn (see below: 'sport involved'). The correct answers are to be found on page 173.

Sentences

1. 'That's quite normal here: it's always happening, just (P,F,T,C, 3,3,3,6).'
2. After his appalling gaffe concerning the spelling of 'tomato' the Vice President was out of the (R,7) for the White House.
3. 'We couldn't do anything about it. It just happened. That was the way the cookie crumbled: it was the rub of the (G,5).
4. The bill was rejected by the House at the first full debate, thus falling at the (F,H,5,6).
5. It certainly was not the gentlemanly thing to do – it certainly was not (C,7).
6. She had done it all on her own initiative, off her own (B,3), so to speak.
7. Were the two of them really progressive, or did they just act like it? Certainly there were some colleagues who claimed, or at least insinuated, that the two were just (K-J,4-4) liberals.
8. She really had a difficult start to her new job – no preparation, just thrown in the (D,E,4,3).
9. At best he'll get a severe reprimand, at worst he'll be sacked: one way or the other, he's due for the (H,J,4,4).
10. The postmodern novel with its intricate narrative ploys, multiculturalism, dense intertextuality and polysemic language was a real challenge, something to really (W,7) with.
11. He was the ideal exam candidate, quick-witted and with the gift of the gab – never (S,7) for an answer.
12. The government has changed its position on state pensions utterly, done a complete (S,10).
13. Come on, old chap! Be fair! Do the right thing! (P,T,G,4,3,4).
14. They were in a tricky situation, on a (S,W,6,6).
15. The exercise couldn't beat me! I was more than a (M,5) for it!
16. His attempt to get to university was a total flop – failing to get into the Sixth Form to even start on his 'A'-Levels, he did not as much as get to (F,B,5,4).

Sport Involved

1. golf / 2. athletics / 3. golf / 4. athletics / 5. & 6. cricket / 7. gymnastics / 8. swimming / 9. field athletics / 10. wrestling / 11. cricket / 12. gymnastics / 13. any sport / 14. cricket / 15. any sport / 16. baseball

Field 4: Games and Pastimes

Your Task

Read the text below and then decide which newspaper's position is best characterised by which of the basic idioms of games and sports listed below. The correct answers are to be found on page 173.

Text

When the far-away, fog-ridden, forlorn, forgotten former colony was invaded by a neighbouring power, the national press in the mother country was by no means unanimous as to what should be done. The *Imperial Rag* predicted that if these islands were relinquished then other colonies would soon follow in a chain reaction. The *Daily Letter* also argued that it was up to the government to act and to act fast. The *Commercial Times* went further, calling for ministerial heads to roll – or at least for a government re-shuffle. Meanwhile, the *Dawn* tried to get things moving by starting a campaign for the islands' recapture.

The *Daily Wire*, however, maintained that the government had been caught with its idiomatic trousers down and was now in an utterly hopeless position. Indeed, the precarious position of *both* governments at home – thus the *Bystander* – left neither with any room for manoeuvre. The *Day and Age*, accordingly, predicted a long tussle between the two sides over possession. The *Comet* saw even a drawn-out sea campaign with battleships hunting and eluding each other over the vast arena of the South Atlantic. And for the *Free-Thinker*, recapturing and abandoning the bleak islands were equally unattractive propositions.

As the crisis wore on and hostilities continued, many came to agree with *This Morning* that neither side had a way out. The confident, braying predictions of the *Views of the World* now seemed far from the terrible truth of modern warfare. Closer to reality seemed the *Onlooker*'s picture of two governments groping in the dark. Pity the islanders, cried the *People's Looking-Glass* – the islanders, now innocent victims in the savage sport of power politics. But it was left to the *Old Republican*, quoting the South American sage Borges, to hit the nail on the head: the conflict, it argued, was just like two bald men fighting over a comb. *Vae victis! Vae victoribus!*

The Cast

the *Bystander* / the *Comet* / the *Commercial Times* / the *Daily Letter* / the *Daily Wire* / the *Dawn* / the *Day and Age* / the *Free-Thinker* / the *Imperial Rag* / the *Old Republican* / the *Onlooker* / the *People's Looking-Glass* / *This Morning* / the *Views of the World*

Options

1. a tug-of-war / 2. check-mate / 3. to set the ball rolling / 4. to be snookered / 5. it's a toss-up / 6. to play musical chairs / 7. it's stalemate / 8. the domino effect / 9. to score a bull's eye / 10. the ball's in your court / 11. to play blind man's bluff / 12. to be wide of the mark / 13. to be a pawn in the game / 14. to play hide-and-seek

24

UNIT

Idioms of Religion, Fairy Tale, Myth

Field 1: Biblical Names

Your Task

Imagine you are involved in the mini-dialogues below. Which of the idioms from the Bible listed beneath would best fit which situation? The correct answers are to be found on page 173.

Dialogues

1. – You mean the game's up? We've been betrayed?
– Yes, and by one of our number. Someone here has ***.
2. – Why is she always so self-righteous?
– Ugh! She always was hypocritical. A real ***.
3. – And are you still undecided, still the ***?
– Well, I must confess to being less than convinced. I'm sorry.
4. – How generous! And who's the ***?
– Well, we don't know. A completely anonymous donor.
5. – I suppose you're the oldest child: you behave like it.
– Quite wrong: I'm the ***. Your psychology's not so hot after all.
6. – They're bosom friends, aren't they?
– Oh, yes! Thick as thieves! A real *** pair.
7. – And then the skunk made sexual advances to her? But he's 73!
– And as ugly as sin! But it's ***! Choir master or not!
8. – There'll be one hell of a row about this, if it gets out!
– You bet! The vicar'll ***!
9. – ***! I don't trust him an inch.
– Nor do I. There must be something behind it. And something nasty.
10. – What?! Preston from the 4th Division beat the League leaders!
– Yup! That's the F.A. Cup for you! It often causes an upset, a ***.
11. – A very confused and confusing case, Sir. An unenviable task.
– Yes, and morally disturbing. We need *** today, I'm afraid.
12. – *The Prelude* is to poetry what *Der Nachsommer* is to the novel!?
– Both certainly demand *** from time to time. But there are rewards.

Options

A. the old Adam / B. a Benjamin / C. to raise Cain / D. a David and Goliath situation / E. David and Jonathan / F. the patience of Job / G. the kiss of Judas / H. to play Judas / I. a pharisee / J. the Good Samaritan / K. the wisdom of Solomon / L. a doubting Thomas

> *There are many phrases in the* King James Bible *which have entered the general idiom of the language (sometimes with minor changes in grammar or emphasis).*

DAVID CRYSTAL, *Cambridge Encyclopaedia of the English Language* (1995)

Field 2: The Bible

Your Task

Complete the crossword opposite, made up of idioms derived from the Bible, noting that the first letter of each major word and the number of letters in each word are given. The correct answers are to be found on page 173.

Clues

1. Their suffering cannot leave one unmoved. No man is an island. One cannot (4,2,2,3,5,4).
2. 'This will sort out the good from the bad, the (5,4,3,5).'
3. There are many, many of them. Vast numbers. They're (6)
4. The victim's mother wished no mercy. No clemency. She demanded (2,3,3,2,3).
5. 'Those are our regulations and principles, our (3,12), so to speak.'
6. It was a hotbed of vice, crime and carnality, a real (5,3,8).
7. It came like a welcome gift from the gods, like (5,4,6).
8. 'But that type of attitude was outdated even in my grandma's time! It's antediluvian! It (4,3,4,3,3)!'
9. 'Well, it is not easy to find the straight and narrow path of righteousness, you know. '(6,2,3,4)'. Many, many go astray.'
10. The failure of the Faculty to establish amical working conditions led to a good number of key members of staff leaving – a mass (6).
11. 'It must be appalling working in your multilingual Brussels ministry.' – 'Yes, it's often just like the (5,2,5).'
12. But no-one was kind enough to offer them accommodation. No one opened the door in welcome. There was (2,4,2,3,3).
13. 'Away, you wicked tempter! Be gone temptation! (3,6,2,5)!'
14. 'Were your folks annoyed?' – 'And how! I harvested the (6,2,5)!'
15. The three newly-appointed experts were inevitably dubbed by the newspapers the (5,4,3).
16. It was a bitter experience to live entirely on the cold charity of the wealthy, on the crumbs (4,3,4,4,5).
17. The yuppies went out in search of money, money, money. 'Get rich quick' was their motto. They worshipped (3,6,4).
18. In their materialism, they had totally forgotten that life contains also other values and aspirations, that man does not live (2,5,5).
19. 'One really must get down to work. One must (4,2,4,5).'
20. The tests were to weed out the less able, to separate the (5,4,3,5).
21. He's so arrogant, he always looks as if he thinks he could (4,2,5).
22. We must not strike back. We must learn to (4,3,5,5).
23. 'Ugh, what a total and utter hypocrite he is, a real (6,9)!'
24. Of course, he protested he was not to blame and, as always, washed (3,5,2,9).

Key Phrase: After years of misfortune, they needed some-one to take them to the promised land, (2,4,[4],3,2,3,10).

Crossword

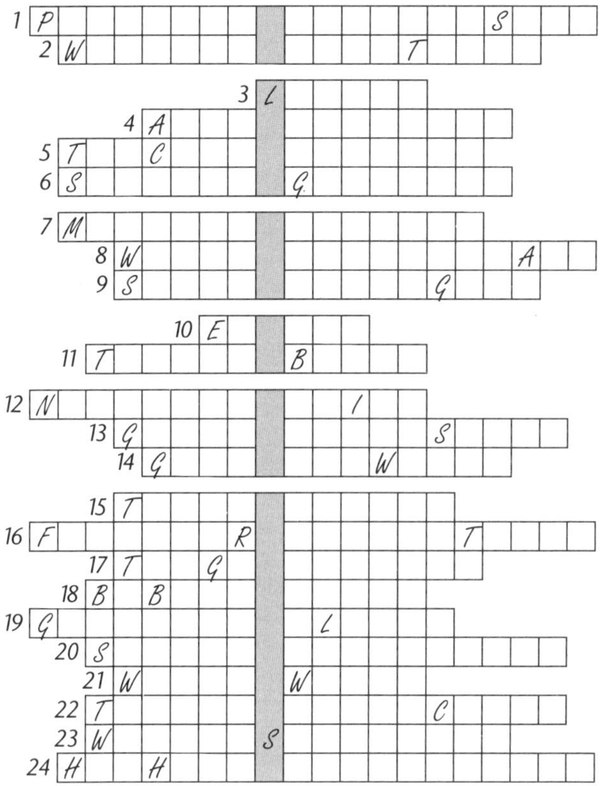
1 P S
2 W T
3 L
4 A
5 T C
6 S G
7 M
8 W A
9 S G
10 E
11 T B
12 N I
13 G S
14 G W
15 T
16 F R T
17 T G
18 B B
19 G L
20 S
21 W W
22 T C
23 W S
24 H H

Field 3: The Bible II

Your Task

Imagine you are involved in the mini-dialogues below. Which of the idioms from the Bible listed beneath would best fit which situation? The correct answers are to be found on page 174.

Dialogues

1. – It seems that the government's days are numbered now, eh?
– Yes, after that last heavy bye-election defeat ***.
2. – Did you pluck up courage and see the professor?
– Yes, I was *** yesterday. Actually, she was quite charming.
3. – It seems your advice ***. They haven't changed their policy.
– That's their funeral! ***! I don't know why I bother!
4. – But I've got to eat in the *Mensa* tomorrow and Friday.
– Oh, come on! You must pay the photocopying fee! ***!
5. – Why is she so modest? She could do so much with her talents.
– Yes! 'This little light of mine ...' But she's always ***.
6. – And they all rushed into the stadium, trampling others underfoot?
– Yes, like the ***. Extraordinary. Bizarre.
7. – You know, this sherpa's the ***.
– Yes, splendid chap! We'd be lost without him, utterly lost.
8. – And then, after months of debauchery he runs home to Daddy, I suppose, and asks for a Eurocard Gold?!
– Yes, he's bloody good at playing the ***.
9. – We've got to be realistic: it's no use ***.
– Yes, I suppose you're right. There are certain constraints.
10. – You're the archetypal eager beaver autodidact – an insatiable thirst for more!
– Well, you know, when you've ***, it's hard to stop.
11. – Fallen on hard times, old boy? Not much money in the kitty?
– Too true. Got to tighten the proverbial belt. After ***.
12. – So there'll be a feast?
– Oh, yes! No cost spared! We're ***.
13. – They never see their own faults, do they?
– No! They never see the ***.
14. – If everyone gives a little – the *** – it'll make all the difference.
– Absolutely. Many a mickle makes a muckle.

Options

A. the beam in one's own eye / B. to eat from the tree of knowledge / C. the Gadarene swine / D. to give unto Caesar that which is Caesar's / E. to hide one's light under a bushel / F. to kill the fatted calf / G. to kick against the pricks / H. to be in the lion's den / I. (to cast) pearls before swine / J. the years of plenty, the lean years / K. the prodigal son / L. the salt of the earth / M. to fall on stony ground / N. the widow's mite / O. the writing is on the wall

Field 4: Myth

Your Task

Complete the crossword below, made up of idioms derived from classical myth. The correct answers are on page 175.

Crossword

Clues

1. 'Ooh! Sue! Just look at that guy over there! What muscles! How broad-shouldered! How well-endowed! Ooh! What a tan! Ooh! Mmm! What an (6)!'
2. His hatred of his father was seen as an (7,7) acquired in early youth from seeing his mother maltreated.
3. 'We are looking for a man or woman already accustomed to going through problems not round them, a managerial manager capable of cutting the (7,4) of business.'
4. 'You look as if the (5,2,8) were hanging over you.' – 'It is. My C 17th exam's next week and I'm ignorant about the Great and Glorious Revolution.'

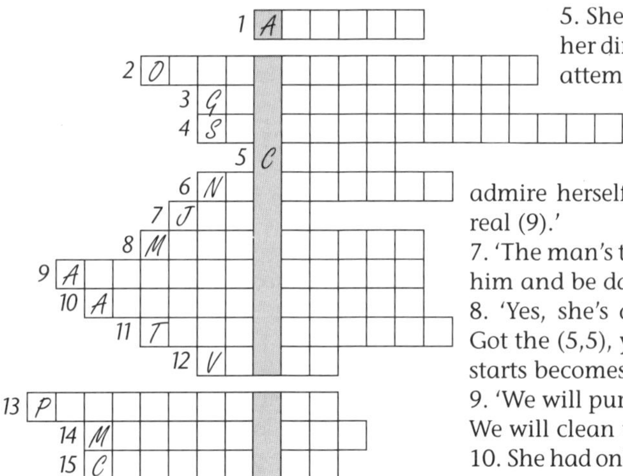

5. She loved to play (5): each of her dinner parties was a blatant attempt at match-making, at bringing together what she saw as lonely souls.
6. 'She wants only to admire herself in others' eyes – she's a real (9).'
7. 'The man's two-faced, a real (5). Trust him and be damned.'
8. 'Yes, she's a millionaire twice over! Got the (5,5), you see. Every project she starts becomes a money-spinner!'
9. 'We will purge corruption and waste. We will clean up the (6,7).'
10. She had only one weakness, one (8,4). But it proved her undoing.
11. The lecturer was viewed with suspicion by her elder colleagues. Would she prove a (6,5) bringing in the unwanted complications of deconstruction, psycho-linguistics and radical feminist criticism?
12. Shapely, and firm in her shapes, she was a (5) in blue jeans.
13. They feared the new leader would bring not only the benefits of democratisation but also the (8,3) of the untried Third Way.
14. 'Your great-grandfather's still alive! He must be as old as (10)!
15. Seeing himself as a warning voice appealing to a somnolent and complacent population, he signed his newspaper column '(9)'.

Key Phrase: 'This is a harsh and doctrinaire measure which takes no regard of individual needs. It is, Mr Speaker, (1,11,3) if ever there was one.'

Field 5: Fairy Tale

Your Task

Read the text below and then decide which of the phrases underlined would be better expressed by which of the phrases derived from fairy tale listed beneath. The correct answers are to be found on page 175.

Text

Old Uncle Don had travelled far and long. Over the hills and a long way off. And as a (1:)person returning home after a prolonged absence he had his tales to tell – tales about where he had been and tales about what had happened while he was away.

When Uncle Don was telling his stories, you needed (2:)a broad imagination to follow him. To listen to him was to feel one had finally arrived at (3:)the very place of one's dreams.

For as a young man Uncle Don had (4:)felt the allure of Empire. And the excitement of Empire, it seemed, had left him (5:)forever young. The allure of Empire? No. Of the imperial lands.

With a gleam in his eye, he could tell of the (6:)untold riches of oriental markets, of the (7:)hidden wealth discovered only by the boldest traveller. Of the Indian hill stations and Burma, of Fiji, Tonga and Nauru.

And of how he himself had left England just a (8:)dull, unappealing youth and had developed overseas into a (9:)handsome suitor. And even seeing Uncle Don at eighty you could see the truth of that tale at least.

But where did he find his (10:)unsuspecting bride? Assuredly not in England. England, in Uncle Don's accounts, was at best the (11:) friendly benefactor of his youth – she who granted him the chance to get away. More often it was the land to which he returned, only to see it as (12:)a sham, an impostor. Uncle Tom was the archetypal traveller who has travelled so far and long that he can see his own country as a foreign land. And that foreign England was the (13:) unseemly figure of power suppressing the (14:)spurned but lovely child of the colonies. It was the (15:)naive, jejune experimenter aghast at the consequences of its actions or – worse – the unsuspecting villain (16:)destroying its most precious possession.

Yes, Uncle Don was our Scheherazade – but he was less a Kipling than a Conrad.

Options

A. the Aladdin's cave / B. the Cinderella / C. the crock of gold / D. the Emperor who has no clothes / E. the fairy godmother / F. to kill the goose that lays the golden eggs / G. a Peter Pan / H. to follow the Pied Piper / I. a Prince Charming / J. Rip van Winkle / K. seven league boots / L. a Sleeping Beauty / M. the sorcerer's apprentice / N. an ugly duckling / O. the ugly sister / P. where the rainbow ends

25

UNIT

Idiomatic Structures IV

Field 1: The 'To be + in' Construction

Your Task

Read the twenty alliterative biographies below and then decide which life is best characterised by which of the 'to be + in' idioms listed beneath. The correct answers are to be found on page 175.

Biographies

1. Annabelle is acutely and anxiously agitated.
2. Bad boy Bert is in his boss's bad books.
3. Caroline is being completely and carefully cared for.
4. Charles is our chosen chairperson.

5. Deirdre is in a dire and dreadful dilemma.
6. Fred is firing on all four cylinders, really in fine form.
7. Grousing Gertrude is not in good spirits.
8. Hearty he-man Harry is in top health.

9. Ingrid is in the ideal industry for her initiative and input.
10. Can't-catch-it Kay hasn't a clue.
11. 'Life-is-lousy' Lew is in low spirits.
12. Nervy Norbert never knows what not to do.

13. Patricia perpetually gains publicity.
14. Rupert is in an 'orribly rigid and restrictive routine.
15. Sandy is sick, seemingly sickening for something for sure.
16. Tracy is faced with a tricky and teasing problem.

17. Vincent indulges in vapid, vain fantasies.
18. Wendy was there when the wayward wretch was apprehended.

Options

He or she is in ...

A. a bad way / B. the chair / C. the clouds / D. the dark / E. the dog-house / F. the doldrums / G. the dumps / H. one's element / I. fine fettle / J. a flat spin / K. a flutter / L. good hands / M. the kill / N. the limelight / O. the pink / P. a rut / Q. the soup / R. a tight squeeze

Field 2: Verb Pairs

Your Task

Join each of the twenty-six verbs on the left with the verb on the right with which it is normally associated in an idiomatic verb pair. Then fit each pair to its definition on the right. (Note that the connecting word is 'and' except where stated.) The correct answers are to be found on page 175.

Verbs

	and	
TO AID	HAW	A. call an early election
TO BOW	BE DAMNED	B. make concessions
CARP	BEAR IT	C. take life easy
CHOP	MUDGE	D. create or ruin
CUT	DEAL	E. utilise public transport

FETCH	MAR	F. react furiously
FORGIVE	BE SEEN	G. get up and enjoy life
FUDGE	SCRAPE	H. mug; crash and drive off
GRIN	DINE	I. select carefully
HIT	CAVIL	J. print and not fear the consequences

HUFF	RUN	K. kow-tow
HUM	RIDE	L. bid ecstatic farewell
LIVE	CHOOSE	M. be parsimonious
LOVE IT	RAVE	N. give evasive answers
MAKE OR	SHINE	O. lavish hospitality on

MAKE OR	BREAK	P. take a blow lightly
PARK	LEAVE IT	Q. exert great effort
PICK	SCRAPE	R. keep altering policy
PUBLISH	CHANGE	S. do dogsbody jobs
RANT	FORGET	T. show grace

RISE	LEAVE IT	U. criticise mercilessly
SCRIMP	LET LIVE	V. prevaricate
SEE	PUFF	W. accept or reject
TAKE IT OR	RUN	X. treat life as a spectacle
WHEEL	ABET	Y. assist criminal
WINE	CARRY	Z. be decisive, one way or the other

Field 3: Noun Pairs II

Each of the forty nouns in the left-hand columns below is commonly used with one of the nouns in the right-hand column in a noun pair construction. Fit the idioms together and check your answers on page 175, before going on to Part II below and overleaf. Note that for simplicity's sake this exercise is divided into two halves A and B, the latter being the more demanding.

Nouns

Section A

	AND	
ALL		BOUNDS
BREAD		THRUST
CHEEK BY		JETSAM
CUT		GO
DOOM		GLOOM
FLOTSAM		SUNDRY
GET-UP		GRAB
HEAD		NECK
HIGH DAYS		OUTS
INS		BUTTER
LEAPS		TATTERS
MEAT		BONE
NECK		NONSENSE
RAGS		BRANCH
ROOT		SHOUL-DERS
SKIN		GO
SMASH		HOLIDAYS
STUFF		POTATOES
TOUCH		MEANS
WAYS		JOWL

Section B

	AND	
ALARUMS		JOAN
BOBBING		*origo*
BOX		CRY
DARBY		KIN
FITS		TUMBLE
fons et		TRIBULATIONS
GOODS		COX
HEWERS OF WOOD		STARTS
HUE		FILE
KITH		HIS WIFE
MOVER		EXCURSIONS
P'S		CRY
RANK		SHAKER
ROUGH		Q'S
SCYLLA		CHARYBDIS
SLAP		CHATTELS
STRESS		TICKLE
TRIALS		STRAIN
TWEEDLE-DUM		PEERING
THE WORLD		DRAWERS OF WATER
		TWEEDLEDEE

Sentences

Part II Section A

1. The children of the shanty town were dressed in ___.
2. Another broken window at another jeweller's. Yet another ___.
3. 'Cynthia, do try to eat, dear. You'll be nothing but ___ soon.'
4. After nine years in the job, she knew all the ___ of the system.
5. 'Charles wore the suit on special occasions only – only on ___.'
6. 'Whatever happened to your energy and *joie de vivre*? You used to have so much ___.' – 'I know, but one day it just got up and went!'
7. She was the outstanding candidate – ___ above the rest.
8. After a storm the beachcombers were soon out among the ___.
9. The essential, basic ___ issues had been dealt with.
10. The secret police had ___ of making their detainees talk.
11. 'Utter rubbish! ___!'

12. She loved lively argument, the ___ of debate.
13. 'It was ___ , but we just made it with literally seconds to spare.'
14. The report was terribly depressing – all ___ .
15. 'We must eradicate the complete drug supply network, ___.'
16. The polls suggest that the election will be close, a ___ race.
17. The modern edifice was out of place, standing ___ with the pub where Shakespeare had exchanged witticisms with Ben Jonson.
18. 'How's your paper?' – 'Unprofound, rather ___ , actually.'
19. During her year abroad, her language ability advanced by ___.
20. She was so happy at her exam result – and so drunk – that she went through the *Philosophikum* distributing champers to ___.

Sentences

Section B

1. 'No. No. Not Blackpool, dear. Not at Easter. The place will be packed, chock-a-block. ___ go to Blackpool at Easter!'
2. 'With the parties so similar there's not much choice: It's ___!'
3. 'Our success as a party does not depend on convincing our own MPs but on selling our policies to the party ___ and to the voters.'
4. They were an inseparable couple – married for almost seventy-five years and still going strong. The ___ of Much-Mirebury-in-the-Moor.
5. 'Blood is thicker than water, Marmaduke. I don't feel really at ease unless I'm among my own ___. Strangers begin next door.'
6. The cutting of the professorial post caused such a ___ among the student body that the Senate was forced to reverse its decision.
7. 'Insufferably arrogant, she saw herself as the ___ of all wisdom.'
8. 'Why so miserable today, Wilbur? Why so downcast?' – 'Ach, nothing. Alas. Ach. Just the ___ of this earthly life.'
9. The police arrested both people concerned: the prostitute for ___ and the driver of the car for kerb-crawling.
10. 'We're just the lowest of the low in their eyes, the ___.'
11. 'And be careful when you speak to Aunt Agatha. She lays great emphasis on the correct behaviour. So mind your ___!'
12. Rugby is not the gentlest of games. But who minds a bit of ___?
13. 'A good secretary must be like a good bridge. Both must be able to withstand the ___ of day-by-day comings and goings.'
14. Democratisation was a stop-go process, proceeding by ___.
15. On the university trip to Sri Lanka there were several ___ – four bags left in Colombo, three participants sick and two arrested.
16. 'They share the workload – like ___ , really – the one stepping in when the other's too busy or ill and vice versa.'
17. 'With me it's boredom or migraine. They're the ___ of my life.'
18. With her many connections and creative ideas she became a real ___ in the cultural world, the organiser of many memorable events.
19. After his bankruptcy, all his ___ went to the state receiver.
20. He was never a great lover, always preferring a little ___ in the back seat to longer sessions in the cornfield.

Field 4: Portmanteau Words

Your Task

A portmanteau word is a word such as 'brunch' or 'Reaganomics' made out of two words telescoped together. Construct correct portmanteau words from each of the word-pairs beneath and then match each with the fitting definition on the right.

Word pairs

ad hoc	+	bureaucracy
American	+	Asian
automobile	+	hypochondriac
'bonking'	+	blockbuster
breath	+	analyser
catalogue	+	magazine
chocolate	+	alcoholic
docklands	+	cockney
education	+	entertainment
estimate	+	guess
evangelism	+	television
garbage	+	technology
goat	+	sheep
inflation	+	boom
inflation	+	stagnation
influenza	+	affluence
information	+	commercial
intelligentsia	+	privilege
mock	+	cockney
motorcar	+	cavalcade
pharmaceutics	+	farm
plug	+	documentary
quality newspaper	+	lollipop
rock	+	documentary
ship	+	hijacker
suburb	+	slum
twig	+	igloo
van	+	hooligan
work	+	alcoholic

A. procession of cars
B. chocolate addict
C. urban sprawl
D. rough calculation
E. farm for GM foods
F. sheep/goat cross
G. to seize a ship
H. refuse science
I. film on rock music
J. police vehicle for soccer trouble-makers
K. work addict
L. advert-cum-film
M. privileged stratum
N. test for drink-driver
O. Asian living in US
P. film plug
Q. glossy sales catalog
R. Bakker-like TV use
S. prosperity disease
T. lengthy novel with oodles of sex
U. impromptu firm management structures
V. pseudo East-Ender
W. inhabitant of new London docklands
X. inflation due to upswing
Y. teaching disguised as fun
Z. temporary home of eco-protester
AA. quality newspaper going down-market
BB. downturn due to inflation
CC. car worryguts

(Answers on page 176.)

Field 5: British Proverbs II

Your Task

Below are thirty British proverbs, each of which, however, has been cut in half, the halves then being jumbled up. Connect the beginning on the left with the correct ending on the right and state the proverb's meaning. The correct answers are to be found on page 176.

Proverbs

1. a rolling stone
2. a new broom
3. you may lead a horse to water but
4. more haste,
5. no news
6. still waters
7. every man for himself and
8. you can't make an omelette
9. a miss is
10. a stitch in time
11. you can't teach an old dog
12. you scratch my back and I'll
13. it takes all sorts to
14. make hay while
15. any port
16. example is
17. first thrive then
18. man proposes,
19. no man is
20. happy is the country which
21. sow the wind and you'll
22. East or West,
23. one man's meat is
24. what can't be cured must
25. anything for
26. dead men
27. he goes long barefoot that
28. he that fights and runs away
29. Christmas comes but
30. fear the Greeks even when

A. is good news
B. has no history
C. the devil take the hindmost
D. in a storm
E. saves nine
F. be endured
G. home's best
H. a quiet life
I. less speed
J. sweeps clean
K. without breaking eggs
L. run deep
M. wive
N. God disposes
O. once a year
P. as good as a mile
Q. lives to fight another day
R. you cannot make him drink
S. better than precept
T. gathers no moss
U. tell no tales
V. scratch yours
W. waits for a dead man's shoes
X. make a world
Y. new tricks
Z. reap the whirlwind
AA. they bring gifts
BB. a hero to his own valet
CC. the sun shines
DD. another man's poison

For further British proverbs see page 36.

Revision IV

Exercise 1: Idiomatic Aphorisms

Your Task

Each of the following aphorisms contains one or more idioms learned in the foregoing twenty-four chapters. Translate or paraphrase the sentences and then compare your versions with the master translations on page 176.

Aphorisms

1.Modesty is the only sure bait when you angle for praise. PHILIP STANHOPE, EARL OF CHESTERFIELD
2. A politician is an animal who can sit on the fence and yet keep both ears to the ground. H. L. MENCKEN
3. If the creator had a purpose in equipping us with a neck, he surely meant us to stick it out. ARTHUR KOESTLER
4. War is capitalism with the gloves off. TOM STOPPARD
5. If you see a bandwagon it is too late. JAMES GOLDSMITH
6. Damn it all, you can't have the crown of thorns and the thirty pieces of silver. ANEURIN BEVAN
7. He who slings mud usually loses ground. ADLAI STEVENSON
8. Show me a congenital eavesdropper with the instincts of a Peeping Tom and I'll show you a dramatist. KENNETH TYNAN
9. The structure of a play is always the story of how the birds come home to roost. ARTHUR MILLER
10. The English statesman is bribed not to be bribed. He is born with a silver spoon is his mouth so that he may never afterwards be found with the silver spoons in his pocket. G. K. CHESTERTON
11. Stretched on the rack of a too easy chair. ALEXANDER POPE
12. If there are cat-calls ... you are sure at least that the audience is still there. CARYL BRAHMS & S. J. SIMON
13. The only man who wasn't spoiled by being lionised was Daniel. HERBERT TREE
14. Vote Labour and you build castles in the air. Vote Conservative and you can live in them. DAVID FROST
15. If it be true that 'good wine needs no bush', 'tis true that a good play needs no epilogue. WILLIAM SHAKESPEARE, *As You Like It*
16. I don't see how an epigram, being a bolt from the blue, with no introduction or cue, ever gets itself writ. WILLIAM JAMES
17. Most great men of the past were only there for the beer. A. J. P. TAYLOR
18. When all is rotten, it's a man's duty to cry 'stinking fish'. A. H. WHITEHEAD

Exercise 2: Idiomatically Different

Your Task

Each of the following aphorisms derives its strength from deliberately modifying one or more of the idioms learned in the foregoing twenty-four chapters. Point out what is modified and then state the sense of the aphorism. The correct answers are to be found on page 177.

Aphorisms

1. Time wounds all heels. GROUCHO MARX
2. A fool and his books are soon parted. HOLBROOK JACKSON
3. 'Pushing up theses', that is the euphemism which men of letters use for being dead; a long littleness of dons lies ahead of us, unless we have been afflicted with the curse of lucidity. CYRIL CONNOLLY
4. The poet makes silk dresses out of worms. WALLACE STEVENS
5. My motto is 'publish and be sued'. RICHARD INGRAMS

6. One's impossible, two is dreary. / Three is company safe and cheery. STEPHEN SONDHEIM
7. Education is the process of casting false pearls before real swine. IRWIN EDMAN
8. Personally, I have no bone to pick with graveyards. SAMUEL BECKETT
9. Of course you can get a quart into a pint pot – you can get a couple of gallons into it, if you stay till closing time. PATRICK SKENE CATLING
10. He's the kind of bore who's here today and here tomorrow. BINNIE BARNES

11. The early worm gets the bird. ERNEST MANDELBAUM
12. Those whom the gods love grow young. OSCAR WILDE
13. The humorist runs with the hare; the satirist hunts with the hounds. FATHER KNOX
14. Our ideas: They are for the most part like bad sixpences and we spend our lives in trying to pass them on one another. SAMUEL BUTLER II
15. You can lead a whore to culture but you can't make her think. DOROTHY PARKER

> *Since [...] Phrases [...] used in ordinary conversation contract a kind of Meanness by passing through the Mouths of the Vulgar, a Poet should take particular Care to guard himself against Idiomatick Ways of Speaking.*

ADDISON, *The Spectator No. 285* (1712)

Answers

Gerade die Einfachheit dieser Idiome bringt für die Lernenden eine gewisse Schwierigkeit; sie sind z.T. wieder dissoziiert und ungestützt, insofern als ihre Bedeutung aus den Teilen nicht erkenntlich wird. [...] Sie müssen deshalb sorgfältig einzeln gelernt werden. Da dies bis heute noch nicht systematisch genug getan wird, sind in diesem Punkte grobe Übersetzungsfehler häufig.
ERNST LEISI, CHRISTIAN MAIR, *Das heutige Englisch: Wesenszüge und Probleme* ^{8}1999

Unit 1 Idioms of the Cosmos and Earth

Page 7: The Heavens and Heavenly Bodies

Answers: 1. planet 2. star 3. a) sky b) earth 4. world 5. sunny 6. sun 7. moonlight 8. world 9. ray of sunshine (*ironic*) 10. a) moon b) sky c) space 11. world 12. mooning 13. a) world b) moon 14. moonlight 15. a) moonshine b) starry

Page 8: Astronomy and Astrology

Answers: 1. zenith 2. eclipse 3. stars 4. lucky stars 5. shooting star 6. earth 7. meteoric 8. orbit 9. star-studded 10. mooned 11. nothing on earth 12. satellite 13. in the ascendant 14. heaven and earth 15. wax and wane 16. galaxy 17. nadir 18. skies
Key Phrase: Her star is on the wane.

Page 9: Features of World Geography

Answers: A. field B. to peak C. island D. the tip of the iceberg E. straits F. hill G. range H. slough I. an Everest J. oasis K. tide L. slope M. the four winds N. up the creek O. ocean P. pond Q. coast R. landslide S. pass T. channel U. the lie of the land V. hills W. summit X. mountain

Page 10: Countries and Nations

Answers: 1. Indian 2. Dutch 3. a) Greek b) Greek 4. China 5. French 6. Dutch 7. Dutch 8. Spain 9. Greek 10. French 11. bohemian 12. Dutch 13. Russian 14. French 15. Greek 16. Sheba 17. Dutchman 18. Gallic 19. Welsh 20. Turks 21. Teutonic

Cultural Background
Indian Summer The phrase derives not from India, but from C 18th New England. The local American Indians ascribed such splendid late summer weather to the benevolent God Cautantowwit.
Dutch Courage This reference to the courage which comes from alcohol is one of several anti-Dutch phrases (cf. 17) to enter the English language during the intense Anglo-Dutch rivalry of the C 17th.
Greek gift a reference to the Troy myth and to one of the oldest of still extant proverbs – *timeo Danaos et dona ferentes*
Yes, and I'm the Queen of Sheba *Wer das glaubt, wird selig!* The Queen of Sheba visits Solomon in I Kings, X, i–xiii (that story being also one of hearing and believing).
Welsh rabbit a traditional poor man's dish of pre-melted butter and cheese, mixed with ale, on toast. 'Welsh' denoted inferior quality – cf. 'Welsh comb' for the hand. Some insist on 'rarebit', but there are many examples of meat words used jocularly to hide 'lesser' foods.
Young Turk a radical anti-Establishment figure. The Young Turks emerged in 1889, attempting to overthrow the then Ottoman sultan, whose régime had helped earn Turkey the title 'sick man of Europe'.

Page 11: Areas, Cities, Towns, Rivers

Answers: 1. U 2. P 3. G 4. F 5. S 6. B 7. V 8. C 9. J 10. D 11. N 12. W 13. I 14. X 15. K 16. R 17. M 18. O 19. H 20. A 21. L 22. E 23. T 24. Q

Cultural Background

Dunkirk spirit a reference to the 'little miracle' of Dunkirk, where in May 1940 the 'little ships' brought back the British army stranded on the French beaches by the German advance.

to send to Coventry to give the cold shoulder. In the English Civil War, Coventry was a parliament stronghold, in which royalists would be *personae non gratae*.

Bedlam a short form of 'Bethlehem' – the priory of St Mary of Bethlehem having cared for the mentally ill since the C 14th. On dissolving the monasteries, Henry VIII donated the hospital to the City of London. Today the institution is Bethlehem Royal Hospital.

the Wapping Revolution In 1986, press baron Rupert Murdoch effectively ended the old Fleet Street (see p. 12) by moving his newspaper empire to a new high-tech centre at Wapping in the refurbished London Docklands. Other papers soon followed suit.

Bow Bells To be a genuine cockney one should have been born within the sound of the bells of London's St Mary-le-Bow Church.

Bristol fashion Ships from Bristol, one of the great Atlantic-going (and slave) ports of the C 18th, were notoriously spick and span. Other echoes of Bristol's past include the quality sherry, 'Bristol cream'.

beyond the Pale 'uncivilised'. The Pale was the double-ditch palisade around the English colony in Dublin. Beyond the Pale, English (and later Protestant) writ did not run.

I'm from Missouri I'm a no-nonsense sceptic. The phrase allegedly goes back to 1899 when one Willard Vandiver used the now legendary words to demand proof for their claims from political speech-makers in Philadelphia.

coals to Newcastle From Roman times on, Newcastle, with its vast under-sea mines, has been a centre of the British coal industry.

Fiddling while Rome burns an activity attributed to the much-hated Roman emperor Nero during the great fire of 64 A.D., when, however, he was not in the city.

Babel The essential myth of the origin of the world's multi-lingualism is to be found in Genesis, Chapter XI, 1-9. 'Babel', and the English 'babble' are derived from the Hebrew 'balal' (to confuse).

See Naples and die! a reference both to the fabled beauty of Naples and its location and to the nearby town of Mori (It. 'to die'), where thousands did indeed once die of typhoid and cholera.

to Shanghai The practice of 'pressing' able-bodied men into naval service – a practice legal for the king's navy but illegal for the merchant navy – was common in the C 18th and early C 19th. The far-away town of Shanghai is a synecdoche for the ensuing long voyages.

Page 12: Specific Streets

Answers: 1. C 2. J 3. D 4. A 5. L 6. B 7. M 8. G 9. F 10. E 11. I 12. K 13. H

Cultural Background
Threadneedle Street location of the Bank of England since 1734. The Bank itself was founded in 1694 to meet the financial requirements arising from Britain's new-found strategic/imperial ambitions under William and Mary.
Damascus Road scene of the conversion of the pharisee Saul/St Paul to Christianity – cf. Acts IX, 3-19
Carey Street site of the Courts in Bankruptcy off the Strand, London
Christopher Street parade gay pride parade defiantly commemorating an incident of anti-homosexual harassment in the gay stronghold of Christopher St, Greenwich Village, New York, in 1963.
Whitehall road between Westminster and Trafalgar Square housing the major British ministries
Fleet St traditional home of the British national press until the Wapping revolution (see p. 11). Fleet St emerged as, and long remained, the press centre on account of its closeness to the scribes of St Paul's Cathedral, the government press, the Thames, the law courts, parliament, St James and the City. By 1850, 'Fleet Street' was a metaphor for the national press. Britain's first daily, the *Daily Courant* (1702), was sold from a tavern on Fleet Bridge.
Downing St traditional home of the British Prime Minister (No. 10) and the Chancellor of the Exchequer (No. 11) since the 1730s. Under Tony Blair, the PM and Chancellor exchanged homes.
Harley St long-established London centre of British specialist doctors
Grub St traditional C 18th London home of impoverished hack writers, centred around the no longer existent Grub St, in Moorfields. Gissing's naturalist novel *New Grub Street* (1891) has been translated into German as *Zeilengeld.*

Unit 2 Idioms of Time and Number

Page 13: Long and Longish Durations

Answers: 1. a month of Sundays 2. took years off them 3. autumn of life 4. many moons ago 5. to call it a day 6. light years away 7. silly season 8. it has had its day 9. small hours (ScotE.: 'wee hours') 10. since the year dot 11. set the agenda 12. be on nights 13. hidden agenda 14. an unearthly hour 15. for aeons and aeons 16. living will 17. for donkey's years
Key Phrase: from (the) cradle to (the) grave

Cultural Background
for donkey's years for years and years. The phrase is a corruption of 'for donkey's ears' – an ass's ears being indeed long.

Page 14: Time Idioms involving 'Time'

Answers: 1. F 2. A 3. N 4. B 5. C 6. D 7. L 8. Q 9. O 10. H 11. E 12. I 13. P or J 14. M 15. G 16. R 17. K 18. J or P

Page 15: Low Numbers – Nought to Nine

Answers: 1. nine 2. nines 3. six 4. a) seven b) two c) one 5. a) two b) three 6. zero 7. fives 8. a) two b) two 9. a) one b) two 10. a) six b) half a dozen 11. seven 12. a) one b) two c) one d) eight 13. one 14. two 15. seven 16. one 17. a) one b) two 18. two 19. nine 20. fours 21. three

Cultural Background
nine days' wonder short-lived sensation. Cf. the proverb 'A wonder lasts nine days and then the puppy's eyes are open'.
plus-fours knickerbockers. The term is tailors' slang, a reference to the four extra inches of material used in the trouser leg to give the 'baggy' effect.

Page 16: Further Low Numbers

Answers: 1. C 2. D 3. C 4. A 5. A 6. A 7. B 8. A or B 9. A 10. C 11. B

Cultural Background
at sixes and sevens in confusion. The idiom originates from the world of dicing.

Page 17: Number in Dialogue and Proverb

Answers: 1. C 2. A 3. I 4. E 5. D 6. B 7. K 8. F 9. L 10. H 11. O 12. N 13. M 14. G 15. J

Page 18: Higher Numbers – Ten and Above

Answers: 1. a hundred-and-one 2. forty 3. sixty-four thousand 4. million 5. fifty-fifty 6. dozen 7. eleven 8. 22 9. thirty 10. thousand 11. a) hundred b) forty 12. four hundred

Cultural Background
Sixty-four thousand dollar question The phrase began life as the 'sixty-four dollar question' in the American Radio quiz programme 'Take It or Leave It' broadcast from 1942 on. The present form is the name of the subsequent television version of the show.
a baker's dozen thirteen for twelve. Traditionally, on buying twelve rolls or cakes from a British baker one receives a thirteenth free. This may derive from the baker's fear of being found to have sold under weight. The thirteenth loaf was called the 'inbread' or 'vantage loaf'.
Catch-22 from the late Joseph Heller's anti-war novel of the same name (1961)
thirty pieces of silver the payment of Judas
the four hundred the wealthiest and most exclusive people. Mrs Astor was *the* New York hostess of America's Gilded Age.

Page 18: Ordinal Numbers

Answers: A. seventh heaven B. third degree burns C. fifth column D. eighth wonder of the world E. for the umpteenth time F. to come off second best G. to second-guess H. at the eleventh hour I. first class J. fourth estate

Cultural Background
fourth estate The invention of the phrase is credited to the C 18th conservative thinker Edmund Burke (1729–97), who allegedly said: 'There are three estates in Parliament, but in the reporters' gallery yonder there sits a fourth estate, more important than they all'. The first three estates are monarchy, lords and commons. In the 1960s, PM Harold Wilson spoke of the trade unions as a 'fifth estate'.

Unit 3 Idioms of Colour

Page 19: The Basic Colours

Answers: Part A: A. blue B. blue C. red D. green E. purple F. grey G. purple H. green I. blue J. red K. yellow L. red M. browned N. brown O. purple P. white Q. crimson R. white S. red T. red U. green V. pink W. blue X. green Y. white Z. red AA. green BB. golden CC. silver DD. grey
Part B: 1. red carpet 2. great white hope 3. pink elephants 4. red herrings

Cultural Background
blue stocking bookish woman more interested in learning and things academic than in marriage, children etc. The origins of the phrase are unclear, some pointing to Britain, others to France, others again to the *della calza* of 1590 Venice. The original English blue stockings gathered at the lush and sparkling London *soirées* of Elizabeth Montagu from *c.* 1750 – 1790 and included Fanny Burney, Hester Chapone, Hannah More and *femmes savantes* from across the Channel. Montagu, the 'Queen of the Blues' (Dr Johnson), was vain but not licentious. She discouraged drink and gambling, offering instead good food and *esprit* served with coffee, tea or chocolate – as lauded in Hannah More's poem, 'The Bas Bleu'. Though in some ways emancipated, the original blue stockings did not share all the ideals of their modern counterparts, nor indeed of such contemporaries as Mary Wollstonecraft (of whose great *Vindication of the Rights of Women* (1792) More said that its very title was so ridiculous that she had no intention of reading it).
yellow cowardly. Yellow has various meanings in various European cultures, ranging from jealousy through inconstancy and adultery to treachery and heresy.
grey matter the brain cells. The active part of the brain is composed of grey tissue containing the nerve endings.
pink elephants hallucinations induced by alcohol. In the C 19th the idiom was 'pink spiders'. The modern version is so well-known that the pink elephant is today the symbol for Alcoholics Anonymous.
red herring deliberate distraction. During the training of hounds for fox-hunting, a (strongly-smelling) red herring would be drawn across the trail of the fox. Hounds thus learnt not to be misled.

Page 20: Colourful Phrases

Answers: 1. J 2. C 3. K. 4. O 5. I 6. R 7. T 8. S 9. L 10. D 11. H 12. P 13. B 14. Q 15. M 16. N 17. E 18. F 19. A 20. G

Cultural Background

to worship the golden calf worship money. The calf was a molten divine image created by Aaron for the Israelites but rejected by Moses – see Exodus, XXXII, *passim*.

scarlet woman harlot. The term derives from Revelation, XVII, 1–6. Hence the title of Nathaniel Hawthorne's *The Scarlet Letter* (1850).

to take up the white man's burden to do one's 'imperial duty'. The notorious term originates in Kipling's poem 'The White Man's Burden' (1899).

Page 21: Black and White Together

Answers: 1. M 2. G 3. Q 4. V 5. I 6. a) J b) B 7. R 8. a) K b) D 9. E 10. W 11. N 12. C 13. B 14. O 15. S 16. P 17. L 18. F 19. a) H b) Q 20. X 21. U 22. a) T b) A

Cultural Background

Black Maria police van, so named after Maria Lee, a prodigiously strong free black woman who repeatedly came to the aid of the Boston, Mass. police force in the early 1800s. British 'Black Marias' came into being in the 1830s.

a white knight a hero, champion, rescuer. The term derives not from the mediaeval period but from the figure in Lewis Carroll's *Alice Through the Looking Glass* (1865) and owes something to the similar 'knight in shining armour' (see p. 96). In recent years, a 'white knight' has taken on a further, parallel meaning – a company or individual who rescues a company from a hostile take-over bid.

blackleg strike-breaker, non-union worker. The idiom seems to come from the sphere of gambling, where it denoted a swindler at cards.

whiter than white suspiciously pure. The idiom stems from soap-powder advertising – cf. 'squeaky clean' from the shampoo ad.

to blackball to exclude from a club/organization. The term derives from the rapidly expanding London club scene of the C 18th: members voted with white and black balls to signify acceptance or rejection of a new applicant.

to show the white feather from the British national sport of the C 18th, cock-fighting, where the strongest cocks, descended from the Indian red jungle fowl, had no white feathers

Page 22: Sophisticated Shades

Answers: 1. B 2. A 3. B 4. C 5. B 6. D 7. A 8. C 9. C 10. D

Cultural Background

to cry blue murder probably a corruption of the French curse *morbleu*

the thin red line The phrase originated in 1854 at the Battle of Balaclava during the Crimean War. By 1899 the poet Frederick Ward could write of 'the thin red line/ That girdles round the globe'. Britain's Second Empire, however, was held together by its navy.

Unit 4 Idioms of Weather

Page 23: Idioms of the Wind

Answers: 1. C 2. I 3. F 4. D 5. A 6. H 7. B 8. E 9. J 10. G

Page 24: Essential Weather

Answers: Across 2. bluster 8. blow hot and cold 9. windfall 10. freeze 13. storm 14. cool 15. cut ice 16. thaw 17. wind 18. hail 20. ice 23. breezes 24. heat 25. hazy 26. cloud
Down 1. frosted 3. lull before the storm 4. snowball 5. foggiest 6. under the weather 7. fog 11. thin ice 12. cold 15. calm 19. air 21. thunder 22. haze

Page 25: Weather, Hot and Cold

Answers: 1. heated 2. cold 3. hothouse 4. hotbed 5. hot 6. hot 7. cold 8. cold 9. heat 10. hot 11. hothead 12. cool 13. sang-froid 14. temperatures 15. hot 16. hot 17. cold 18. hot 19. cold 20. cold 21. heat 22. hot 23. cold 24. coolly 25. hot-line

Cultural Background
hot-line immediate, intimate contact. The hot-line was the telephone link established between Washington and the Kremlin following the Cuba Crisis of 1962 with its threat of nuclear war. The first use of the term in literature is perhaps in Ted Hughes.

Page 26: More Extreme Weather

Answers: 1. cloud nine 2. snowballed under 3. by storm 4. weather eye open 5. thin air 6. ray of hope 7. rainy day 8. on ice 9. driven snow 10. fair weather 11. squalls 12. weather-cock 13. drop in the ocean 14. lightning 15. heavy weather
Key Phrase: come rain or shine

Cultural Background
on cloud nine Yes, the exultant English go higher. There were, allegedly, nine orders of angels.
squalls sudden and sharp wind gusts – one of the countless British idioms derived from the country's long nautical tradition.

Unit 5 Idioms of the Natural World

Page 27: Basic Nature

Answers: Annabelle: F Basil: E Charlotte: C Daniel: G Enid: Q Freddy: I Georgina: D *or perhaps* O Hubert: B Ingrid: H Jeremy: J Kay: M Lew: L Margaret: O *or perhaps* D Nigel: P Olive: N Patrick: K

Cultural Background
to sow one's wild oats to indulge in sexual adventures before marriage. 'Wild oats' are the long grass which grows as a weed in cornfields.

Page 28: Natural Dialogue

Answers: 1. E 2. G 3. J 4. M 5. H 6. F 7. A 8. B 9. C 10. I 11. D 12. L 13. N 14. K

Page 29: The Gardening Life

Answers: 1. G 2. B 3. N 4. P 5. K 6. D 7. A 8. E 9. I 10. M 11. O 12. H 13. C 14. J 15. F 16. L

Cultural Background
to go on the stump to deliver rousing election speeches from a soap-box etc. The '(tree) stump' in question is any high point of advantage used for public speaking – a very British tradition, last tellingly used by John Major in the general election of 1992.

Page 30: Trees and Bushes

Answers: Across 3. cleft stick 5. big stick 7. leaf 8. sap 11. sapling 13. bush 14. *see* 5 15. trunk 16. willowy 20. bushy 21. trunk 22. oak 23. stem 24. hedge
Down 1. stump 2. birch 4. leaf through 6. willow 7. log 9. family tree 10. husk 12. nut 17. ivy 18. bush 19. core

Cultural Background
leather on willow The cricket bat is traditionally made of the pliable willow wood, the cricket ball of leather around a cork core wrapped in twine.

Unit 6 Idiomatic Structures

Page 31: Pairs of Adjectives

Answers: 1. D 2. S 3. J 4. C 5. I 6. M 7. V 8. E 9. K 10. G 11. H 12. F 13. O 14. R 15. U 16. P 17. A 18. B 19. a) N b) T 20. L 21. Q

Cultural Background
spick and span The idiom derives from the world of ships – a spick being a nail or spike, and a span a new, untreated plank.

Page 32/33: The 'as ... as' Construction

Answers: as ... 1. a) black as a cinder b) dry as tinder 2. sober as a judge 3. good as gold 4. a) snug as a bug in a rug b) fresh as a daisy 5. bright as a button 6. a) pale as death b) right as rain 7. brown as a berry 8. cool as a cucumber

9. keen as mustard 10. a) dead as a doornail b) large as life 11. mad as a hatter 12. fit as a fiddle 13. bold as brass 14. pretty as a picture 15. poor as church mice 16. hard as nails 17. steady as a rock 18. blind as a bat 19. drunk as a lord 20. deaf as a post 21. happy as the day is long 22. dead as mutton 23. a) patient as Job b) wise as Solomon 24. warm as toast

Cultural Background
as mad as a hatter From the C 17th on, the use of mercury to process the felt (*Filz*) employed in hat-making did indeed tend to give hatters tremors, disorders, sleeplessness and hallucinations.

Page 34: The 'Verb + Like' Construction

Answers: A4 / B3 / C18 / D24 / E12 / F22 / G25 / H14 / I19 / J7 / K1 / L20 / M15 / N5 / O21 / P13 / Q11 / R2 / S16 / T8 / U26 / V9 / W24 / X17 / Y6

Cultural Background
to live like fighting cocks *in Saus und Braus leben.* With cock-fighting one of the most lucrative of sports, contestants kept their fighting fowl very well.

Page 35: Eponyms I

Answers: 1. S: a Bailey bridge 2. J: a biro 3. O: bloomers 4. T: bowdlerisation 5. Q: the bowler hat 6. H: the/to boycott 7. N: Braille system, Braille, to Braille 8. P: the cardigan 9. C: the diesel (engine) 10. K: garibaldi biscuits 11. R: Geiger counter 12. AA: gerrymandering 13. W: to have Hobson's choice 14. Y: hooligan, hooliganism 15. D: Belisha beacon 16. F: Luddite, Luddism 17. V: Malthusianism 18. L. mackintosh, 'mac' 19. G: a maverick 20. X: to mesmerise, mesmerising, mesmerisation 21. B: to pasteurise, pasteurisation 22. A: a plimsoll (cf. also the Plimsoll line) 23. E: a Pyrrhic victory 24. I: a quisling 25. M: a sandwich 26. U: a Spoonerism 27. Z: wellington boots ('Wellies')

Cultural Background
Bailey bridge The quickly assembled bridge, which could support heavy vehicles such as tanks, was a key factor in World War II. Field Marshall Montgomery even claimed, 'Without the Bailey bridge we should not have won the war.'
biro This invention also, patented in 1938, came to the fore in World War II, assisting aircraft navigators writing at great heights.
bowdlerise Dr Bowdler was the editor of the *Family Shakespeare* (1818), which claims to contain nothing which 'cannot without propriety be read aloud in a family'. Recent research suggests that the first edition of this was, however, the work of Bowdler's sister.
boycott During one of the many land and rent wars in the Irish past, Capt. Boycott, a landlord for the Earl of Erne in Co. Mayo around 1880, was ostracised when he refused to accept lower rents.
cardigan In the deep cold of the Russian winter, the Earl of Cardigan prescribed this garment for his cavalrymen at Balaclava. Cardigan led the now infamous, once lauded, Charge of the Light Brigade – cf Tennyson's poem of that name and

the mutterings of Mr Ramsay in Virginia Woolf's *To the Lighthouse* (1927). Note that the village of Balaclava gave its name to the still popular snug-fitting woollen hood.

garibaldi The connection between the renowned biscuit and the soldier-hero of the Italian *Risorgimento* (1860-61) is unclear.

gerrymander The term and practice, though originating in Massachusetts, were perhaps most notorious and fateful in Northern Ireland politics on the local council level between 1921 and 1968.

Hobson's choice The C 16th and 17th Cambridge liveryman allowed his customers to ride not any of his forty horses but only the horse which, on a rotation principle, was nearest the stable door. The practice presumably paid off: visitors to Cambridge can still admire Hobson's Conduit, a water supply which he (and others) donated to the city.

hooligan Patrick Hooligan – his real name may have been the very Irish Houlihan – was a London criminal of the 1890s, head of a rowdy family and with a coterie of rowdy supporters.

Luddite Ned Ludd destroyed job-threatening stocking frames around 1779. His name was then adopted by similarly-minded groups in the Midlands and Northern England textile industry from 1810 to 1817. The Industrial Revolution saw several such movements, including those of 'Captain Swing' in the agricultural sector.

Malthusianism Thomas Malthus published his controversial *Essay on the Principle of Population* in 1798, a time of rapid demographic increase. He saw war, famine, disease or sexual restraint as remedies.

maverick someone who does not follow the herd. The Texan rancher did not brand all his cattle and claimed any unbranded stock roaming free in the neighbourhood as his own.

plimsoll/Plimsoll line Plimsoll, elected MP for Derby in 1868, campaigned for ship safety. In 1876, the Plimsoll line, marking the point to which a ship may be loaded, was adopted. The rubber-soled canvas shoe for sailors – later worn also by generations of English school-children in the gym – was named a 'plimsoll' since its rubber surround was said to recall the Plimsoll line.

sandwich So addicted was the Earl of Sandwich (1718-92) to gambling (a major force in the emergence of organised British sports in the latter C 18th) that he asked his valet to create a portable meal which would allow him to eat while still at the gaming tables.

spoonerism The Revd William Archibald Spooner (1844-1930), was Dean of New College and a nervous public speaker. Among his alleged slips of tongue are the – perhaps apocryphal – 'The Lord is a shoving leopard' and 'You have hissed all my mystery lectures'.

wellington The 1st Duke of Wellington, British victor in Northern India, in the Peninsular War and at Waterloo, and anti-Reform PM in the troubled years 1828-30, in fact wore a leather boot which covered the knee and was cut away behind. The modern wellington, however, is of waterproof rubber and stops short of the knee.

Page 36: British Proverbs I

Answers: 1. It's no use crying over spilt milk 2. Absence makes the heart grow fonder 3. A bad workman blames his tools 4. Actions speak louder than words 5. Don't cross your bridges until you come to them 6. All good things come to an end 7. It's an ill wind that blows nobody any good 8. All's fair in love and war 9. Cross the stream where it is narrowest 10. The early bird catches the worm 11. It's easy to be wise after the event 12. All roads lead to Rome 13. A creaking gate hangs long 14. Honesty is the best policy 15. As you make your bed, so you lie on it 16. Forbidden fruit is sweetest 17. Time heals all wounds 18. Those whom the gods love die young 19. Fine words butter no parsnips 20. Beggars can't be choosers 21. All work and no play makes Jack a dull boy 22. A fool and his money are soon parted 23. Fools rush in where angels fear to tread 24. Every dog has its day 25. It's a long lane that has no turning 26. Penny wise, pound foolish.

Revision I

Page 37: Literary Lives

Answers: 1. cut down 2. range 3. white heat 4. ascendant 5. Gallic 6. true blue 7. drunk as a lord 8. meteoric 9. a) zenith b) marking time 10. galaxy 11. blue-stocking 12. green old age 13. rolling stone 14. blueprint 15. gild the lily 16. thorn

Page 38: Making Tracks

Answers: 1. trunk 2. peaked 3. winds 4. tape 5. wind 6. seven 7. rough 8. Bedlam 9. zenith 10. autumn 11. agenda 12. wood 13. pruned 14. branch 15. lopped 16. heaven 17. earth 18. channel 19. Rubicon 20. light years 21. the year dot 22. square one 23. pass 24. day 25. line

Unit 7 Idioms of Insects, Birds and Fish

Page 39: The Birds of the Air

Answers: 1. a) ostrich b) swans 2. swan 3. stormy petrel 4. night bird 5. turkey 6. a) duck b) bird 7. a) crowing b) geese c) swans 8. a) ducks b) drakes 9. ducklings 10. jay 11. magpie 12. crow 13. lark 14. albatross

Cultural Background

albatross a burdensome worry. The role of the albatross as a token of ill weather or ill fortune is memorably celebrated, and given a Romantic, gaia-oriented turn, in Coleridge's 'The Rime of the Ancient Mariner' (1798).

to jay-walk to cross the street paying no heed to traffic signals etc. The term originated in Boston, Mass. around 1917. A 'jay' is a country bumpkin not up to life in the town, but that term derives from the much-maligned, bright-feathered, chattering bird.

Page 40: Insects

Answers: 1. B 2. D 3. A 4. D 5. B 6. C 7. C 8. B 9. A ('garibaldis') 10. D

Page 41: Insects, Molluscs and Invertebrates

Answers: 1. worm 2. termites 3. moths 4. flies 5. crickets 6. drones 7. bee-line 8. beetled 9. wasp 10. flea-bites 11. flies 12. snail's pace 13. sluggishly 14. flies 15. bugs 16. hornets' nest

Page 42: Fish, Shellfish and Fishing

Answers: Part 1 1. salmon 2. a) fish b) red herring 3. fish 4. sardines 5. caviar 6. whelk 7. crabs 8. shark 9. cockles 10. a) sprat b) mackerel 11. whale 12. a) small fry b) minnows c) tiddlers
Part 2 1. cry 'stinking fish' 2. fishing fleet 3. rose to the bait 4. fishing for compliments 5. cast his/her nets widely 6. hooked 7. fishy 8. angling for 9. fish in murky waters 10. a) trawling for b) fish out of water

Cultural Background
neither fish, flesh, fowl nor good red herring neither the one thing nor the other. Fish was traditionally the food of the monks, flesh that of the commoners, red herring that of the poor. These herrings, left in brine for a week and then cured over oak smoke, were a standard part of the English diet, especially on the east coast. The kipper, still much loved in the 'full' British breakfast or at high tea, is a milder, yellow variety.
the fishing fleet The term was indeed used especially for young British women sent to India to capture an eligible young husband during the years of the Raj in the second half of the C 19th.

Unit 8 Idioms of Larger Animals

Page 43: The Basic Animal in Man

Answers: 1. bats 2. lion-hearted 3. toad 4. monkey 5. mule 6. pig 7. donkey 8. rat 9. dark horse 10. bull-necked 11. hog 12. ratty 13. pig-headed 14. sheep 15. ass
Key Phrase: snake in the grass

Page 44: Essential Animals

Answers: Part A A. fox B. chameleon C. turtle D. ferret E. scapegoat F. stag G. mole H. buck I. hedgehog J. tiger K. ape L. lynx M. lion N. badger O. lemmings P. crocodile Q. crocodile R. hare S. hare T. hare U. wolf V. rat W. elephantine X. lionize Y. hog Z. hound AA. donkey BB. wild cat CC. dinosaur DD. chicken

Part B 1. rat race 2. a) culture vultures b) eager beavers 3. white elephant 4. bull in a china-shop 5. hide like a rhinoceros 6. wolf from the door 7. tiger economies

Cultural Background
tiger economies The recent term designates the more successful economies of East Asia – Hong Kong, Singapore, South Korea, the Philippines etc. – which boomed spectacularly, if unevenly, in the 1990s.

Page 45: Puzzling Animals

Answers: 1. D 2. B 3. C 4. A 5. A 6. C 7. B 8. C 9. A 10. B 11. B

Page 46: Animals of the Farm

Answers: A. 4 B. 3 C. 12 D. 10 E. 14 F. 7 G. 6 H. 8 I. 13 J. 11 K. 1 L. 5 M. 9 N. 2

Page 47: Farmyard, Pasture and Field

Answers: 1. L 2. E 3. K (pigged) 4. J 5. A 6. K 7. C 8. H 9. I 10. P 11. G 12. O 13. G 14. M 15. O 16. D (foxed) 17. O (wolves) 18. B 19. F 20. N

Cultural Background
wild goose chase a reference to the grey lag-goose, allegedly the last species of goose to leave Britain each year and head north to breed. The geese fly in an extended, fixed V, never catching up those ahead.

Page 48: Pets

Answers: 1. P 2. J 3. G 4. K 5. A 6. H 7. E 8. M 9. L 10. N 11. I 12. B 13. F 14. C 15. O 16. D

Pages 49/50: Animals in Proverb and Saying

Answers: (for both parts together) 1. 14U 2. 1Y 3. 8O 4. 21Q 5. 10N 6. 13E 7. 26Z 8. 6X 9. 2M 10. 11B 11. 22K 12. 17J 13. 9R 14. 4G 15. 19L 16. 7D 17. 5P 18. 18A 19. 27BB 20. 20H 21. 28DD 22. 30CC 23. 23C 24. 15S 25. 12I 26. 16F 27. 24W 28. 3V 29. 29AA 30. 25T

Unit 9 Idioms of the Human Body

Page 51: Body and Life

Answers: 1. hand 2. chin 3. head 4. teeth 5. limb 6. knuckles 7. knee 8. finger 9. brow 10. eyelid 11. eye 12. sinews 13. arm 14. flesh 15. flesh 16. hair 17. neck 18. vein 19. kidney 20. faced 21. foot 22. thumbs

Cultural Background
the sinews of war money. The idiom derives from Cicero's *nervos belli pecuniam*, echoed, for example, in Beaumont and Fletcher's *Fair Maid of the Inn*, I, i.

Page 52: The Basic Body I

Answers: Part A A. elbow B. head C. eye to eye D. eyeball to eyeball E. nose F. mouth G. ear H. tooth I. mouth J. teeth K. tongue L. arm M. hand N. palm O. leg P. bile Q. figure R. guts S. livered T. thumbnail U. skeleton V. heel W. feet X. leg Y. spine Z. kneed AA. back BB. bosom CC. chin DD. head
Part B 1. ugly head 2. right arm 3. bloody nose 4. back teeth 5. cold blood 6. brave face 7. sore thumb

Page 53: The Basic Body II

Answers: 1. elbow 2. tongue 3. face 4. brains 5. stomach 6. nose 7. ears 8. chest 9. head over heels 10. bellyful 11. hair 12. head or tail 13. fist 14. foot 15. shin 16. shoulder 17. finger 18. leg 19. toes 20. skinned 21. skeleton 22. heart 23. bones 24. lip-service 25. neck
Key Phrase: wear one's heart on one's sleeve

Page 54: The Essential Body

Answers: Agatha: 15 Basil: 21 Cecily: 8 Derek: 2 Eileen: 13 Freddy: 22 Gertrude: 16 Hubert: 12 Iris: 3 Julian: 20 Kathy: 14 Lionel: 1 Matilda: 17 Norbert: 19 Olivia: 5 Pete: 4 Roger: 10 Susan: 7 Tim: 11 All of them: 9 Everyone: 18 the Will: 6

Page 55: The Anglo-German Body

Answers: 1. J 2. L 3. F 4. R 5. N 6. C 7. P 8. A 9. O 10. E 11. H 12. G 13. Q 14. D 15. B 16. I 17. K 18. M

Page 56: The Puzzling Body

Answers: 1. C 2. C 3. B 4. A 5. A 6. D 7. D 8. B 9. A 10. B 11. C 12. B

Unit 10 Idioms of Clothing

Page 57: Basic Clothing

Answers: 1. pants 2. cap 3. belt 4. collar 5. mantle/cloak 6. hat 7. jacket 8. boots 9. trousers 10. shirt 11. clogs 12. cap 13. sleeve 14. tie 15. bra 16. sock 17. kilt 18. blanket 19. escutcheon 20. umbrella 21. coat

Cultural Background
old school tie 'Old boys', the former pupils of Public Schools, do indeed still at times wear the tie of their old boys' associations as a mark of prestige. Ties, of which there can be a prodigious variety at any one school, are of great iconographic significance there also.

Page 58: Essential Clothing

Answers: 1. shirt 2. boot 3. crown 4. hat 5. shoes 6. trousers 7. cuff 8. buttonhole 9. collar 10. knickers 11. cap 12. socks 13. heeled 14. pocket 15. sleeve 16. garters 17. a) *and* b) belt 18. skirt 19. stitch 20. Sunday best 21. altogether
Key Phrase: It was run on a shoestring

Page 59: Literary Clothing and Fabric

Answers: cloak – glove – pocket – coat – wool – spur – coat-tails – boot – feather – cap – boots – veil – frills – boots – shoes – patch – gauntlet – boot – wool – pocket – hat

Cultural Background
run the gauntlet *Spießruten laufen.* The idiom stems from the ancient punishment.

Page 60: Anglo-German Clothing

Answers: 1. H 2. N 3. A 4. L 5. J 6. O 7. P 8. M 9. Q 10. B 11. E 12. G 13. D 14. F 15. R 16. I 17. K 18. C

Unit 11 Idioms of Food and Drink

Page: 61 Cooking

Answers: 1. a) scorcher b) bakingly 2. cooking 3. hard-boiled 4. grilled 5. simmering 6. stew 7. larding 8. broil 9. stirring up 10. boil 11. brewing 12. mincing 13. cook 14. half-baked 15. simmer

Page 62: Bread, Cake and Pastries

Answers: 1. breadwinner 2. pies 3. humble pie 4. pudding 5. sliced bread 6. gingerbread 7. piece of cake 8. loaf 9. on toast 10. dough 11. apple pie 12. crumb 13. in a bun 14. hot cakes 15. breadline
Key Phrase: a slice of the cake

Page 63: Fruit

Answers: 1. pear 2. plum 3. fig 4. apple 5. gooseberry 6. raspberry 7. bananas 8. apple 9. cherry 10. apple 11. plummy 12. lemons 13. banana 14. grape 15. sour grapes

Cultural Background
to play gooseberry to chaperone two self-engrossed lovers. Brewster surmises that this idiom of obscure origin derives from the idea that the chaperone does something harmless (like picking gooseberries) while the lovers engage in more intense activity.
to give s.o. the raspberry to make a vulgar noise signalling disapproval. This is a classic example of Cockney rhyming slang: raspberry tart = fart.
to hear on the grapevine *durch Mundpropaganda hören.* The entanglements of the grapevine are a symbol for information of intangible and untraceable origin.

Page 64: Vegetarian Foods

Answers: 1. A 2. D 3. J 4. F 5. E 6. H 7. L 8. C 9. B 10. I 11. M 12. G 13. K

Cultural Background
full of beans full of energy. The term was originally used of horses in need of exercise – as in Shakespeare's *A Midsummer Night's Dream.*
to spill the beans to tell the truth. This began life as early C 20th American slang, perhaps referring to the American country fair game of guessing the number of beans in a jar. 'Spill the beans' was a request to the game's organiser to pour out the beans and count them.
couch potato a TV addict and simultaneous junk food-consumer. The term seems to originate in the America of the 1970s, when cartoonist Robert Armstrong illustrated the common pun 'a boob-tuber' (meaning TV addict) by drawing a potato on a sofa.
to be in one's salad days to be young. Cf. Shakespeare's *Anthony and Cleopatra,* I,v 'my salad days/ When I was green in judgement'. Hence also the title of the renowned American musical of the 1950s.

Page 65: Puzzling Foodstuffs

Answers: 1. B 2. B 3. A 4. C 5. C 6. B 7. B 8. A 9. D 10. B

Cultural Background
Dead Sea Fruit The idiom refers to the apples of Sodom on the Dead Sea coast, which, according to ancient writers, were magnificent to behold but crumbled into ashes when touched.
above the salt a throw-back to the days of large dinner parties, when social standing was marked by one's position at table in relation to the centrally positioned salt cellar.

Page 66: Drinking

Answers: Alfred: 10 Beatrice: 13 Charles: 3 Daphne: 7 Edward: 14 Faith: 8 Gertrude: 9 Harry: 6 Isabelle: 11 Jason: 12 the Ruby Wedding guests: 4, 5 the two families: 1 milk: 2

Cultural Background
to have a lot of bottle to have great power or 'oomph'. The idiom was popularised in the 1980s by the now-legendary advertising campaign of the British Milk Marketing Board featuring the East End boxer Henry Cooper ('Our 'Enry') and the triple-glottal-stop, 'estuary English' slogan, 'Milk's Got a Lot of Bottle'.
to splice the main brace to celebrate with a drink. 'Splicing the main brace' – repairing one of the major ropes on a ship – was so arduous a task that its completion was traditionally celebrated by a round of rum 'stood' by the captain.
to be on the wagon be teetotal. The 'wagon' referred to is the water wagon of the purveyor of drinking water in the Middle Ages.

Page 67: Essential Drinks

Answers: 1. whiskey 2. drink 3. lager 4. milk 5. milk 6. cocktails 7. apéritif 8. a) tonic b) pick-me-up 9. tea 10. champagne 11. elixir 12. wine 13. drank 14. watery 15. watering 16. groggy 17. potion 18. juicy 19. water 20. water 21. wine 22. Chardonnay

Cultural Background
Chardonnay socialist a 'pinko', Third Way socialist – a reference to the alleged favourite wine of Tony Blair and his friends
groggy tired or slightly inebriated. 'Grog' and 'groggy' derive from the nickname of Admiral Sir Edward Vernon (1684-1757) – 'Old Grog' – who gave diluted spirits to his sailors to reduce drunkenness and brawling on his vessels.

Page 68: Last Drinks

Answers: 1. tea 2. champagne 3. beer 4. rum 5. wine 6. barrel 7. milked 8. bottle 9. ferment 10. this bitter cup 11. cuppa 12. mud 13. water 14. pint 15. drink 16. juice 17. pinta 18. dribs and drabs 19. milk and water 20. small beer 21. dregs 22. waters
Key phrase: the milk of human kindness

Unit 12 Idiomatic Structures II

Page 69: The 'To be + on' Construction

Answers: 1. A *or* J 2. S 3. I 4. N 5. E 6. R 7. Q 8. J *or* A 9. K 10. H 11. B 12. L 13. P 14. D 15. G 16. O 17. C 18. S, M 19. T 20. F

Cultural Background
on tenterhooks in suspense, nervy. Tenterhooks were originally right-angled hooks on a wooden frame, or 'tenter', used to stretch new cloth during the drying process.

Page 70/71: Idioms of Noun Pairs

Answers: 1. R4 2. D26 3. N8 4. F27 5. I9 6. GG1 7. W15 8. B14 9. E20 10. Z6 11. H2 12. L29 13. O31 14. M23 15. V18 16. FF12 17. Q19 18. Y16 19. J28 20. BB11 21. K32 22. X5 23. DD21 24. G22 25. P10 26. A25 27. a) C30 b) U3 28. S13 29. CC33 30. T7 31. AA17 32. EE24

Page 72: Idioms Involving Internal (Half-) Rhymes

Answers: 1. F 2. E 3. P 4. D 5. L 6. G 7. S 8. Q 9. I 10. B 11. M 12. K 13. W 14. U 15. C 16. N 17. H 18. A 19. O 20. V 21. J 22. T 23. X 24. R

Page 73: The Pejorative

Answers: 1. F 2. H 3. O 4. K 5. P 6. A 7. R 8. S 9. B 10. Q 11. N 12. G 13. M 14. Z 15. C 16. J 17. BB 18. X 19. T 20. E 21. I 22. V 23. DD 24. AA 25. U 26. CC 27. W 28. L 29. D 30. Y

Cultural Background

blurb short publicity note on book-cover. In the early C 20th it was customary to decorate US books with a female figure. To promote his book *Are You a Bromide?* (1907) Gelett Burgess drew a sweeter-than-sweet female, whom he called Miss Belinda Blurb. His book was successful and the name stuck.

bumph This is a typical piece of Royal Air Force slang, said to have originated among the young air crews of World War II. It is a contraction of the vulgar 'bum fodder' (*Arschfutter*).

tree-hugger a term derived from the pro-environment activists of the 1990s, who climbed up trees in an attempt to prevent their felling for by-pass developments and the like.

Page 74: The 'Verb + Adverb' Construction

Answers: 1. N 2. P 3. Y 4. Z 5. AA 6. M 7. E 8. K 9. U 10. A 11. C 12. D 13. a) L b) V 14. J 15. H 16. I 17. a) X b) R 18. F 19. a) W b) G 20. T 21. B 22. S 23. O 24. Q

Revision II

Page 75: Historical Moments

Answers: 1. backs 2. face 3. palms 4. Lion's 5. stormy petrel 6. a) shilly-shallied b) bull c) horns 7. war horse 8. brewing 9. dyed-in-the-wool 10. a) sluggish b) dinosaurs 11. a) small fry b) minnows (*or*: tiddlers) 12. boots 13. fist

Page 76: In the Family

Answers: 1. cow 2. kid [gloves] 3. gauntlet 4. bone 5. mince 6. bull 7. geese 8. swans 9. bile 10. fly[-on-the-wall] 11. goings-on 12. ferrets 13. skeletons 14. beans 15. drone 16. bodice 17. eye-opener 18. silk purse 19. sow's ear 20. albatross 21. dinosaur 22. carpet 23. bench 24. wild goose

Unit 13 Idioms of Travel and Transport

Page 77: Essential Paths

Answers: 1. a) tracks b) road 2. track *or* lane 3. rut 4. way 5. dead-end 6. trail 7. track 8. ways 9. garden path 10. streets 11. highway 12. way 13. half-way 14. one-track 15. avenue 16. cross-roads 17. lane 18. street

Page 78: Further Ways

Answers: 1. way 2. streets 3. side-tracked 4. way 5. way 6. road 7. way 8. way 9. street 10. way 11. way 12. road 13. track 14. track 15. inroads 16. a) line b) path

Page 79: Means of Human Transport

Answers: 1. cart 2. lorry 3. jet 4. bus 5. tandem 6. apple-cart 7. trolley 8. coach and horses 9. tank 10. coach 11. rocket 12. bus *or* boat 13. skates 14. train 15. driving force 16. railway 17. cart 18. gravy train 19. omnibus 20. wagon
Key Phrase: to jump on the bandwagon

Cultural Background
the man on the Clapham omnibus the man on the street. Clapham in the late C 19th was a standard middle class London suburb just south of the Thames. (Like so many London areas it later went downhill before being 'gentrified' in the late C 20th.)

Page 80: Ships, Boats and Navigation

Answers: 1. C 2. G 3. F 4. O 5. M 6. K 7. A 8. D 9. B 10. E 11. N 12. L 13. H 14. I 15. J

Cultural Background
to batten down the hatches The hatches are the doors above a ship's cargo holds. They have to be firmly secured – 'battened down' – before any storm.
clear blue water The term became current in the mid-1990s to denote clear ideological differences between Conservative and New Labour. 'Clear water' is the distance between two ships; blue is traditionally the Conservative colour.
to make up leeway to make up for time wasted, catch up. 'Leeway' is the distance between a ship's intended course and its present position.

Unit 14 Idioms of Buildings

Page 81: Doors, Floors, Fences

Answers: 1. M 2. D 3. N 4. J 5. I 6. F 7. B 8. A 9. C 10. G 11. L 12. K 13. H 14. E 15. O

Page 82: Basic Buildings

Answers: 1. cottage 2. pigsty 3. shop 4. brewery 5. shacked 6. pier 7. coop 8. hall of fame 9. china shop 10. stable 11. bridge 12. museum 13. mint 14. dog-house 15. ivory tower 16. madhouse
Key Phrase: a tower of strength

Cultural Background
to talk shop to talk about one's everyday work. The idiom goes back to the days when 'shop' meant not only *Laden* but also a part of a factory. This sense, derived from 'work-shop', survives in such key phrases as the 'shop-floor' or the 'shop-steward'.
ivory tower The phrase comes from the French *tour d'ivoire*, a term coined by Sainte-Beuve for the secluded retirement from life of the writer Alfred de Vigny. By the early C 20th the term was in common use in English: Henry James took it as the title of a novel unfinished at his death in 1916.

Page 83: Parts of Buildings

Answers: 1. B 2. D 3. D 4. A 5. A 6. *all four meanings are current* 7. C 8. C 9. A 10. D 11. C 12. C

Page 84: Buildings in Headlines

Answers: 1. N 2. B 3. G 4. I 5. C 6. L 7. E 8. A 9. H 10. J 11. O 12. K 13. D 14. F 15. M

Unit 15 Idioms of the Household

Page 85: Furniture

Answers: 1. O 2. I 3. N 4. L 5. E 6. H 7. G 8. J 9. D 10. F 11. C 12. P 13. K 14. B 15. A 16. M

Page 86: Household Goods

Answers: 1. sieve 2. brush 3. bucket 4. whisked 5. mug 6. pot 7. kettle 8. pan 9. grill 10. wooden spoon 11. pots 12. fork 13. sink 14. dish 15. silver spoon 16. broom 17. frying pan 18. candle 19. panned 20. kitchen sink 21. sponge **Key Phrase:** She's got a lot on her plate.

Cultural Background

to kick the bucket die. The 'bucket' here is not a water container but the beam from which pigs were hung to be slaughtered. As the pigs hung dying, their trotters could be said to be 'kicking the bucket'.

to get the wooden spoon to come last. The idiom seems to derive from a custom practised at the Cambridge University graduation ceremony in the Middle Ages. Graduands were summoned to receive their degrees in order of merit, a large wooden spoon being meanwhile lowered from the ceiling so as to land in the lap of the last.

Page 87: Utensils and Furnishings

Answers: 1. B 2. C 3. C 4. A 5. B 6. B 7. D 8. A 9. D 10. B 11. B 12. C 13. A

Cultural Background

mug shot a police photo. This is a 'mug' in the common slang sense of a *Visage* – cf. also 'mug-faker' (*Straßenfotograf*), 'ugly mug' (*häßliche Fratze*), to mug (*küssen, schmusen*)

Page 88: Containers

Answers: 1. bucketing 2. bundle 3. basket 4. can 5. box 6. package 7. coffers 8. coffin 9. bag 10. bundle 11. basket 12. packet 13. drawer 14. parcel 15. pot 16. pot 17. bag 18. bag

Unit 16 Family and Proper Names

Page 89: The Essential Family

Answers: 1. mother and father 2. fathers 3. baby 4. twinned 5. grandmother 6. uncle 7. family 8. merry widow 9. country cousins 10. mother's milk 11. child's play 12. daddy 13. wife 14. brain-child 15. Aunt Sally 16. cry-baby 17. a) father b) son 18. family 19. golf widow 20. sugar daddy 21. how's your father 22. baby

Page 90: Puzzling Names

Answers: 1. D 2. C 3. A 4. B 5. D 6. C 7. B 8. C 9. A 10. C 11. D 12. B 13. A 14. B 15. D 16. D

Cultural Background

to do sweet Fanny Adams to do nothing at all. Fanny Adams, a Hampshire girl, was murdered in 1812, her body being found dismembered in the River Wey. Subsequently sailors tastelessly used her name to describe a meal of tinned mutton they disliked. The phrase thereafter meant something of little value, and has since taken its current meaning.

the real Mackoy The phrase derives from the Scottish whisky firm Mackay, which advertised its product from 1870 as 'the real Mackay'. The switch to 'Mackoy' came when the phrase was consciously adopted and adapted by the US welterweight boxer, Kid McCoy.
a Tommy Atkins The name 'Thomas Atkins' was used by the British army on sample enlistment forms as early as 1815. By World War I it had become a standard phrase for the average private, the British soldier also being called a 'Tommy' – cf. Kipling's poem of that name. Hence also, incidentally, the German idiom '*eine treulose Tomate*' – a reference to the faithless English soldier lovers after the end of the Second World War.
Davy Jones's locker In sailors' mythology, Davy Jones is the spirit of the sea, his 'locker' being the sea's depths. 'Jones' is perhaps a corruption of the Jonah in the Bible. The phrase first occurs in print in 1726 and is found subsequently in Smollett, Scott, Dickens and Stevenson.
a Paul Pry The name is that of the eponymous, over-inquisitive protagonist in John Poole's farce of 1825.
a peeping Tom When Lady Godiva famously rode naked through the streets of Coventry to save the town from high taxes, all citizens were required to keep their shutters closed. All complied – except the tailor Tom, who was then allegedly struck blind.
to give a Roland for an Oliver Roland and Oliver were two of the legendary twelve worthy knights of Charlemagne, who once fought an evenly-matched duel of inordinate length.

Page 91: Names in Dialogue

Answers: 1. I 2. A 3. K 4. F 5. E 6. B 7. M 8. G 9. J 10. L 11. D 12. N 13. H 14. C

Cultural Background
all my eye and Betty Martin untrue, or utter nonsense. The phrase, of obscure origin, is sometimes said to be a garbled version of a Latin prayer *O mihi, beate Martine* – 'grant unto me, oh blessed Martin'. No such established prayer, however, has been found.
Bob's your uncle everything will be fine. The uncle in question is perhaps PM Robert Cecil, Lord Salisbury, who made certain that his nephew Arthur Balfour received important posts in government.
to bogart to keep to oneself. The reference is to the telling use of cigarettes by actor Humphrey Bogart.
Charlie's dead Your petticoat is showing. This whispered message, common in the days of petticoats, is of obscure origin, Charlie being perhaps no more than an easy name to say *sotto voce*.
Queen Anne is dead Don't tell stale news. Queen Anne, England's second constitutional monarch, following on William and Mary, died in 1714, thus ushering in the Hanoverian dynasty. The phrase is first found in a ballad of 1722.

Page 92: The Name 'Jack'

Answers: 1. F 2. M 3. N 4. P 5. H 6. J 7. Z 8. B 9. S 10. V 11. L 12. K 13. BB 14. X 15. E

Cultural Background
Jack 'Jack' is the pet-form of the common name 'John' and can simply have the meaning of 'man' – as in such professions as 'steeplejack' or 'cheapjack'. 'Every man Jack' means simply 'everybody'. No other English name has engendered so many idioms. It is noteworthy that even the British flag is commonly called the 'Union Jack'.

Unit 17 Idioms of Professions, Tools and Money

Page 93: Craftsmanship

Answers: 1. benchmarks 2. hallmark 3. nail 4. vice 5. hammering 6. hammer 7. tongs 8. spade 9. spade 10. axe 11. brass tacks 12. two pins 13. rakes 14. spanner 15. nail 16. hinges 17. hammered 18. nailed

Cultural Background
a hallmark characteristic feature. The term derives from the practice of the Goldsmith's Co., which developed stamped marks to identify the genuineness, quality and origin of gold and silver products.

Page 94: Puzzling Tools

Answers: 1. B 2. D 3. A 4. A 5. D 6. D 7. C 8. C 9. D 10. D 11. B 12. B

Page 95: Key Professions

Answers: 1. hatter 2. butchered 3. nurse 4. pilot 5. broker 6. tailor 7. cowboy 8. trooper 9. potter 10. tinker 11. thieves 12. judge 13. doctored 14. bandit 15. shepherd 16. soldier 17. ploughman's 18. lawyer 19. busman's 20. trooper 21. jockeying 22. hewer 23. drawer 24. spy 25. cobble 26. baker's **Key Phrase:** the poacher turned gamekeeper

Cultural Background
cowboy reckless operator. The idiom seems to have started life in the US around 1942, meaning a reckless driver. 'To cowboy' (to drive recklessly) entered British English in 1988. As an adjective, 'cowboy' means unreliable, 'fly-by-night' – e.g. a 'cowboy travel agent'.

Page 96: Profession and Class

Answers: 1. a) actress b) bishop 2. gentleman's 3. high priests 4. doctor 5. beggars 6. villain 7. yeoman 8. cleaners 9. fisherman 10. hunter 11. tinker 12. soldier 13. knight 14. nursed 15. marines 16. pilot

Cultural Background
as the actress said to the bishop The idiom is used to point up a self-conscious and slippery *double entendre*.
yeoman('s) service faithful, stalwart fulfilment of duty. A yeoman was either a small, middle-class landowner, who owned free land worth 40s. and so had the right to serve on juries and vote for the knight of the shire, or a servant in the royal household. Hamlet says of his ability to 'write fair' that 'It did me yeoman's service' – see *Hamlet*, V, ii, 36. Later the extinct class was celebrated in the well-known song 'The Yeomen of England'.

Page 97: Essential Money

Answers: 1. P 2. U 3. E 4. N 5. I 6. J 7. T 8. K 9. L 10. B *or* Q 11. R 12. D 13. C 14. F 15. M 16. H 17. A 18. O 19. G 20. S

Cultural Background
widow's mite a tiny amount of money, but much to its giver. See Mark XII, 41-44.
sterling of solid value. A 'sterling' was originally an English silver penny. Sterling silver is of the quality fixed for British coinage (92½% silver, 7½% copper).

Page 98: Money, Money

Answers: 1. E 2. A 3. F 4. C 5. G 6. D 7. L 8. N 9. H [put my money where my mouth is] 10. O [see the colour of your money] 11. I [spends money like water] 12. K 13. J [throw money at it] 14. B 15. M [not made of money]

Cultural Background
pin money a trifling amount of money. This is an interesting example of an idiom which has markedly changed its meaning over the centuries. In the C 14th and C 15th 'pin money' was an amount left in a will to pay for the then expensive and desirable pins. Later it became the allowance for a wife – a meaning it still has in Jane Austen.

Unit 18 Idiomatic Structures III

Page 99: The 'Verb + like' Construction II

Answers: 1. H1 2. B5 [i.e. to get on very well] 3. I6 4. L12 5. A13 6. K16 7. M15 8. J14 9. N7 10. E11 11. D3 12. C10 13. G4 14. F2

Page 100/101: The 'as ... as' Construction II

Answers: 1. 10AA 2. 23F 3. a) 30V b) 24T 4. 3DD 5. 9W 6. 29C 7. 14D 8. 15E 9. 21K 10. 27N 11. a) 11M 12. a) 5I b) 26BB 13. 6O 14. 4P 15. 16CC 16. 13J 17. 22G 18. 18H 19. a) 19Y b) 7R 20. 8U 21. 1L 22. 12Z 23. 28S 24. a) 17Q b) 25X c) 20B 25. 2A

Page 102: Common Abbreviations

Answers: 1. a) as soon as poss(ible) b) pretty damn quick 2. no bloody good! 3. absent without leave 4. a) bed and breakfast b) hot and cold (water) 5. gin and tonic 6. very important person(s)(') 7. waste paper basket 8. Thank God it's Friday 9. a) *répondez s'il vous plaît* b) bring a bottle 10. sweet fuck all (i.e. nothing at all) 11. a) for your infomation b) please turn over 12. disc jockey 13. a) nuclear b) genetically modified 14. (on the) quiet 15. apex/arse over tip/tit (*the latter being, of course, more vulgar*) 16. bloody fool

Page 103: Eponyms II

Answers: 1. X: a baedeker 2. W: a clerihew 3. T: Boolean algebra 4. Z: the bowie knife 5. M: a busby 6. EE: caesarean section 7. B: catherine wheel 8. D: a cicerone 9. AA: Custer's last stand 10. BB: a (local) derby 11. C: a derrick 12. Q. a doyley 13. CC: Fabianism 14. V: Ferris wheel 15. E: a Mickey Finn 16. U: Freudian slip 17. S: Gallup poll 18. Y: to galvanize (into action) 19. F: greengage 20. H: Hansard 21. G: a hoover, to hoover/do the hoovering 22. DD: to stonewall 23. J: lynch justice 24. N: tar macadam (tarmac) 25. R: a bloody Mary 26. a nosey Parker 27. I: a peeler *and* a bobby 28. L: Ritziness; ritzy; to go on the Ritz 29. FF: shrapnel 30. O: levis 31. P: grog, *also* groggy 32. A: a silly-billy

Cultural Background

a clerihew The good clerihew combines apparent 'primitiveness' – e.g. its *aabb* rhyme scheme and two couplets of differing length – with knowing wit. Clerihew Bentley's own best-known effort reads:

Sir Christopher Wren
Said, 'I'm going to dine with some men.
If anybody calls,
Say I'm designing St Paul's.'

E. C. Bentley also wrote the major (anti-)detective novel *Trent's Last Case* (1913), memorably analysed by Sir Frank Kermode in 'Novel and Narrative' (1972).

busby The modern term is derived from the – large and bushy – busby wig of the C 18th. This in turn owes its name to the hair of the famous headmaster of Westminster School. Among Busby's pupils, incidentally, were Dryden, Locke and Sir Christopher Wren.

catherine wheel St. Catherine was tortured on a spiked wheel, although it failed to kill her – she was subsequently beheaded. Oddly, this instrument of torture has become the rather attractive firework, much beloved at 5 November celebrations.

Custer's last stand a hopeless situation. George Armstrong Custer, a distinguished figure from the American Civil War, fought his last stand in less meretricious circumstances against the Sioux tribes in Dakota territory. Hopelessly outnumbered and isolated, he ordered his men to shoot their horses and use the carcasses as a final palisade. Not one escaped with his life.

Fabian Quintus Fabius Maximus earned the nickname 'Cunctator' (the hesitator) through his delaying tactics, which successfully halted Hannibal's advance

on Rome in 217 B.C. The Fabian Society, founded in 1884, believed in 'gradualism' and 'permeation' rather than revolution and so named themselves after him. Their symbol was the snail. Their attitudes are both symptom and cause of the fact that the British socialist party, the Labour Party, was the last to be established in Europe (some 30 years after the SPD).
Mickey Finn The Chicago bar-keeper of the 1890s gained notoriety by first plying lonely customers with a drugged drink and then robbing them. They would awake in a side-alley, poorer but with little recollection to make them any wiser.
gallup poll George Horace Gallup developed his methods first for advertising, but then found that he was highly successful in predicting the result of the 1936 American presidential election.
Hansard Luke Hansard printed his *Journal of the House of Commons* from 1774 on, shortly after reporting the debates in the House became legal at all. Hansard is still printed overnight so as to be available by breakfast time. It is the symbol of the continuing debate- and word-orientation of the British parliament.
to lynch to administer mob justice. Capt. William Lynch (1742–1820) organised extra-court trials in Pennsylvania Co., Virginia – see Edgar Allen Poe's account in an editorial of the *Southern Literary Messenger* in 1836.
to stonewall to put up obdurate resistance. General Jackson's US Confederate troops famously stood like a stone wall against Federal forces at the first Battle of Bull Run in 1861.
tarmac The best British roads on the eve of the Industrial Revolution were still the Roman roads of some 1500 years earlier. (Hence the key early importance of the canal.) The Scot MacAdam (1756–1836) and Th. Telford (1757–1834) – the 'Colossus of Roads' – were the essential reformers here.
nosey parker very inquisitive person. The idiom is said to originate in the inquisitive nature of Archbishop Parker. Some cite his long nose.
peelers Sir Robert Peel (1788-1850) was the first British Conservative PM *proprement dit*. His Tamworth Declaration of 1834, the first Conservative manifesto, stressed constitution and law and order. Appropriately, first in Ireland and later in London, he established police forces, whose members became known as 'peelers'. The affectionate 'bobby', current to-day, stems from his Christian name.
silly-billy The unfortunate prompter of the term seems to have been William IV (1765–1837), the former Duke of Clarence, known for his lax and poor performance as a monarch.

Page 104: Idiomatic Threesomes

Answers: 1. between you, me and the gatepost 2. hop, skip and jump 3. been there, seen that, got the T-shirt 4. cool, calm and collected 5. hook, line and sinker 6. stuff, nonsense and rubbish 7. Tom, Dick and Harry 8. high, wide and handsome 9. dead, gone and buried 10. morning, noon and night 11. lock, stock and barrel 12. rag, tag and bobtail 13. the long and the short and the tall 14. bell, book and candle

Cultural Background
lock, stock and barrel three parts of the standard door lock
hook, line and sinker three parts of traditional fishing tackle. One should not forget that fishing is still, statistically, the most popular sport in Britain.
high, wide and handsome one of the countless cricketing idioms in English – see Unit 23. It is used to describe the flight of the ball after a splendid shot, probably a 'six'.
bell, book and candle three elements employed in excommunication
rag, tag and bobtail the riffraff
the long and the short and the tall everybody – immortalised in the First World War song 'Bless Them All' and later in Willis Hall's play (1959) which takes the idiom as its title.

Revision III

Page 105: Literary Lives

Answers: 1. home truths 2. midnight oil 3. sea change 4. ropes 5. hallmarks 6. boot 7. hinges 8. a) trail b) way 9. avenue 10. benchmarks 11. a) object b) water 12. weight in gold 13. simple Simons 14. household 15. curtains

Cultural Background
benchmark point of reference, criterion. A benchmark was originally a notch cut by surveyors to assist them in their work By the 1880s it had assumed a metaphoric significance. It is currently much used in the sense of an independent gauge of the power of a computer system.

Page 106: Idiomatic Gossip

Answers: 1. you, me [and the] gatepost 2. how's your father 3. sin 4. [something] the cat brought in 5. Queen Anne 6. coot 7. every Jack [has his] Jill 8. shelf 9. shacked 10. cottage 11. write home about 12. Mackoy 13. marines 14. tiles 15. blanket 16. knife *or*: boot 17. Jack Robinson 18. Pete['s sake] 19. hole in the head 20. rough house 21. knife 22. axed 23. all my eye [and] Betty Martin 24. Adam 25. a) drain b) spout 26. window 27. coach [and] horses 28. hewers [of] wood [and] drawers [of] water 29 [brain-]child 30. skates 31. bus *or*: boat 32. boat 33. paddle [our own] canoe(s).

Unit 19 Idioms of the Law, Justice and History

Page 107: The Basic Law

Answers: 1. O 2. D 3. L 4. B 5. R 6. G 7. C 8. Q 9. I 10. A 11. P 12. F 13. E 14. M 15. J 16. H 17. K 18. N

Page 108: The Law Courts

Answers: 1. kangaroo courts 2. justice 3. trial 4. rack 5. guillotine 6. jury 7. brief 8. racked 9. trial 10. pleading 11. brief 12. sentence 13. court 14. plead 15. counsel 16. case

Cultural Background
kangaroo court an unofficial court of law which judges unfairly. Originally, a mock trial held by prisoners in jail. Cf. 'to kangaroo' – to convict unjustly.

Page 109: Crime and Punishment

Answers: 1. plea 2. clue 3. tribunal 4. penalty 5. bar 6. judgement 7. advocate 8. rough justice 9. bench 10. stay of execution 11. justice 12. *cause célèbre* 13. case 14. verdict 15. poetic justice 16. warrant 17. brief 18. dock 19. pilloried 20. reprieve
Key Phrase: play *advocatus diaboli*

Page 110: British and American History

Answers: 1. B 2. M 3. F 4. P 5. R 6. J 7. K 8. O 9. N 10. D 11. E 12. G 13. H 14. A 15. Q 16. I 17. L 18. C

Cultural Background
'We are not amused' the legendary response of Queen Victoria is found in her *Notebooks of a Spinster Lady*, 2 Jan 1900. That this should be her best-known remark, however, is part of the continuing misapprehension of both her and her age. Her journals, in fact, repeatedly contain the phrase 'I was very much amused'.
the Black Hole of Calcutta In 1756 relations between the British East Indian Co. and the natives in Bengal were at breaking point. Nawab Siraj-ud-Dawlah forced the British garrison in Calcutta to surrender and imprisoned overnight some 140 captives in a cell intended for four. Only 22 men and one woman survived to tell the tale.
to play King Cnut/Canute to attempt to stop the unstoppable. Cnut, Danish King of England 1016–35, once demonstrated that not even a king could hold up the march of the sea's waves, drawing for all and sundry the message: 'Let all men know how empty and worthless is the power of kings, for there is none worthy of the name, but He whom heaven, earth and sea obey by eternal laws.'
crusade The four crusades of 1096–9, 1147–9, 1187–92 and 1202–04 have been called 'the first examples of European overseas imperialism'. They are a reflection also of how much the then England was at one with the European mainland.
as queer as Dick's hatband very awkward or odd. 'Hat-band' is British slang for 'crown'. The Dick in question was Richard Cromwell, son of Oliver, but a son who emphatically did not wish to take up his father's role on the latter's death in 1658. After eight disastrous months, in which he earned the nickname 'Queen Dick', he fled the country.
Geronimo! Here we go! Geronimo (1829–1909) spearheaded the resistance of the Apaches to the US government and famously eluded some 5,000 troops for some

five months over 1,600 miles of territory. The word was shouted by World War II paratroopers as they jumped, perhaps in recollection of Geronimo's renowned leaps.
to dine with Duke Humphrey to go without food. Humphrey Plantagenet (1391–1447), Duke of Gloucester, was the youngest brother of Henry V and long-time Protector of the infant Henry VI. When the latter came of age, Humphrey fell out of favour, was imprisoned and starved to death in the Tower.
to read the Riot Act to give a severe talking to. In the tense years of Jacobite plotting which followed the Great and Glorious Revolution, after the '08 rising and before the '15, a Riot Act was passed in 1714 forbidding assemblies of twelve or more. When the appropriate section of the Act was read, groups had to disperse within an hour or risk the death penalty.
Sinatra Doctrine belief in state self-determination. In a major departure from the centralist Brezhnev Doctrine of 1968, the Soviet foreign ministry announced in 1991 that it would allow former Soviet-dominated states to go their own ways. The reference is of course to Frank Sinatra's famous song 'My Way', whose final lines run: 'The record shows I took the blows / and did it my way!'
Go West, young man! Seek adventure and gain through personal initiative. The phrase was coined by the Terre Haute Express in 1851 in an attempt to encourage westwards expansion in the US. Mae West starred in a film of the same name in 1936, which was followed in 1940 by *Go West, young woman.*

Unit 20 War, Weapons and Peace

Page 111: War in Dialogue

Answers: 1. O 2. B 3. I 4. A 5. D 6. J 7. C 8. E 9. H 10. G 11. M 12. F 13. L 14. K 15. N

Page 112: Puzzling Weaponry

Answers: 1. B 2. D 3. D 4. B 5. A 6. D 7. B 8. C 9. A 10. B 11. *all four meanings are current*

Cultural Background
flak repeated criticism. 'Flak' is an abbreviation of *Fliegerabwehrkanone*.
to spike someone's guns thwart or counter criticism. 'Spiking' a gun involved plugging the vent of a cannon to render it incapable of firing.

Page 113: Doing Battle

Answers: 1. L 2. G 3. D 4. M 5. C 6. J 7. A 8. O 9. F 10. N 11. H 12. E 13. P 14. I 15. B 16. K

Page 114: Weapons II

Answers: 1. daggers 2. swords 3. sabre 4. guns 5. battle-axe 6. hatchet 7. bomb 8. lance 9. artillery 10. bolt 11. stiletto 12. cudgels 13. bombshell 14. gun 15. longbow 16. pole-axed

Unit 21 Idioms of Books and Literature

Page 115: Words

Answers: 1. B 2. O 3. J 4. K 5. M 6. D 7. I 8. A 9. H 10. N 11. C 12. L 13. G 14. E 15. F

Page 116: Books and Their Parts

Answers: 1. lines 2. chapter 3. book with seven seals 4. leaf 5. article 6. column 7. encyclop(a)edic 8. passage 9. chapter and verse 10. compendious 11. open book 12. dictionary 13. copybook 14. good books 15. portfolio 16. volumes 17. reams and reams 18. index
Key Phrase: It's a closed book to me

Cultural Background
reams and reams a great amount of paper. A ream was 20 quires or 480 sheets of paper (sometimes 500, to allow for wastage).

Page 117: Puzzling Books and Words

Answers: 1. A 2. D 3. C 4. B 5. A 6. D 7. A 8. B 9. A 10. B 11. B 12. A

Page 118: Literature

Answers: 1. Micawber 2. Scrooge 3. quixotic 4. kafkaesque 5. like Hamlet without the Prince 6. Walter Mitty 7. epic 8. Jekyll and Hyde 9. Waiting for Godot 10. Vicar of Bray 11. hamletesque 12. Lilliputian 13. dickensian 14. Frankenstein's monster 15. faustian 16. pickwickian

Cultural Background
a Jekyll and Hyde a person with two distinct personalities. The term derives, of course, from R. L. Stevenson's *The Strange Case of Dr Jekyll and Mr Hyde* (1886), a renowned variant on the *Doppelgänger* motif and a study of the ego/id and good/evil conflicts in man.
a Micawber an eternal optimist. Wilkins Micawber in Dickens' *David Copperfield* (1849-50) is forever repeating the words 'Something will turn up, Mrs Micawber'.
the Vicar of Bray a political/religious turncoat. The central figure in a well-known English C 18th folk-song, the Vicar of Bray claims to have kept his post from the reign of Charles II to George I by altering his beliefs to suit the times – a story perhaps based on Symon Symonds of Bray, parson there from Henry VIII to Elizabeth I.
Walter Mitty the protagonist in James Thurber's renowned short-story *The Secret Life of Walter Mitty* (1939) and an archetypal Mr Suburbia, beneath whose humdrum, hen-pecked exterior lies a hankering for the limelight, for the virile and for violence.

Unit 22 Theatre and Music

Page 119: Essential Instruments

Answers: 1. fiddled 2. whistling 3. a) bell b) fiddle c) drum 4. drum 5. whistle 6. pipe 7. whistle 8. fiddling 9. drummed 10. trumpet 11. whistle 12. drum

Page 120: Musical Instruments II

Answers: 1. whistle 2. trumpet 3. strung 4. stops 5. second fiddle 6. concertina 7. harp 8. bell 9. soft-pedal 10. fiddlesticks 11. fiddle 12. drum 13. clarion 14. pipe
Key Phrase: He's on the fiddle

Page 121: The Stage

Answers: 1. A 2. C 3. W 4. D 5. CC 6. GG 7. M 8. I 9. G 10. HH 11. Z 12. O

Cultural Background
to put through the hoop to subject to harsh initiation/discipline – a reference to the training of circus animals

Page 122: The Stage II

Answers: 1. L 2. K 3. J 4. M 5. O 6. G 7. P 8. E 9. F 10. N 11. B 12. C 13. I 14. A 15. H 16. D

Cultural Background
the backdrop (or 'backcloth') background – from the painted cloth hung at the back of a scene or stage
the limelight *Rampenlicht* a C 19th lighting technique, which focussed in on one character leaving the others in comparative blackness. It was made by heating lime in an oxyhydrogen flame and gave a bright white (not lime-green) light.
wait in the wings The wings (or coulisses) are the side-scenes of a stage, where actors habitually wait for their cues

Unit 23 Idioms of Sport and Games

Page 123: The Game of Cards

Answers: 1. ace 2. good hand 3. play 4. trump 5. bad deal 6. house of cards 7. re-shuffle 8. trumps 9. cards 10. better deal 11. suit 12. on the cards 13. hand 14. trump card 15. joker **Key Phrase**: a game of patience

Page 124: Boxing

Answers: 1. sparring partner 2. packs a punch 3. the gloves were off 4. put my hat in the ring 5. won hands down 6. pull its punches 7. threw in the towel

8. Box his ears 9. fighting fit 10. knock-out 11. round one to Labour 12. below the belt 13. the knock-out punch 14. throw up the sponge 15. out for the count 16. punch-bag

Page 125: This Sporting Life

Answers: 1. par for the course 2. running 3. green 4. first hurdle 5. cricket 6. bat 7. knee-jerk 8. deep end 9. high jump 10. wrestle 11. stumped 12. somersault 13. play the game 14. sticky wicket 15. match 16. first base

Cultural Background
par for the course average. Each golf course has its 'par' – the number of strokes required by a scratch player to complete all 18 holes.
It's not cricket – like the concepts of 'fair play', a 'fair ball', a 'fair catch' and the idioms 'play up' (= behave manfully) and 'play the game' (= do the decent thing) – is a product of the high and late Victorian ages with their intense sporting ethos closely linked to the phenomena of the Public Schools and the Empire.
stumped at a loss. To be 'stumped' at cricket is one of the slightly less common ways of being dismissed as a batsman.
on a sticky wicket in difficulties. The 'wicket' is the actual playing area at cricket. A 'sticky wicket' is a damp, rain-affected one, on which it is notoriously difficult to bat.

Page 126: Games and Pastimes

Answers: the *Bystander*: 2 *or* 7; the *Comet*: 14; the *Commercial Times*: 6; the *Daily Letter*: 10; the *Daily Wire*: 4; the *Dawn*: 3; the *Day and Age*: 1; the *Free-Thinker*: 5; the *Imperial Rag*: 8; the *Old Republican*: 9; the *Onlooker*: 11; the *People's Looking-Glass*: 13; *This Morning*: 7 *or* 2; the *Views of the World*: 12

Cultural Background
to be snookered to be unable to act. A snooker player is 'snookered' when the balls are so situated that a clear shot is impossible.

Unit 24 Idioms of Religion, Fairy Tale, Myth

Page 127: Biblical Names

Answers: 1. H 2. I 3. L 4. J 5. B 6. E 7. A 8. C 9. G 10. D 11. K 12. F

Page 128/9: The Bible

Answers: 1. pass by on the other side 2. sheep from the goats 3. legion 4. an eye for an eye 5. ten commandments 6. Sodom and Gomorrah 7. manna from heaven 8. went out with the Ark 9. strait is the gate 10. exodus 11. Tower of Babel 12. no room in the inn 13. Get behind me, Satan 14. grapes of wrath 15. three wise men 16. from the rich man's table 17. the golden calf 18. by bread alone 19. gird up one's loins 20. wheat from the tares 21. walk on water

22. turn the other cheek 23. whited sepulchre 24. wash his hands in innocence
Key Phrase: to lead [them] out of the wilderness

Cultural Background
pass by on the other side from the parable of the Good Samaritan – see Luke X, 30-37
legion – see Luke VIII, 30
an eye for an eye the Old Testament doctrine, see Exodus, XXI, 24; for the contrasting New Testament doctrine, see Matthew, V, 38
the Ten Commandments – see Exodus, XX
manna from heaven the miraculous food found by the Israelites on their journey out of Egypt – Exodus, XVI
strait is the gate – see Luke XIII, 24
no room in the inn from the Christmas story, Luke II, 7
Get behind me Satan! Christ's response to Peter's suggestion that He would not lead a life of suffering – see Matthew, XVI, 23
the grapes of wrath a Bible-based idiom derived, in this form, from the religious rhetoric of Julia Howe's extraordinary 'Battle Hymn of the Republic' (1861), from which comes also the title for Steinbeck's novel of that name (1939)
three wise men Caspar, Balthazar, Melchior, the Magi from the Christmas story – see Matthew II, 1-12
crumbs from the rich man's table – see Matthew, XV, 27
man does not live by bread alone – see Luke IV, 4
to gird up one's loins prepare for action, *die Lenden schürzen* – see Luke XII, 35
to walk on water – see Matthew XIV, 22-36
to turn the other cheek the central doctrine of the Sermon on the Mount – see Matthew, V-VII
whited sepulchre *getünchtes Grab*, hypocrite – see Matthew XXIII, 27
to wash one's hands in innocence from the story of Pontius Pilate – see Matthew XXVII, 24

Page 130: The Bible II

Answers: 1. O 2. H 3. a) M b) I 4. D 5. E 6. C 7. L 8. K 9. G 10. B 11. J 12. F 13. A 14. N

Cultural Background
the beam in one's own eye – see Luke VI, 41 or Matthew, VII, 5
to eat from the tree of knowledge from the Fall myth, Genesis III
the Gadarene swine – see Matthew VIII, 28-34
give unto Caesar ... – Matthew XXII, 21; Mark XII, 17
hide one's light under a bushel see Mark IV, 21
kill the fatted calf from the parable of the prodigal son – see Luke XV, 30
kick against the pricks *wider den Stachel löcken* – see Acts IX, 5
the lion's den from the story of Daniel, Book of Daniel, VI
to cast pearls before swine see Matthew, VII, 6
the years of plenty, from the story of Jacob and Pharaoh, Genesis XLI, 14-36

the salt of the earth see Matthew V, 13
to fall on stony ground see the parable of the sower, Matthew, XIII, 1-23
the writing is on the wall from the story of Belshazzar's feast – see Daniel V

Page 131: Myth

Answers: 1. Adonis 2. Oedipus complex 3. Gordian knot 4. sword of Damocles 5. Cupid 6. Narcissus 7. Janus 8. Midas touch 9. Augean stables 10. Achilles heel 11. Trojan horse 12. Venus 13. Pandora's box 14. Methuselah 15. Cassandra **Key Phrase**: a Procrustean bed

Page 132: Fairy Tale

Answers: 1. J 2. K 3. P 4. H 5. G 6. A 7. C 8. N 9. I 10. L 11. E 12. D 13. O 14. B 15. M 16. F

Unit 25 Idiomatic Structures IV

Page 133: The 'To be + in' Construction

Answers: 1. J *or perhaps* K 2. E 3. L 4. B 5. Q 6. I 7. G *or* F 8. O 9. H 10. D 11. F *or* G 12. K *or perhaps* J 13. N 14. P 15. A 16. R 17. C 18. M

Cultural Background
in the doldrums in depression. The doldrums are that part of the Atlantic where neither the NE nor the SE trade winds blow, ships consequently becoming becalmed and their crews listless, despondent.

Page 134: Verb Pairs

Answers: A. cut and run B. wheel and deal C. live and let live D. make or mar E. park and ride F. rant and rave G. rise and shine H. hit and run I. pick and choose J. publish and be damned K. bow and scrape L. love it and leave it M. scrimp and scrape N. fudge and mudge O. wine and dine P. grin and bear it Q. huff and puff R. chop and change S. fetch and carry T. forgive and forget U. carp and cavil V. hum and haw W. take it or leave it X. see and be seen Y. aid and abet Z. make or break

Page 135/6: Noun Pairs II

Answers: Section A: 1 rags and tatters 2. smash and grab (raid) 3. skin and bone 4. ins and outs 5. high days and holidays 6. get-up and go 7. head and shoulders 8. flotsam and jetsam 9. meat and potatoes 10. ways and means 11. stuff and nonsense 12. cut and thrust 13. touch and go 14. doom and gloom 15. root and branch 16. neck and neck 17. cheek by jowl 18. bread and butter 19. leaps and bounds 20. all and sundry
Section B: 1. the world and his wife 2. Tweedledum and Tweedledee 3. rank and

file 4. Darby and Joan 5. kith and kin 6. hue and cry 7. *fons et origo* 8. trials and tribulations 9. bobbing and peering 10. hewers of wood and drawers of water 11. P's and Q's 12. rough and tumble 13. stress and strain 14. fits and starts 15. alarums and excursions 16. Box and Cox 17. Scylla and Charybdis 18. mover and shaker 19. goods and chattels 20. slap and tickle

Cultural Background

flotsam and jetsam *Treibgut, Strandgut* the former is wreckage found floating on the sea, the latter has been cast up onto the shore.

Tweedledum and Tweedledee an idiom first used for the rival composers Händel and Bononcini, but of course popularised by the podgy identical twins in Lewis Carroll's *Through the Looking Glass* (1872).

Darby and Joan the archetypal happily-married couple first saw the light of day in a song by Henry Woodfall published in the *Gentleman's Magazine* of 1735. A 'Darby and Joan Club' is a club for the elderly.

Box and Cox The two names stem from J. M. Morton's farce *Box and Cox* (1847). The two are lodgers inhabiting the same room but unaware of each other since while the one works the other sleeps and vice versa.

Page 137: Portmanteau Words

Answers: 1. U: adhocracy 2. O: Amerasian 3. CC: autochondriac 4. T: bonkbuster 5. N: breathalyser 6. Q: magalogue 7. B: chocoholic 8. W: dockney 9. Y: edutainment 10. D: guesstimate 11. R: televangelism 12. H: garbology 13. F: geep 14. X: boomflation 15. BB: stagflation 16. S: affluenza 17. L: infomercial 18. M: priviligentsia 19. V: mockney 20. A: motorcade 21. E: pharm 22. P: plugumentary 23. AA: qualipop 24. I: rockumentary 25. G: shipjack 26. C: slurb 27. Z: twigloo 28. J: hoolivan 29. K: workaholic

Page 138: British Proverbs II

Answers: 1. T 2. J 3. R 4. I 5. A 6. L 7. C 8. K 9. P 10. E 11. Y 12. V 13. X 14. CC 15. D 16. S 17. M 18. N 19. BB 20. B 21. Z 22. G 23. DD 24. F 25. H 26. U 27. W 28. Q 29. O 30. AA

Revision IV

Page 139: Idiomatic Aphorisms

Answers: 1. Wenn man nach Lob fischt, ist die Bescheidenheit der einzig sichere Köder.

2. *Probably untranslatable – a paraphrase loses the pun and thus the point*: Ein Politiker ist ein Wesen, das keine Position bezieht und dennoch die Ohren gespitzt hält.

3. Wenn der Schöpfer eine Intention hatte, als er uns mit einem Hals versah, so wollte er, daß wir uns mit unseren Meinungen weit hinauslehnen.

4. Der Krieg ist Kapitalismus mit harten Bandagen.

5. Wenn man einen Trend wahrnimmt, ist es bereits zu spät.

6. Verdammt, man kann nicht beides haben: die Dornenkrone und den Judaslohn.
7. Wer Dreck schleudert, verliert gewöhnlich an Boden.
8. Zeigen Sie mir einen Menschen mit der Veranlagung eines Lauschers und den Neigungen eines Spanners, und ich zeige Ihnen einen Dramatiker.
9. Die Struktur eines Stückes ist immer die Geschichte davon, wie das Vergangene die Gegenwart heimsucht.
10. Der englische Staatsmann wird dafür bestochen, daß er unbestechlich bleibt. Privilegien werden ihm in die Wiege gelegt, damit er sie sich nicht später verschafft.
11. Auf der Folterbank eines allzu behaglichen Sessels.
12. Wenn man ausgepfiffen wird ..., so weiß man zumindest, daß die Zuschauer noch da sind.
13. *Probably untranslatable – a paraphrase loses the pun*: Der einzige, der nicht dadurch verdorben wurde, daß man ihn feierte, war Daniel.
14. Wählt man Labour, so baut man Luftschlösser. Wählt man die Konservativen, so kann man drin wohnen.
15. Wenn es stimmt, daß das gute Weinlokal kein Aushängeschild nötig hat, so stimmt es auch, daß ein gutes Stück keinen Epilog braucht.
16. Ich verstehe nicht, wie ein Epigramm, das ja ein Blitz aus heiterem Himmel ohne jegliche Einführung oder Stichwort ist, je niedergeschrieben wird.
17. Die meisten großen Männer der Vergangenheit waren nur da, um sich zu amüsieren.
18. Wenn alles grundverdorben ist, so ist es Mannespflicht zu schreien: „Hier stinkt's zum Himmel!"

Page 140: Idiomatically Different

Answers: 1. a witty inversion of 'Time heals all wounds' – see page 36/17
2. adaptation of 'A fool and his money are soon parted' – see page 36/22
3. play on 'pushing up daisies' – see page 27/B
4. adaptation of 'You cannot make a silk purse out of a sow's ear' – see page 46/14
5. play on 'publish and be damned' – see page 134
6. adaptation of 'One's company, two's a crowd' – see page 15/5
7. play on 'to cast pearls before swine' – see page 139/I
8. play on the phrase 'to have a bone to pick with s.o.' – see page 54
9. cf the proverb 'You can't put a quart in a pint pot' – see page 68
10. adaptation of 'here today and gone tomorrow' – see page 31/5
11. triple play on words: adaptation of 'The early bird gets the worm' – see page 36/10 – and reference to both 'to be a worm' (a contemptible person) and 'to get/give s.o. the bird' – see page 39/6b.
12. adaptation of 'Those whom the gods love die young' – see page 36/18
13. reference to 'to run with the hare and hunt with the hounds' – see page 46/F7
14. play on the phrase 'to turn up like a bad penny' – see page 97/17A
15. play on the proverb 'You can lead a horse to water, but you cannot make him drink' – see page 138/3. (Dorothy Parker had been challenged to include the word 'horticulture' in an aphorism.)

Literatur

In den letzten Jahren ist die Anzahl der auf dem Markt zur Verfügung stehenden idiomatischen Wörter- und Handbücher – technologiebedingt – sprunghaft angestiegen. Der Vorwurf Nidas, die Lexikographen hätten sich nur sporadisch-kursorisch mit dem Phänomen der Idiomatik auseinandergesetzt (s. S. 77), ist damit weitgehend entkräftet. Unter der Vielzahl der nunmehr leicht zugänglichen Werke sind folgende Klassiker und Newcomer als weiterführende Lektüre besonders zu empfehlen.

Wörterbücher englischer Idiome

Cambridge International Dictionary of Idioms. Cambridge: CUP 1998.

CLARK, John O. E.: *Word Wise: A Dictionary of English Idioms.* London: Harrap 1988.

COWIE, A. P.: *Oxford Dictionary of English Idioms.* Oxford: OUP 1993.

FERGUSSON, Rosalind: *The Cassell Dictionary of English Idioms.* London: Ward Lock 1999.

GULLAND, Daphne M. u. HINDS-HOWELL, David G.: *The Penguin Dictionary of English Idioms.* Harmondsworth: Penguin 1986.

HENDRICKSON, Robert: *Facts on File Encyclopaedia of Word and Phrase Origins.* New York: Facts on File 1987.

KIRKPATRICK, E. M. u. SCHWARZ, C. M.: *The Wordsworth Dictionary of Idioms.* Ware: Wordsworth 1993.

SEIDL, Jennifer u. MCMORDIE, W.: *English Idioms and How to Use Them.* Oxford, New York: OUP 1978.

Wörterbücher amerikanischer Idiome

Longman Dictionary of American English Idioms. London: Longman 1999.

SPEARS, R.: *NTC American Idioms Dictionary.* New York: National Textbook Company 1996.

SPEARS, R.: *NTC's Thematic Dictionary of American Idioms.* New York: National Textbook Company 2000.

WHITFORD, H. C.: *Handbook of American Idioms and Idiomatic Usage.* New York: Prentice Hall 1987.

Historische Wörterbücher englischer Idiome

CARVER, Craig: *A History of English in Its Own Words.* New York: HarperCollins 1991.

CLAIBORNE, Robert: *Loose Cannons and Red Herrings: A Book of Lost Metaphors.* New York: Norton 1988.

DUNKLING, Leslie: *Dictionary of Curious Phrases: The Origin and Meaning of Metaphorical Phrases.* Glasgow: HarperCollins 1998.

EVANS, Ivor H., ed.: *Brewer's Dictionary of Phrase and Fable.* New York: Harper and Row 1989.

Historische Wörterbücher amerikanischer Idiome

AUTCHER, Dorothy: *Dictionary of Historical Allusions and Eponyms.* Santa Barbara, Denver, Oxford: ABC-Clio 1998.

MISH, Frederick C.: *The Merriam-Webster New Book of Word Histories.* Springfield IL: Merriam-Webster 1991.

Slang-Wörterbücher

AYTO, John u. SIMPSON, John: *The Oxford Dictionary of Modern Slang.* Oxford, New York: OUP 1992.

PYTHIAN, B. A.: *A Concise Dictionary of English Slang.* London: Hodder and Stoughton [3]1986.

BURKE, David: *Street Speak 1: The Best of American Slang and Idioms.* New York: Caslon 1999.

Wörterbücher der Neuprägungen

KNOWLES, Elizabeth u. ELLIOTT, Julia: *The Oxford Dictionary of New Words.* Oxford, New York: OUP 1997.

PYTHIAN, B. A. u. COX, Richard: *A Concise Dictionary of New Words.* London: Hodder and Stoughton 1996.

Eponym-Wörterbücher

BEECHING, Cyril: *A Dictionary of Eponyms.* London: Clive Bingley 1979.

HENDRICKSON, Robert: *Dictionary of Eponyms: Names that Became Words.* New York: Stein and Day 1985.

MANSER, Martin H.: *The Wordsworth Dictionary of Eponyms.* London: Sphere Books 1986.

Sprichwort-Wörterbücher

TITELMAN, Gregory: *Random House Dictionary of Proverbs and Sayings.* New York: Random House 1996.

Wörterbücher der Idiome: Englisch-Deutsch

SCHEMANN, Hans: *German/English Dictionary of Idioms.* London: Routledge 1996.

SCHEMANN, Hans: *English/German Dictionary of Idioms* – Supplement. London: Routledge 1997.

Spezialwörterbücher zu Teilbereichen der Idiomatik

ACHTEMEIER, Paul J.: *Harper's Bible Dictionary.* San Francisco: Harper and Row 1985.

JEANS, Peter D.: *Ship to Shore: A Dictionary of Everyday Words and Phrases Derived from the Sea.* Santa Barbara, CA: ABC-CLIO 1993.

MERCANTATE, Anthony S.: *Facts on File Encyclopaedia of World Mythology and Legend.* New York: Facts on File 1988.